Weapons and Equipment of the Warsaw Pact

INTRODUCTION

The Warsaw Pact (more formally, the "Treaty of Friendship, Co-operation, and Mutual Assistance") was formed on 14th May 1955. Officially, it was created in response to the formation of NATO in 1949, and the re-armament and integration of West Germany into NATO. Another, unacknowledged motive was a Soviet desire to control Eastern European military forces. The Warsaw Pact was disbanded at a meeting of defence and foreign ministers on 25th February 1991. The Soviet Union was dissolved the following December.

The signatories of the Warsaw Pact were:
Albania
Bulgaria
Czechoslovakia
German Democratic Republic (DDR)
Hungary
Poland
Romania
Soviet Union

In 1962, Albania supported China over the Soviet Union in the Sino-Soviet split. They severed relations with the Soviet Union and ended active participation in the Warsaw Pact. In 1968, Albania protested the invasion of Czechoslovakia, and later that year they formally withdrew from the treaty.

The Soviet military had a deeply ingrained culture of secrecy, to the point that soldiers were not told the designations of the vehicles they used. Whereas most Western armies believed that crews should be familiar with their own specific vehicle, the Soviet army believed that once a soldier had been taught to drive a tank or fire a gun, he would be able to drive any tank or fire any gun. It was common for a subset of a unit's vehicles to be used for training, allowing the remaining vehicles to be kept in better condition. If a vehicle was especially secret, the soldiers would be trained on a different model, while the secret vehicle was kept in storage. In time of war, the soldiers would be given a short time for familiarisation.

Warsaw Pact weapon systems tended to be simpler and less expensive than their Western counterparts. This was partly due to the experience of the Second World War, when the German advance meant that Soviet factories were overrun or had to be moved. During that war, simple weapons that did not require complex industrial processes, and which could be produced in great quantities, were highly valued. Western planners generally assumed that a third world war in Europe would be over quickly, but Soviet planners wanted to be able to continue production even after extensive damage had been inflicted on the country. User comfort was a much lower priority for Soviet designers than their Western counterparts, but ease of use was of the utmost importance. Warsaw Pact armies consisted primarily of short-term conscripts, and many Soviet soldiers spoke and read little to no Russian. Thus, it was important that the weapon systems should be rugged, simple to use, and easy to maintain.

In a similar vein, Warsaw Pact tactics tended to be much simpler than those in the West. Although it is easy to dismiss such straightforward tactics, it should be borne in mind that they were based on the experience gained during the Second World War, when a large Soviet army had defeated a smaller but technically superior German army. In the event of another war in Europe, the numerically superior Warsaw Pact armies would have faced smaller, technically superior NATO armies.

Combat experience in Afghanistan highlighted some shortcomings in vehicle designs. The Soviet army was organised and equipped for a large-scale war in Western Europe or China. It was ill-equipped for fighting a counter-insurgency war in a mountainous region like Afghanistan. Vehicle crews often had difficulty engaging targets high above them due to the limited elevation of their weapons. This experience led to vehicle armament being given greater maximum elevation, to allow engagement of targets on high ground. This had the secondary effect of allowing some limited use against helicopters.

Warsaw Pact combat engineering equipment was simple, rugged, and supplied in larger quantities than in the West. Combat experience in Afghanistan and in the Middle East showed it to be effective. The conscription system used by Warsaw Pact armies meant that training time was limited. This in turn meant that individual engineers were trained on specific tasks, and were less flexible than their Western counterparts. This was offset to some extent by the quantity of equipment that was provided to them. Both peacetime exercises and experience in Afghanistan demonstrated that the Soviet army's engineers were an effective force. The non-Soviet Warsaw Pact armies were not tested in combat, save for the invasion of Czechoslovakia in 1968. Their engineers' training was based on the Soviet model, and their equipment was similar if not identical, although often not as modern. This suggests that they would have been similarly effective, although the older equipment may have had a negative impact.

Artillery was very important to the Soviet army, and the Russian army before it. They sometimes referred to it as the "god of war", and were deservedly proud of the artillery arm. During the Second World War, most artillery pieces were towed, with only multiple rocket launchers being developed as mobile systems. The only self-propelled guns were tank destroyers and assault guns designed for direct fire, rather than artillery guns and howitzers intended to provide indirect fire support.

Multiple rocket launchers (MRLs) were pioneered by the Soviet Union during the Second World War, when they were officially known as Guards Mortars, but commonly known by the nickname Katyusha. The ease of construction compared to tube artillery (which requires complex tools for rifling barrels) meant that mass production was possible even after many of the armaments factories had been overrun by the German army. The relative ease of manufacture of mortars meant that they were also widely employed during the Second World War and afterwards, with very large calibre weapons being developed.

A note on armour thickness: sloping armour increases the thickness of armour that a weapon has to penetrate. The effectiveness of sloping can be calculated using the formula $T_{eff}=T/Cos(x)$, where T is the thickness of the armour plate, x is the angle from vertical, and T_{eff} is the effective thickness. The increase in effectiveness for various angles is given below:

10°: 1.02
20°: 1.06
30°: 1.15
40°: 1.31
50°: 1.56
60°: 2.00
70°: 2.92
80°: 5.76

In the above list and throughout this book, armour angles are given in degrees from the vertical: so 0° is vertical, and 90° is horizontal. To illustrate the dramatic effect that increasing the angle can have, consider the frontal hull armour of the T-62 tank. The armour was 102mm thick. The upper part was at an angle of 60° from vertical, the lower part 54° from vertical. A shell striking the upper part would have to pass through 204mm of armour, twice the thickness of the actual armour plate. The effective thickness of the lower part was 174mm — still significantly more than vertical armour, but much less than the upper, because of just 6° difference in angle. In the vehicle listings, where the armour is at an angle, the effective armour thickness is listed in square brackets.

Tanks

The wartime T-34/85 was considered by many to be one of the best, if not the best, tank design of the Second World War. Despite development of new tanks with larger, more powerful guns, the T-34/85 was kept in service with the Soviet army until the 1960s, with some Soviet client states keeping it in service for many more years. The T-44 was accepted into service in late 1944 as an improvement on the T-34. This had some teething problems, and was only produced in limited numbers, but formed the basis for the later T-54.

In the late 1950s, Khrushchev, a proponent of missiles over guns, ordered designers to investigate the possibility of tanks armed with missiles instead of guns. Despite widespread opposition to the idea, work continued after Khrushchev's removal from power, and eventually led to the deployment of gun-launched anti-tank missiles such as the AT-8 Songster.

The Soviet Union exported many tanks during the Cold War, to Warsaw Pact nations as well as other countries. The T-54 and T-55 in particular were widely exported. Care should be taken when comparing the effectiveness of exported tanks against Western tanks. Export models, especially those exported to non-communist countries, were not always of an equivalent standard to domestic tanks, and the operating country would sometimes choose to use cheaper, locally-produced ammunition rather than buying ammunition from the Soviet Union. In addition, the armour on export models of the T-72 was less effective than that fitted to domestic models.

It is interesting to note that by the mid-1970s the Soviet army had three largely similar tanks in production: the T-64, T-72, and T-80. Despite the communist system of government, there were three major competing tank design bureaus, and each used political influence to get their own design into service with the Soviet army.

Western analysts predicted that the use of composite armour would change the shape of Soviet tank turrets from the curved shape previously used, to an angular shape similar to the British Challenger or US M1 Abrams. Turret shapes did become less curved with the introduction of composite armour on the T-64, but they remained far less angular than those of Western tanks fitted with composite armour.

T-34/85

The original T-34, armed with a 76mm gun, entered service in 1940. Many changes were introduced during the Second World War, the main one being the replacement of the 76mm gun with an 85mm weapon, the new vehicle designated the T-34/85. It was still an important tank at the end of the war, and production continued in the Soviet Union until 1950. Czechoslovakia began production in 1951, followed by Poland in 1953, with the Polish vehicles incorporating several improvements. In the 1960s, some T-34/85s were taken out of storage and fitted with the same wheels and engines as the T-54, as well as mountings for a deep-wading snorkel.

The hull of the T-34/85 was of all-welded construction. The driver sat at the front left, with a bow machine gunner to his

T-34/85

right. The fighting compartment was behind them, and the engine and transmission at the rear. The commander and gunner were on the left in the turret, with the loader on the right. All three were provided with periscopes; the loader had a hatch, and the commander had a cupola. On some models, the cupola could be traversed through 360°, and one model allowed the commander to line up the gun on a target.

External fuel tanks could be fitted to the sides and rear to provide additional range, and would be used before using the fuel in the internal tank. There was no NBC system or night-fighting equipment fitted.

The original main armament was the D5-T85 gun, but this was soon replaced by the ZIS-S53. Two 7.62mm DTM machine guns were fitted: one mounted co-axially with the main armament, and one on the right side of the front hull. These were fed from 63-round magazines. Some countries fitted a 12.7mm DShKM anti-aircraft machine gun on the turret roof.

Specifications: T-34/85

Crew: 5
Combat weight: 32 tonnes
Length: 6.19m (8.08m including gun)
Width: 3m
Height: 2.74m
Ground clearance: 0.38m
Maximum road speed: 55km/hour
Maximum road range: 300km
Gradient: 60%
Vertical obstacle: 0.73m
Trench: 2.5m

Armament:
1x 85mm ZIS-S53 gun
2x 7.62mm DTM MG

Armour:
Hull front: 46mm @ 60° [Effective: 92mm]
Hull side: 46mm @ 40° [Effective: 60mm]
Hull rear: 47mm @ 50° [Effective: 73mm]
Hull top: 20mm
Belly: 20mm
Turret front: 90mm
Turret mantlet: 250mm
Turret sides: 75mm
Turret rear: 60mm
Turret top: 20mm

T-44

Development of the T-44 was complete by 1944, but it was not produced in large numbers. Armed with the same 85mm gun

T-44

as the T-34/85 in a similar turret, it had a new hull, which was both easier to manufacture and provided better protection. The engine was improved, but the new transmission was unreliable. By the end of the war, it was becoming increasingly obvious that the 85mm gun was insufficient. It could not penetrate the King Tiger's armour, and could only penetrate the German Panther at under 500m. Possibly of greater concern, the Soviets had acquired an American M26 Pershing under Lend-Lease, and they soon discovered that the 85mm gun could not penetrate the M26's armour.

The Soviet army had a 100mm gun available, the D-10, which had been proven in the SU-100 tank destroyer. Experiments were carried out fitting D-10s in both T-34s and T-44s, the vehicles being designated T-34-100 and T-44-100, respectively. Both were found to be workable designs, but by this time progress on the T-54 had reached the prototype stage. Designed from the outset for the 100mm gun, this was clearly a better design, and so no further work was done on the T-34-100 or T-44-100.

SPECIFICATIONS: T-44

Crew: 4
Combat weight: 32 tonnes
Length: 6.07m (7.65m including gun)
Width: 3.25m
Height: 2.46m
Ground clearance: 0.51m
Maximum road speed: 53km/hour
Maximum road range: 350km
Armour: Up to 120mm

ARMAMENT:
1x 85mm ZIS-S53 gun (58 rounds)
2x 7.62mm DTM MG

IS-3

The IS-3 was developed as an improvement of the wartime IS-2, with a new turret and hull. Limited production began in the spring of 1945, but it was never used in combat. IS series heavy tanks were included in Soviet tank and mechanised divisions until the late 1950s, as well as being deployed in limited numbers by non-Soviet Warsaw Pact armies. Later, they were only assigned to special units, and were removed from Soviet combat units entirely by the late 1960s.

The driver's compartment was in the front, with the fighting compartment in the centre and the engine in the rear. The driver sat in the centre of his compartment, with a single-piece hatch cover with integrated periscope. The commander and gunner were in the left of the turret, with the loader to their right. The

Tanks and Combat Vehicles of the Warsaw Pact | 13

IS-3

commander had a cupola, and a hatch was provided for the loader.

Long-range fuel tanks could be fitted on the rear hull sides. The IS-3 had no NBC protection or night-vision equipment. The main armament was a 122mm D-25 gun, which had a double-baffle muzzle brake. A 7.62mm DTM machine gun was mounted co-axially with the main armament, and a 12.7mm DShKM machine gun was fitted to the roof for anti-aircraft use.

Specifications: IS-3

Crew: 4
Combat weight: 45.8 tonnes
Length: 6.77m (9.75m including gun)
Width: 3.07m
Height: 2.44m
Ground clearance: 0.46m
Maximum road speed: 37km/hour
Maximum road range: 150km
Gradient: 60%
Vertical obstacle: 1m

Armament:
1x 122mm D-25 (28 rounds)
1x 7.62mm DTM MG (1,500 rounds)
1x 12.7mm DShKM MG (250 rounds)

Armour:
Turret front: 160mm
Turret side: 100mm
Mantlet: 200mm
Hull glacis: 120mm @ 55° [Effective: 209mm]
Hull sides: 60mm @ 60° [Effective: 120mm]
Hull top: 25-45mm
Hull rear: 60-90mm
Belly: 20-35mm

IS-10/T-10

After the end of the Second World War, development of the IS series of heavy tanks continued, eventually culminating in the IS-10, armed with a 122mm D-25TA gun. It was accepted for service in 1952, but the tank was renamed the T-10 after Stalin's death in 1953.

T-10M

The hull was made of rolled armour, divided into three compartments. The driver was in the front, the fighting compartment in the centre, and the engine in the rear. The turret was cast steel. The gunner and commander were positioned to the left of the gun, the loader to the right. Armament consisted of a 122mm D-25TA gun with a double-baffle muzzle brake, a 12.7mm DShKM co-axial machine gun, and another 12.7mm DShKM anti-aircraft machine gun at the loader's hatch.

In 1956, the T-10A added stabilisation for the main gun in the vertical plane. In 1957 the T-10B added stabilisation in both vertical and horizontal planes, and two infra-red searchlights, one to the right of the main armament and one forward of the commander's hatch. The T-10M was introduced later in 1957. This version had NBC protection and a new M-62-T2 gun with a multi-baffle muzzle brake. The 12.7mm DShKM machine guns were replaced with 14.5mm machine guns (KPVT in the co-axial mount, KPV at the loader's hatch). The T-10M was produced at two different plants, with incompatible parts, until 1962, when a single design was finally settled on. From 1963, T-10Ms were fitted with deep-wading snorkels, and from 1967 they were supplied with APDS and HEAT ammunition.

Specifications: IS-10/T-10 (T-10M in parentheses)

Crew: 4
Combat weight: 50 tonnes (52 tonnes)
Length: 7.04m (9.88m including gun) (10.6m including gun)
Width: 3.56m
Height: 2.25m (2.43m)
Ground clearance: 0.43m
Maximum road speed: 42km/hour
Maximum road range: 250km (420km with long-range fuel tanks)
Gradient: 62.5%
Vertical obstacle: 0.9m
Trench: 3m

Armament:
1x 122mm D-25TA gun (30 rounds) (1x 122mm M-62-T2, 30 rounds)
2x 12.7mm DShKM MG (1x 14.5mm KPV, 1x 14.5mm KPVT)

Armour:
Hull front upper: 120mm @ 60° [Effective: 240mm]
Hull front lower: 100mm @ 55° [Effective: 174mm]

Hull side: 90mm @ 60° [Effective: 180mm]
Hull rear upper: 60mm @ 30° [Effective: 69mm]
Hull rear lower: 30mm @ 50° [Effective: 47mm]
Hull top: 35mm
Belly: 20mm
Turret front: 250mm
Turret mantlet: 250mm
Turret sides: 75-115mm
Turret rear: 60mm
Turret top: 30mm

PT-76

After the Second World War, the Soviet army decided that it needed a new light tank and armoured personnel carrier. Both were to be amphibious and share automotive components. This requirement led to the PT-76 light tank and BTR-50P APC. Prototypes were completed in 1950, and the PT-76 entered service the following year. The original PT-76 lacked NBC protection and infra-red night-vision equipment.

The PT-76 was fully amphibious, the only preparation for swimming being to switch on the electric bilge pumps (a manual pump was also fitted for emergency use) and erect the trim vane at the front of the hull. In the water, the vehicle was propelled by a pair of water jets, and steered by closing a hatch over one of the jets.

Main armament was an unstabilised 76.2mm D-56T gun, with a 7.62mm SGMT mounted co-axially. In 1962, the PT-76B was introduced, with the D-56T replaced by a 76.2mm D-56TM gun. The D-56TM was stabilised in both vertical and horizontal planes, had a bore evacuator, and a double-baffle muzzle brake in place of the slotted muzzle brake on the D-56T. The PT-76B also

PT-76B

had NBC protection for the crew, a modified hull shape to improve buoyancy in the water, and a pair of auxiliary fuel tanks, each with a capacity of 95 litres.

Starting in 1967, overhauled PT-76s had the co-axial SGMT machine gun replaced with a newer PKT machine gun. Improved communication systems and infra-red night-vision equipment were also fitted.

SPECIFICATIONS: PT-76B

Crew: 3
Combat weight: 14.6 tonnes
Length: 6.91m (7.63m including gun)
Width: 3.14m
Height: 2.26m
Ground clearance: 0.37m
Maximum road speed: 44km/hour
Maximum road range: 370km

Gradient: 70%
Vertical obstacle: 1.1m
Trench: 2.8m

ARMAMENT:
1x 76.2mm D-56TM gun (40 rounds)
1x 7.62mm SGMT MG (later 1x 7.62mm PKT) (1,000 rounds)

ARMOUR:
Hull front upper: 11mm @ 80° [Effective: 63mm]
Hull front lower: 14mm @ 45° [Effective: 20mm]
Hull side: 14mm
Hull rear upper: 7mm
Hull rear lower: 7mm @ 45° [Effective: 10mm]
Hull top: 7mm
Belly: 5mm
Turret front: 17mm @ 35° [Effective: 21mm]
Turret mantlet: 11mm @ 33° [Effective: 13mm]
Turret sides: 16mm @ 35° [Effective: 20mm]
Turret rear: 11mm @ 35° [Effective: 13mm]
Turret top: 8mm

T-54

Design work on the T-54 began in 1944. The first prototype was built in 1945, with low-rate production starting in 1947. Full production started in 1953. Initially, the T-54 did not have NBC protection, though this was added to later models and retrofitted to existing vehicles. Turret traverse and gun elevation was manual.

Main armament was an unstabilised 100mm D-10T gun, with a 7.62mm SGMT machine gun mounted co-axially with the main armament. A second 7.62mm SGMT machine gun was positioned in a fixed mount at the centre of the glacis plate, operated by the driver. A 12.7mm DShKM anti-aircraft machine gun was mounted at the loader's hatch.

In 1955, the T-54A replaced the unstabilised D-10T with the 100mm D-10TG, which had a fume extractor, stabilisation in the vertical plane, and powered elevation (but not traverse). This model also introduced a snorkel for deep wading and an automatic fire-suppression system. The T-54A was manufactured in Czechoslovakia and Poland as well as the Soviet Union.

The T-54B, introduced in 1957, added an infra-red searchlight and driving lights. This model was fitted with the 100mm D-10T2S gun, stabilised in both vertical and horizontal planes. All of these improvements were retrofitted to earlier models. The Poles designated this variant the T-54AM, and this designation was sometimes erroneously used in the West to identify Soviet vehicles of this type.

The TO-54 variant mounted a flamethrower in place of the co-axial machine gun, with a maximum range of around 160m. The T-54AK was a command variant of the T-54A, with extra communications equipment and a reduced ammunition load. The Poles made the T-54AD command version, which had an extension on the turret rear to accommodate the extra radios.

Some T-54As and T-54Bs were upgraded to the same specification as the T-55M, and were designated T-54M.

SPECIFICATIONS: T-54

Crew: 4
Combat weight: 36 tonnes
Length: 6.04m (9m including gun)
Width: 3.27m
Height: 2.4m
Ground clearance: 0.43m

© Vitaly V. Kuzmin

T-54

Maximum road speed: 50km/hour
Maximum road range: 510km (720km with long-range fuel tanks)
Gradient: 60%
Vertical obstacle: 0.8m
Trench: 2.7m

ARMAMENT:
1x 100mm D-10T, D-10TG, or D-10T2S gun (34 rounds)
2x 7.62mm SGMT MG (3,000 rounds)
1x 12.7mm DShKM MG (500 rounds)

ARMOUR:
Hull front upper: 97mm @ 58° [Effective: 183mm]
Hull front lower: 99mm @ 55° [Effective: 173mm]
Hull side upper: 79mm
Hull side lower: 20mm
Hull rear: 46mm

Hull top: 33mm
Belly: 20mm
Turret front: 203mm
Turret sides: 150mm
Turret rear: 64mm
Turret top: 39mm

T-55

The T-55, introduced in 1958, was a development of the T-54 with a new turret mounting the 100mm D-10T2S gun, stabilised in both vertical and horizontal planes. The 12.7mm anti-aircraft machine gun was removed, 100mm ammunition stowage was increased, and an improved engine was fitted.

In 1961, the T-55A added radiation shielding and protection from nuclear fallout. The 7.62mm SGMT was replaced with the 7.62mm PKT, and the bow-mounted MG was removed. This was the first Soviet tank to be able to create smoke by injecting fuel into the exhaust, a common feature in later tanks. An NBC protection system and night-vision equipment for driver, commander, and gunner were fitted.

During the 1970s, a 12.7mm DShKM anti-aircraft machine gun was fitted to the loader's hatch on new and existing T-55s.

During the early 1980s, three new models of T-55 were introduced: the T-55M, T-55AD, and T-55MV. The T-55AD was fitted with the Drozd missile-defence system, the T-55MV had explosive reactive armour (ERA). The T-55AD and T-55M also had laminated appliqué armour added to the hull glacis plate.

T-55

All three new models had a range of other improvements:
- Thermal sleeve for the main gun barrel
- AT-10 Stabber gun-launched ATGM
- Improved fire-control system with ballistic computer and laser rangefinder
- Laminated appliqué armour on the turret
- Side skirts of steel-reinforced rubber
- Extra belly armour for improved protection against mines
- Improved NBC protection, adding protection from chemical and biological agents
- Napalm protection system
- Smoke grenade launchers
- Improved engine and suspension
- Improved radio (R-173)

A flamethrower variant, the TO-55, saw service with the Soviet army and naval infantry. The co-axial machine gun was replaced by a flamethrower with a maximum range of 200m. 460 litres of fuel were carried for the flamethrower, at the cost of reduced ammunition for the main armament.

Command variants of most T-55 models were produced, these having a "K" suffix (T-55K, T-55MK etc.). Command variants had extra communications equipment and an on-board generator. To make space for this extra equipment, fewer rounds for the main gun were carried.

SPECIFICATIONS: T-55

Crew: 4
Combat weight: 36 tonnes
Length: 6.2m (9m including gun)
Width: 3.27m
Height: 2.35m
Ground clearance: 0.43m
Maximum road speed: 50km/hour
Maximum road range: 460km (650km with long-range fuel tanks)
Gradient: 60%
Vertical obstacle: 0.8m
Trench: 2.7m

ARMAMENT:
1x 100mm D-10T2S gun (43 rounds)
1x 7.62mm SGMT MG (3,500 rounds) (T-55A: 1x 7.62mm PKT MG)
(from the 1970s) 1x 12.7mm DShKM MG (500 rounds)

ARMOUR:

Hull front upper: 97mm @ 58° [Effective: 183mm]

Hull front lower: 99mm @ 55° [Effective: 173mm]

Hull side upper: 79mm

Hull side lower: 20mm

Hull rear: 46mm

Hull top: 33mm

Belly: 20mm

Turret front: 203mm

Turret sides: 150mm

Turret rear: 64mm

Turret top: 39mm

T-62

The T-62 was developed from the T-55. Some components, such as the NBC protection and the fording and fire-detection/suppression systems, were carried over from the T-55. The engine and transmission were also the same, although engine cooling was improved. The T-62 did, however, have a wider turret and a longer, wider hull. The main armament was a 115mm 2A20 smoothbore gun, stabilised on two axes and fitted with a stadiametric rangefinder. After firing, the gun moved to an elevation of +3°30' and automatically ejected the spent case through an ejection port in the turret rear. Unlike later tanks, this was not a full autoloader, and the next round still had to be loaded manually. The T-62 was the first tank to mount a smoothbore gun, although the Soviet army had accepted a smoothbore towed anti-tank gun (the 100mm T-12) into service in 1961. The gun was relatively cheap to manufacture, and the APFSDS ammunition gave greater armour penetration, but was more expensive than traditional APDS. The 115mm APFSDS

T-62

offered penetration of 228mm at 1,000m. By contrast, the T-55's 100mm AP-T round could only penetrate 185mm at the same range.

Early production T-62s had protection against nuclear fallout, but not chemical or biological agents. Later T-62s added a chemical filter to provide protection against these threats. The T-62 was not used as a basis for specialised engineering and recovery vehicles; instead, the cheaper T-55 chassis continued to be used.

During its time in service, a number of improvements were introduced to the T-62. In 1972, the T-62 Model 1972 added a 12.7mm DShKM anti-aircraft machine gun over the loader's position. In 1975, the T-62 Model 1975 added a laser rangefinder over the 115mm gun. In 1983, Model 1975 vehicles were fitted with a new engine and the Drozd missile-defence system. Appliqué armour was added to the glacis plate, and the

R-173 communications system was fitted. These vehicles were designated T-62D.

Also in 1983, the T-62M was introduced. This had appliqué armour on the glacis plate and distinctive horseshoe-shaped armour added to the turret front. Belly armour was added to the hull floor to improve protection against mines, and rubber side skirts were fitted to provide some protection against HEAT warheads. In addition, the fire-control system was improved and a guidance system for the AT-10 Stabber laser beam-riding ATGM was fitted. This fired the same 100mm missile as the T-55, but had extra guiding rings to compensate for the wider barrel. Eight smoke grenade launchers were fitted to the right of the turret, and the R-173 communications system was added. The T-62MV added ERA to the T-62M in place of the appliqué armour on the glacis plate and horseshoe-shaped armour on the turret.

The TO-62 was a flamethrower variant of the T-62. The flamethrower was mounted co-axially with the 115mm main gun, replacing the co-axial machine gun. It had an effective range of around 200 metres.

The T-62K was a command variant, which first appeared in 1973. It had an improved navigation system and an electric charging system, and it carried four fewer rounds of 115mm ammunition. A command variant of the T-62M was also produced, designated the T-62MK.

Specifications: T-62

Crew: 4
Combat weight: 40 tonnes
Length: 6.63m (9.34m including gun)
Width: 3.3m
Height: 2.4m

Ground clearance: 0.43m
Maximum road speed: 50km/hour
Maximum road range: 450km
Gradient: 60%
Vertical obstacle: 0.8m
Trench: 2.85m

ARMAMENT:
1x 115mm 2A20 gun (40 rounds)
2x 7.62mm PKT MG (2,500 rounds)
T-62M: 1x 12.7mm DShKM MG (300 rounds)

ARMOUR:
Hull front upper: 102mm @ 60° [Effective: 204mm]
Hull front lower: 102mm @ 54° [Effective: 174mm]
Hull side upper: 79mm
Hull side lower: 15mm
Hull rear: 46mm
Hull top: 31mm
Belly: 20mm
Turret front: 242mm
Turret sides: 153mm
Turret rear: 97mm
Turret top: 40mm

T-64

The T-64 design introduced some radical changes from previous designs, which led to the engine, transmission, suspension, and automatic loader all being unreliable.

It was powered by a 5TDF multi-fuel engine using opposing pistons, making it relatively small. Main armament was a 115mm 2A21 smoothbore gun with an automatic loader and coincidence optical rangefinder. A 12.7mm NSVT machine gun was fitted to

T-64BV

the turret roof for anti-aircraft use, and could be fired remotely from within the turret. The turret and hull both had steel armour, with ceramic inserts for improved protection against HEAT warheads. Fold-out armoured panels (sometimes referred to as gills) were fitted to the sides to give added protection to the suspension. Two snorkels were carried for deep wading: one was fitted to the turret, the other to the engine. This initial version entered service in 1967, with production limited to about 600, all of which were later rebuilt to the T-64A or T-64B configuration and designated T-64R.

In 1969, the T-64A entered service. The Soviet army had acquired access to an M-60A1 provided by an Iranian defector, and this prompted the replacement of the 115mm gun with a 125mm 2A26M2 smoothbore gun, which had a thermal sleeve and was paired with an improved fire-control system. Smoke dischargers were fitted to the turret, and the turret armour was improved. A self-entrenching blade and fittings for mine-clearing equipment were added to the hull front.

The T-64B entered service in 1976. This had a new type of armour in the hull and turret, which was thinner than that used in previous models, while still giving equivalent levels of protection. Side skirts were fitted to improve protection to the suspension, and it had a napalm-resistant defence system. A new fire-control system was fitted, incorporating a ballistic computer and laser rangefinder. The AT-8 Songster ATGM was added, each tank carrying six missiles. This missile system could also be used against helicopters. Some tanks, designated T-64B1, did not have the AT-8 system. Some T-64Bs were fitted with ERA and designated T-64BV.

A command variant, the T-64AK, was accepted for service in 1973. This variant had an additional HF radio, navigation equipment, and auxiliary generator. It did not have a roof-mounted AA machine gun, and carried a 10m tall telescopic mast which could be deployed when stationary.

All T-64 models incorporated full NBC protection.

Specifications: T-64B

Crew: 3
Combat weight: 39.5 tonnes
Length: 7.4m (9.9m including gun)
Width: 3.38m (4.64m including side skirts)
Height: 2.2m
Ground clearance: 0.38m
Maximum road speed: 75km/hour
Maximum road range: 400km (550km with long-range fuel tanks)
Gradient: 60%
Vertical obstacle: 0.8m
Trench: 2.28m

ARMAMENT:

1x 125mm 2A26M2 gun (36 rounds, 6 missiles)

1x 7.62mm PKT MG (1,250 rounds)

1x 12.7mm NSVT MG (300 rounds)

ARMOUR:

Hull front upper: 200mm @ 68° [Effective: 534mm]

Hull front lower: 100mm @ 60° [Effective: 200mm]

Hull side: 80mm

Hull rear upper: 45mm

Hull rear lower: 20mm @ 70° [Effective: 58mm]

Hull top: 15-30mm

Belly: 20mm

Turret front: 250mm

Turret mantlet: 250mm

Turret sides: 120-200mm

Turret rear: 60mm

Turret top: 30mm

T-72

The T-72 was initially accepted for service with the Soviet army in 1973, and was fully operational by 1975. It had a 125mm 2A26M smoothbore gun with an optical coincidence rangefinder and computer-assisted fire-control system. A 12.7mm NSV anti-aircraft machine gun was mounted on the commander's cupola. Unlike the NSVT fitted to the T-64, it could not be fired remotely from within the turret, and the commander had to open his hatch to operate the weapon. The turret had cast armour, up to 280mm thick, and the glacis plate had 200mm-thick laminated armour. Fold-out armoured panels were fitted to the sides to give added protection against HEAT warheads.

In 1979, the T-72A was introduced. This had a laser rangefinder to replace the earlier optical model, and a 125mm 2A46 smoothbore gun in place of the original 2A26M. Side skirts replaced the fold-out panels, and extra laminate armour was added, particularly to the turret. This model became known as the "Dolly Parton" because of the appearance of the thick extra armour on the turret front. Smoke dischargers were added to the turret, and improved night-vision equipment was fitted.

From 1985, some T-72As were fitted with ERA and designated T-72AV. An export version of the T-72A, designated T-72M, was offered from 1980. This variant was equipped with less-effective armour and a different NBC protection system. In 1982, the T-72M1 was offered for export. This had an additional 16mm armour plate on the glacis and improved turret armour.

The T-72B entered service in 1985, with a new type of composite armour. This was a variant of the armour used on the T-80U, and offered much better protection than earlier versions. This model was nicknamed the "Super Dolly Parton", and also added 20mm of appliqué armour to the glacis plate. It had a 125mm 2A46M gun, capable of firing the AT-11 Sniper laser beam-riding ATGM. Smoke dischargers were fitted on either side of the turret. A variant designated T-72B1 did not have the AT-11 capability. Both T-72B and T-72B1 were sometimes fitted with ERA.

In 1990, the T-72BM entered production, the last variant to enter production before the Soviet Union collapsed. This had the same fire-control system as the T-80U, Kontakt-5 ERA, and the Shtora-1 electronic countermeasures suite. Shtora-1 included optical jammers to defeat SACLOS missiles and a laser warning system to warn the occupants about laser designators and rangefinders. Kontakt-5 was an advanced form of reactive

T-72A

armour, capable of reducing the effectiveness of APFSDS rounds as well as HEAT and HESH warheads.

The T-72K was the commander's variant of the T-72. This had extra radios, and battalion and regimental command vehicles also carried a 10m aerial which could be erected when the vehicle was stationary. Similar variants of the T-72A and T-72B were designated T-72AK and T-72BK, respectively.

All T-72 models incorporated full NBC protection. They all had a self-entrenching blade mounted at the front, an unditching beam at the rear, and fittings for mine-clearing equipment. All models could carry a pair of 200-litre fuel drums at the rear (these could be jettisoned if necessary) and a deep-wading snorkel. Preparation for deep wading took 20 minutes. Once the water obstacle had been crossed, it took two minutes to make the tank ready for action.

Specifications: T-72B

Crew: 3

Combat weight: 46.5 tonnes

Length: 7m (9.5m including gun)

Width: 3.37m (3.59m including side skirts)

Height: 2.2m

Ground clearance: 0.49m

Maximum road speed: 60km/hour

Maximum road range: 480km (550km with long-range fuel tanks)

Gradient: 60%

Vertical obstacle: 0.85m

Trench: 2.8m

Armament:

1x 125mm 2A46M gun (45 rounds, 6 missiles)

1x 7.62mm PKT MG (2,000 rounds)

1x 12.7mm NSV MG (300 rounds)

Armour:

Hull front upper: 220mm @ 68° [Effective: 587mm]

Hull front lower: 100mm @ 55° [Effective: 174mm]

Hull side: 80mm

Hull rear upper: 45mm @ 50° [Effective: 70mm]

Hull rear lower: 20mm @ 55° [Effective: 35mm]

Hull top: 15-30mm

Belly: 20mm

Turret front: 280mm

Turret mantlet: 280mm

Turret sides: 120-300mm

Turret rear: 60mm

Turret top: 45mm

T-80

The T-80 was a similar design to the T-64 and T-72, mounting a 125mm 2A46 smoothbore gun with autoloader. However, it was powered by a gas turbine engine instead of the more traditional diesel. This was expensive and used a great deal of fuel, but provided excellent performance. Initial production of the T-80 started in 1976. Full-scale production began in 1978 with the T-80B. This had improved composite turret armour, and improvements to the fire-control system, including a laser rangefinder to replace the original optical unit. In 1981, the T-80B was deployed to Group of Soviet Forces Germany (GSFG). The T-80B was fitted with the AT-8 Songster radio-controlled ATGM and carried four missiles, which were fired from the main gun.

Two add-on armour upgrades were introduced. In the early 1980s, it was realised that 105mm APFSDS ammunition could penetrate the laminate armour on the glacis plate of the T-80B, and so 20mm of steel appliqué armour was added. In 1983, Kontakt-1 ERA started to be fitted to the T-80 fleet. T-80s with ERA were given a V suffix, and the existing T-80Bs were upgraded to the T-80BV configuration.

The T-80U was introduced in 1985, with a new type of laminate armour, Kontakt-5 ERA, 125mm 2A46M-1 gun, and a new fire-control system. It had the AT-11 Sniper laser beam riding ATGM system with six missiles, fired from the main gun. The gunner was provided with a thermal imaging sight, with a secondary monitor for the commander. The commander could aim and fire the NSVT AA MG from under cover. It also had an auxiliary power unit, which allowed important sub-systems to be powered without running the main engine. Production of this model was relatively limited. In 1988, a T-80U with a diesel

T-80U

engine, the T-80UD, went into production. This sacrificed speed for lower production, fuel, and maintenance costs.

From 1989, the Shtora-1 ECM suite was fitted to the T-80 fleet.

Command variants of the T-80B and T-80BV were designated T-80BK and T-80BVK, respectively. These carried extra communications equipment, but sacrificed the AT-8 Songster ATGM system. The T-80UK was the commander's version of the T-80U. As well as extra communications equipment, it had extra navigation systems, an auxiliary generator, and an improved fire-control system.

All T-80 models incorporated full NBC protection and fire-detection/suppression systems. They all had a self-entrenching blade mounted at the front, an unditching beam at the rear, internal and external communications equipment, and fittings for mine-clearing equipment.

SPECIFICATIONS: T-80B (T-80U IN BRACKETS)

Crew: 3
Combat weight: 42.5 tonnes (46 tonnes)
Length: 7.4m (9.9m including gun) (7m, 9.66m including gun)
Width: 3.4m (3.59m)
Height: 2.2m
Maximum road speed: 70km/hour
Maximum road range: 335km (440km with long-range fuel tanks)
Vertical obstacle: 1m
Trench: 2.85m

ARMAMENT:
1x 125mm 2A46 gun (36 rounds, 4 missiles) (1x 125mm 2A46M-1 gun with 45 rounds, 6 missiles)
1x 7.62mm PKT MG (1,250 rounds)
1x 12.7mm NSVT MG (500 rounds)

ARMOUR:
Hull front upper: 200mm @ 68° [Effective: 534mm]
 220mm [Effective: 587mm] from the early 1980s
Hull front lower: 100mm @ 55° [Effective: 174mm]
Hull side: 80mm
Hull rear upper: 45mm @ 50° [Effective: 70mm]
Hull rear lower: 20mm @ 55° [Effective: 35mm]
Hull top: 15-30mm
Belly: 20mm
Turret front: 450mm
Turret mantlet: 250mm
Turret sides: 120-400mm
Turret rear: 60mm
Turret top: 60mm

TR-77-580 (Romania)

This was a locally built, modified T-55. Outwardly similar to the Soviet tank, it was longer, with six spoked road wheels on each side, and a distinct gap between the first and second wheels. A sheet steel skirt was fitted over the upper part of the running gear on each side.

The 100mm main armament was built in Romania, and was mounted in a locally designed and built cast turret. A 7.62mm machine gun was mounted co-axially with the main armament, and a 12.7mm anti-aircraft machine gun was fitted to the turret roof. Ammunition boxes for the 12.7mm machine gun were fitted on both sides of the turret. An unditching beam was carried at the rear of the hull, with a pair of long-range fuel tanks above it.

Specifications: TR-77-580

Crew: 4
Combat weight: 46 tonnes
Length: 9.25m (including gun)
Width: 3.3m
Height: 2.4m
Maximum road speed: 50km/hour
Maximum road range: 380km

Armament:
1x 100mm rifled gun (50 rounds)
1x 7.62mm MG (3,500 rounds)
1x 12.7mm MG (500 rounds)

Armour:
Hull front: 200mm
Turret front: 320mm

TR-85

TR-85 (ROMANIA)

The TR-85 looked similar to the Soviet T-55, but could be distinguished by the road wheels, since the TR-85 had six, to the T-55's five. It was based on the Soviet tank, with a new suspension and engine. The 100mm main armament was fitted with a fume extractor and thermal sleeve. A laser rangefinder was mounted above the gun mantlet. Boxes of ammunition for the 12.7mm machine gun were mounted on the turret sides and rear, with a stowage box on the turret left. A sheet steel skirt, ribbed for greater strength, protected the upper part of the running gear.

The driver sat at the front left, and was provided with infra-red night-vision equipment. The glacis was fitted with ribs and a splashboard. Two headlamps were fitted on the right side of the glacis. The gunner and commander both had infra-red night sights.

An unditching beam was fitted at the rear of the hull, and two extra fuel tanks could be mounted above it. The TR-85 was provided with NBC protection and a deep-wading snorkel, mounted on the hull rear when not in use.

SPECIFICATIONS: TR-85

Crew: 4
Combat weight: 43.3 tonnes
Length: 9.96m (including gun)
Width: 3.44m
Height: 3.1m
Maximum road speed: 60km/hour
Maximum road range: 310km
Vertical obstacle: 0.9m
Trench: 2.8m

ARMAMENT:
1x 100mm rifled gun (41 rounds)
1x 7.62mm MG (4,500 rounds)
1x 12.7mm MG (750 rounds)

Infantry Fighting Vehicles

The Warsaw Pact started to use infantry fighting vehicles in the late 1960s, when the original BMP-1 went into small-scale production. Most NATO armies only adopted the concept some years later, although West Germany was a notable exception, having deployed the Schützenpanzer 12-3 as early as 1958, followed by the Marder in 1971. In 1969 the introduction of the BMD-1 gave the Soviet airborne forces a similar vehicle specifically designed with their needs in mind, drastically improving their mobility and fire support.

BMP-1

The BMP-1 was first seen by the West on parade in 1967. This model was a pre-production vehicle, and there were several detail changes made before full-scale production began in 1970. Although not the first infantry fighting vehicle, the BMP-1 was certainly an innovative design. Main armament was a 73mm 2A28 smoothbore, low-pressure gun fitted with an autoloader. An AT-3 Sagger ATGM launcher was mounted on top of the gun barrel, and a 7.62mm PKT machine gun was mounted co-axially. Four reload missiles were carried for the AT-3 launcher: two in the turret and two in the hull. The BMP-1 had a vehicle crew of two (driver and gunner). When the infantry section was mounted, the section commander sat behind the driver and commanded the vehicle.

Eight infantrymen were carried in the rear of the vehicle, on outward-facing seats. Firing ports were provided, allowing them to fire while mounted. The infantry could exit via four roof hatches or two rear doors. One BMP-1 in each platoon normally carried an SA-7 Grail surface-to-air missile, which could be fired from the vehicle by opening a roof hatch and standing in the opening.

The BMP-1 was fully amphibious, and when in the water was propelled by its tracks. Preparation for entering the water consisted of erecting the trim vane at the front of the hull, switching on the electric bilge pumps, and replacing the driver's periscope with a taller one so that he could see over the trim vane.

The BMP-1 had full NBC protection, infra-red searchlights, and fittings for the KMT-10 mine-clearing plough. Vehicles in Afghanistan often had extra armour fitted under the driver's and commander's seats to give extra protection against mines, side skirts to protect the suspension, and appliqué armour added to the hull. These vehicles were designated BMP-1D. Some had a stowage box added to the rear hull roof, and a common further modification was the addition of an AGS-17 automatic grenade launcher on the turret roof.

Combat experience with the BMP-1 during the 1973 Yom Kippur War led to some improvements, and in 1979 the BMP-1P entered production. This replaced the AT-3 Sagger launcher with a new, detachable launcher capable of firing AT-4 Spigot and AT-5 Spandrel anti-tank missiles. Both the AT-4 and AT-5 used semi-automatic command to line-of-sight (SACLOS) guidance, which was more accurate and easier to use than the manual command to line-of-sight (MCLOS) guidance used by the AT-3. Unlike the AT-3, however, the new launcher could not be

BMP-1

operated from within the turret. Instead, the gunner had to stand in the open hatch to fire and guide the missile. The NBC protection and fire-fighting equipment was also improved, and six smoke grenade launchers were added to the rear of the turret. Existing BMP-1s were upgraded to the BMP-1P standard.

Command variants of the BMP-1 were the BMP-1K and BMP-1PK. These had extra radios and aerials, but the machine gun firing ports were non-functional. The BMP-1 KShM was a command vehicle used by commanders and staff at the regimental or divisional level. It had extra radios and a large telescopic aerial, but no armament.

SPECIFICATIONS: BMP-1

Crew: 2 + 9 passengers
Combat weight: 13,500kg
Length: 6.74m
Width: 2.94m
Height: 2.15m
Ground clearance: 0.39m
Maximum road speed: 65km/hour

Maximum road range: 600km
Gradient: 60%
Vertical obstacle: 0.8m
Trench: 2.2m

ARMAMENT:
1x 73mm 2A28 gun (40 rounds)
1x 7.62mm PKT MG (2,000 rounds)
1x AT-3 Sagger ATGM (1 + 4 missiles)

ARMOUR:
Hull front upper: 7mm @ 80° [Effective: 40mm]
Hull front lower: 19mm @ 57° [Effective: 35mm]
Hull side upper: 16mm @ 14° [Effective: 16mm]
Hull side lower: 18mm
Hull rear upper: 16mm @ 19° [Effective: 17mm]
Hull rear lower: 16mm @ 19° [Effective: 17mm]
Hull top: 6mm
Belly: 7mm
Turret front: 23mm @ 42° [Effective: 31mm]
Turret sides: 19mm @ 36° [Effective: 23mm]
Turret rear: 13mm @ 30° [Effective: 15mm]
Turret top: 6mm
Turret mantlet: 26-33mm

BMP-2

The BMP-2 was introduced in 1980, and was largely based on the BMP-1, with a similar (though more heavily armoured) chassis. The turret used aluminium armour and was larger than the BMP-1's turret. The commander was seated in the turret, to the right of the gunner. Like the BMP-1, it was fully amphibious and propelled in the water by its tracks. It had full NBC

BMP-2

protection and infra-red night-fighting equipment, and could create smoke by injecting fuel into the engine's exhaust.

The turret had a fully stabilised 30mm 2A42 automatic cannon, with a high elevation giving it some capability against helicopters as well as allowing engagement of targets on high ground. A 7.62mm PKT machine gun was mounted co-axially with the cannon. A launcher for AT-5 Spandrel ATGMs was mounted on the roof, and a ground mount was carried to allow missiles to be fired away from the vehicle. Export vehicles often had the smaller, less effective AT-4 Spigot in place of the AT-5. Three 81mm smoke grenade dischargers were mounted on each side of the turret.

The larger turret meant that the troop compartment had two roof hatches instead of four, and the capacity was reduced from eight infantrymen to seven (one seated behind the driver, where the commander sat in the BMP-1). Firing ports were provided, allowing the infantry squad to fire while mounted, and there were two rear doors. Roughly one vehicle in three carried a gripstock for a man-portable SAM system (SA-7 Grail, SA-14 Gremlin, SA-16 Gimlet, or SA-18 Grouse) and two missiles.

The BMP-2D was introduced in 1982. This model had deeper side skirts, appliqué armour on the hull and turret, and extra armour on the floor to provide greater protection from mines. It could be fitted with the KMT-10 mine-clearing plough. The extra weight of the armour meant that it was not amphibious. From 1986, improved stabilisation, fire-control, and internal communication systems were added to new production vehicles, and these improvements were gradually fitted to existing vehicles.

As with the BMP-1, there was a command variant of the BMP-2, designated the BMP-2K, fitted with additional radios and aerials.

SPECIFICATIONS: BMP-2

Crew: 3 + 7 passengers
Combat weight: 14,300kg
Length: 6.74m
Width: 3.15m
Height: 2.45m
Ground clearance: 0.42m
Maximum road speed: 65km/hour
Maximum road range: 600km
Gradient: 60%
Vertical obstacle: 0.7m
Trench: 2.5m

ARMAMENT:
1x 30mm 2A42 cannon (500 rounds)
1x 7.62mm PKT MG (2,000 rounds)
1x AT-5 Spandrel ATGM (1 + 4 missiles)

ARMOUR:
Hull: 5-19mm
Turret: 23mm-33mm

BMP-3

The BMP-3 entered service in 1990. It used aluminium armour, with spaced steel-aluminium armour on the front and hull floor. Like earlier models, it was amphibious, had full NBC protection, and could create smoke by injecting fuel into the exhaust. Unlike earlier models, it was propelled in the water by two water jets. A self-entrenching blade was fitted under the bow.

BMP-3

A 2A70 100mm rifled gun, 2A72 30mm cannon, and 7.62mm PKT machine gun were mounted in the turret, with a 7.62mm PKT forward-firing machine gun on each side of the hull. The three turret weapons were all mounted in a single assembly, designated 2K23, which was stabilised in the horizontal and vertical planes. A laser rangefinder was fitted, which fed data to a computerised fire-control system. Elevation was -5 to +60°, allowing the 30mm cannon to engage helicopters as well as targets on high ground. The 100mm gun fired HE-FRAG (loaded from an autoloader) and the AT-10 Stabber ATGM (loaded manually).

The BMP-3 had a vehicle crew of three (driver, gunner, commander) and normally carried seven infantrymen (two in the front, five in the rear). If required, an extra two infantrymen could be accommodated in the rear. There were two large rear doors for entry and exit, and two roof hatches above the troop compartment.

Specifications: BMP-3

Crew: 3 + 7 passengers
Combat weight: 18,700kg
Length: 6.72m
Width: 3.15m
Height: 3.57m
Ground clearance: 0.19 - 0.51m (adjustable)
Maximum road speed: 70km/hour
Maximum road range: 800km
Gradient: 60%
Vertical obstacle: 0.8m
Trench: 2.5m
Armour (max): 35mm (estimated)

Armament:
1x 2A70 100mm gun (40 rounds, 8 missiles)
2A72 30mm cannon (500 rounds)
3x 7.62mm PKT MG (6,000 rounds)

BMD-1

The BMD-1 entered service in 1969, and was first seen in public in 1973. It was air-portable by aeroplane (An-12, An-22, Il-76, An-124) or helicopter (Mi-6 and Mi-26), and could also be dropped by parachute. Initially the vehicle and crew were parachuted separately. After tests conducted during the 1970s, this was changed and the vehicle was dropped with the driver and gunner seated inside.

BMD-1

The hull was made of welded aluminium, with the driver in the front centre and the commander in the front left. To the right of the driver was a machine gun operator, who operated the two bow-mounted 7.62mm PKT machine guns. The turret was the same design as that used on the BMP-1. The rear hull, housing the airborne squad, had a single roof hatch with a concertina-type cover. Unlike the BMP-1, the BMD-1 did not have rear doors, so the roof hatch was the only means of entry to, and exit from, the rear compartment.

The BMD-1 was fully amphibious, and was propelled in the water by a pair of water jets at the rear of the hull. A trim vane was erected at the front of the hull before entering the water. It was fitted with a PAZ NBC system, infra-red driving lights and a white-light searchlight, which could be replaced with an infra-red searchlight. Main armament was a 2A28 73mm smoothbore, low-pressure gun fitted with an autoloader. An AT-3 Sagger ATGM launcher was mounted on top of the gun barrel, and a

7.62mm PKT machine gun was mounted co-axially. Two reload missiles were stowed in the turret.

The BMD-1K was the command variant, with extra communications facilities. The BMD-1M was first seen in 1980. This model had improved ventilation, and could be identified by a vent grill on the bow. Another variant, the BMD-1P, had a pintle-mounted launcher for the AT-4 Spigot ATGM instead of the AT-3 launcher. The AT-4 launcher could be fitted with a night sight.

Some vehicles in Afghanistan were fitted with an 82mm mortar in the rear troop compartment, firing rearwards.

SPECIFICATIONS: BMD-1

Crew: 2 + 5 passengers
Combat weight: 7,500kg
Length: 5.4m
Width: 2.63m
Height: 1.62 - 1.97m
Ground clearance: 0.1 - 0.45m
Maximum road speed: 70km/hour
Maximum road range: 320km
Gradient: 60%
Vertical obstacle: 0.8m
Trench: 1.6m

ARMAMENT:
1x 2A28 73mm gun (40 rounds)
3x 7.62mm PKT MG (6,000 rounds)
1x AT-3 Sagger ATGM (1 + 3 missiles)

ARMOUR (MAX):
Hull: 15mm
Turret: 23mm

BMD-2

The first prototype of the BMD-2 was completed in 1985, with production starting in 1989. It was initially believed that they were rebuilt BMD-1s, but in fact the vehicles were new. The hull was similar to that of the BMD-1, though one of the bow-mounted PKT machine guns was removed, leaving only the one on the right side of the hull.

BMD-2

The turret, however, was radically different to that on the BMD-1. Main armament was a 2A42 30mm automatic cannon, stabilised in both vertical and horizontal planes, and capable of engaging helicopters as well as ground targets. An infra-red and white-light searchlight was fitted, and a 7.62mm PKT machine gun was mounted co-axially with the cannon. A pintle mount was fitted to the roof of the turret, on which an AT-4 Spigot or AT-5 Spandrel ATGM launcher was mounted. A ground mount was carried to allow missiles to be launched away from the vehicle itself.

Like the BMD-1, the BMD-2 was air-portable, air-droppable, fully amphibious, and had full NBC protection.

Specifications: BMD-2

Crew: 3 + 4 passengers
Combat weight: 8,225kg
Length: 5.91m
Width: 2.63m
Height: 1.97m
Ground clearance: 0.1 - 0.45m
Maximum road speed: 60km/hour
Maximum road range: 500km
Gradient: 60%
Vertical obstacle: 0.6m
Trench: 1.2m

Armament:
1x 2A42 30mm cannon (300 rounds)
2x 7.62mm PKT MG (3,000 rounds)
1x AT-4 Spigot or AT-5 Spandrel ATGM (1 + 3 missiles)

Armour (max):
Hull: 15mm
Turret: 23mm

BMD-3

The BMD-3 entered service with Soviet airborne units in 1990, then later with naval infantry units. It had a new hull married to the turret of the BMP-2. The hull had aluminium armour, while the turret's armour was steel. The seats for the driver and two front gunners hung from the roof, rather than being mounted on the floor. This arrangement improved crew survivability in the event that the vehicle hit an anti-tank mine.

The hull mounted an AG-17 30mm automatic grenade launcher in the left front, and a 5.45mm RPKS machine gun in the right front. These weapons were operated by two of the mounted infantry, seated to either side of the driver. Both weapons could be quickly removed for use by the dismounted infantry squad.

The two-man turret had a 2A42 30mm automatic cannon, stabilised in both vertical and horizontal planes. It had high elevation and was capable of engaging helicopters as well as ground targets. An infra-red searchlight was fitted, and a 7.62mm PKT machine gun was mounted co-axially with the cannon. An AT-4 Spigot or AT-5 Spandrel ATGM launcher was mounted on the turret roof. Each side of the turret had three 81mm smoke grenade dischargers, and the vehicle could also produce smoke by injecting fuel into the exhaust manifold.

The BMD-3 vehicle crew consisted of driver, gunner, and commander, although the commander normally dismounted with the infantry. Four infantry were carried: two in the front, who operated the AG-17 and RPKS, and two in the rear, who were provided with firing ports in the hull. An extra three infantry could be carried for short distances; these were placed immediately to the rear of the turret, with the roof hatch open.

Like earlier BMD models, the BMD-3 was air-portable, air-droppable, and had full NBC protection. The amphibious capabilities of the BMD-3 were significantly greater than the earlier models—hence the adoption of the vehicle by the naval infantry.

Specifications: BMD-3

Crew: 3 + 4 passengers
Combat weight: 13,200kg
Length: 6.36m
Width: 3.13m
Height: 2.17m
Ground clearance: 0.45m
Maximum road speed: 70km/hour
Maximum road range: 500km
Gradient: 60%
Vertical obstacle: 0.6m
Armour: Proof against small arms and shell splinters

Armament:

1x 2A42 30mm cannon (860 rounds)
1x 7.62mm PKT MG (2,000 rounds)
1x AT-4 Spigot or AT-5 Spandrel ATGM (1 + 4 missiles)
1x AG-17 30mm automatic grenade launcher (550 rounds)
1x 5.45mm RPKS MG (2,160 rounds)

BMP-23 (Bulgaria)

When this was first spotted by the West, it was thought to be based on the 2S1 self-propelled howitzer. In fact, it was based on the MT-LB, which shares many automotive parts with the 2S1.

The welded hull and turret had sufficient armour to provide protection against small arms fire and shell splinters. The driver sat at the front on the left, with one of the infantry squad to his right. He was provided with a hatch cover and three periscopes, one of which could be replaced with a passive night-vision device.

The engine compartment was immediately behind these two men, with roof hatches for access. Behind the engine, a two-man power-operated turret was fitted. The gunner sat in the left of the turret, and the commander in the right. The main armament was an unstabilised 23mm cannon of the same type as used on the ZU-23-2 AA gun. A 7.62mm PKT machine gun was mounted co-axially. A launcher for an AT-3 Sagger ATGM was mounted on the turret roof. This could be fired from within the turret, and a further three missiles were carried as reloads. The gunner had passive night sights, and the commander had a night searchlight, controlled from within the turret.

The BMP-23 could carry six men in the rear infantry compartment, accessed via a pair of rear doors or two roof hatches. Eight firing ports were provided in the rear compartment, three on each side, and one in each door.

The BMP-23 was fully amphibious, propelled in the water by its tracks. Before entering the water, bilge pumps were switched on, the trim vane erected, and the driver's periscope replaced by an extendable one that enabled him to see over the trim vane. It had NBC protection and could lay a smokescreen by injecting diesel into the exhaust.

SPECIFICATIONS: BMP-23

Crew: 3 + 7 passengers
Combat weight: 15,200kg
Length: 7.29m
Width: 2.85m
Height: 2.53m
Ground clearance: 0.4m
Maximum road speed: 61.5km/hour
Maximum road range: 600km
Gradient: 60%
Vertical obstacle: 0.8m
Trench: 2.5m

Armour: Proof against small arms and shell splinters

ARMAMENT:

1x 23mm 2A14 cannon (600 rounds)
1x 7.62mm PKT MG (2,000 rounds)
1x AT-3 Sagger ATGM (1 + 3 missiles)

MLI-84 (ROMANIA)

The MLI-84 was very similar to the BMP-1, although it was larger and heavier than the Soviet vehicle. The most obvious difference was a 12.7mm anti-aircraft machine gun mounted at the right rear of the troop compartment. Where the BMP-1 had four rectangular roof hatches over the troop compartment, the MLI-84 had three. The right rear hatch was replaced with a circular hatch cover, with a 12.7mm DShKM anti-aircraft machine gun mounted on it.

The MLI-84 was fitted with an NBC system and night-vision equipment for the driver, gunner, and commander. It was fully amphibious, propelled in the water by its tracks.

SPECIFICATIONS: MLI-84

Crew: 2 + 9 passengers
Combat weight: 16,600kg
Length: 7.32m
Width: 3.15m
Height: 1.97m
Ground clearance: 0.4m
Maximum road speed: 70km/hour

ARMAMENT:

1x 73mm 2A28 gun (40 rounds)
1x 7.62mm PKT MG (2,000 rounds)

Dismounting from an MLI-84

1x AT-3 Sagger ATGM (1 + 4 missiles)
1x 12.7mm DShKM MG (500 rounds)

ARMOUR:

Hull front upper: 7mm @ 80° [Effective: 40mm]
Hull front lower: 19mm @ 57° [Effective: 35mm]
Hull side upper: 16mm @ 14° [Effective: 16mm]
Hull side lower: 18mm
Hull rear upper: 16mm @ 19° [Effective: 17mm]
Hull rear lower: 16mm @ 19° [Effective: 17mm]
Hull top: 6mm
Belly: 7mm
Turret front: 23mm @ 42° [Effective: 31mm]
Turret sides: 19mm @ 36° [Effective: 23mm]
Turret rear: 13mm @ 30° [Effective: 15mm]
Turret top: 6mm
Turret mantlet: 26-33mm

Armoured Personnel Carriers

Even after the introduction of the BMP series of infantry fighting vehicles in the late 1960s, the Soviet Union continued to produce and use armoured personnel carriers, since these were cheaper to produce and maintain than infantry fighting vehicles. The choice of wheels rather than tracks for many of the APC models made them even more cost-effective in terms of production, maintenance, and training. This, however, came at a cost of decreased off-road mobility.

BTR-40

The BTR-40 was the first mass-produced Soviet APC, and entered service in 1950, based on a lengthened GAZ-63 4x4 lorry chassis. The commander and driver sat in the front, with the eight infantrymen in the open-topped rear. Entry and exit were via two rear doors, and a tarpaulin was carried to provide protection against inclement weather. Three pintle mounts for 7.62mm SGMB machine guns were fitted on the front and sides of the troop compartment. There was no NBC protection.

In 1956, the BTR-40V added a central tyre pressure regulation system to improve off-road mobility. Later production vehicles had two or three firing ports in each side of the hull, and some vehicles had a 4,500kg capacity winch at the front. In 1957,

BTR-40

the BTR-40B was introduced. This had overhead armour for the troop compartment, but could only carry six infantrymen instead of eight.

An NBC reconnaissance variant, the BTR-40Kh, had equipment for setting marker poles with pennants into the ground while crossing contaminated areas. The BTR-40zhd, introduced in 1969, was a rail-scout variant. This was identical to the standard BTR-40, but with extra rail wheels that could be lowered for running on railway lines.

One other variant was produced for use by the East German army. This had a triple AT-3 Sagger launcher in the rear compartment, with overhead cover. This never entered front-line service, but was used as a training vehicle.

Specifications: BTR-40

Crew: 2 + 8 passengers
Combat weight: 5,300kg
Length: 5m
Width: 1.9m
Height: 1.75m
Ground clearance: 0.3m
Maximum road speed: 80km/hour
Maximum road range: 285km
Gradient: 60%
Vertical obstacle: 0.47m
Trench: 0.7m
Armament: 1-3x 7.62mm SGMB MG
Armour: 6-8mm

BTR-152

Production of the BTR-152 started in 1950, and it was accepted for service in the same year. The vehicle was based on a 6x6 lorry chassis (initially the ZIL-151, later the ZIL-157). Up to 17 men could be carried in the open-topped troop compartment, with entry and exit via two doors in the rear. A tarpaulin was carried for protection against inclement weather. The troop compartment had a total of eight firing ports, three on each side and two in the rear. There were three machine gun mounts - one at the front for a 7.62mm SGMB or 12.7mm DShKM machine gun, and one on each side for a 7.62mm SGMB machine gun. There was no NBC protection.

In 1955, the BTR-152V entered service. This was basically the same as the earlier model, but had a central tyre pressure regulation system to improve cross-country performance. In 1962, the BTR-152V1 added a front-mounted winch with a

BTR-152K

capacity of 5,000kg. The BTR-152V3 added infra-red driving lights. The BTR-152K had all the improvements included in the BTR-152V3, plus overhead armour with two roof hatches.

The command variant was designated BTR-152U. It was based on a BTR-152V1 or BTR-152V3, with overhead armour and a higher superstructure to allow command staff to stand upright. Windows were provided (two on the left, one each on the right and rear). Stowage racks were fitted to the roof, and the vehicle usually towed a trailer to carry extra equipment, such as a generator.

SPECIFICATIONS: BTR-152V1

Crew: 2 + 17 passengers
Combat weight: 8,950kg
Length: 6.83m
Width: 2.32m

Height: 2.05m
Ground clearance: 0.3m
Maximum road speed: 75km/hour
Maximum road range: 780km
Gradient: 55%
Vertical obstacle: 0.6m
Trench: 0.69m
Armament: 1x 7.62mm SGMB or 12.7mm DShKM MG

ARMOUR:
Front: 13.5mm @ 35° [Effective: 16mm]
Side: 9mm
Rear: 9mm @ 7° [Effective: 9.1mm]
Top (BTR-152K): 6mm
Belly: 4mm

BTR-50P

The BTR-50P entered production in 1954, based on the same chassis as the PT-76 light tank. It was the standard APC in tank divisions, until it was eventually replaced by the BMP series of infantry fighting vehicles. As late as 1990, there were still twenty-one BTR-50s in service with the Soviet army, all in Central Europe.

The BTR-50P was of all-welded construction, with the driver and commander seated at the front, an open-topped troop compartment for 20 infantrymen in the centre, and the engine at the rear. A pintle mount for a 7.62mm SGMB machine gun was fitted to the front of the troop compartment. There were ramps at the rear of the hull to allow an anti-tank gun or light field gun to be pulled onto the rear deck. The gun could be fired from the rear deck, even while the vehicle was swimming. The BTR-50P was fully amphibious, being propelled in the water by a pair of

BTR-50P

water jets. It had a searchlight, which could be white light or infra-red.

The BTR-50PA was a BTR-50P with the rear ramps removed, and a 14.5mm KPVT machine gun mounted over the commander's position. The BTR-50PK added overhead armour for the troop compartment, and NBC protection. Entry and exit were via roof hatches, and there were firing ports on both sides. The BTR-50PK retained the pintle mount for a 7.62mm SGMB machine gun.

The BTR-50PU was the command variant of the BTR-50. It had overhead armour and seats for four radio operators and four command staff, in addition to the two-person vehicle crew (driver and commander). It had a collapsible map table, a small table for the commander, hammocks, and thermal insulation. In addition to extra radio equipment and associated aerials, it carried four field telephones, a 10-line field telephone switchboard, and four 600m reels of telephone wire.

Specifications: BTR-50PK

Crew: 2 + 20 passengers
Combat weight: 14,200kg
Length: 7.08m
Width: 3.14m
Height: 1.97m
Ground clearance: 0.37m
Maximum road speed: 44km/hour
Maximum road range: 400km
Gradient: 70%
Vertical obstacle: 1.1m
Trench: 2.8m
Armament: 1x 7.62mm SGMB MG (1,250 rounds)
Armour: 6-10mm

BTR-60P

Following a competition between two design bureaus for a new wheeled APC to replace the BTR-152, the BTR-60P was accepted for service in 1960, for use in motor rifle divisions.

The BTR-60P was of all-welded construction, with the driver and commander seated at the front, an open-topped troop compartment in the centre, and a pair of petrol engines at the rear. A pintle mount for a 7.62mm SGMB or PK machine gun was fitted to the front of the troop compartment. Some vehicles had a 12.7mm DShKM machine gun fitted. There were mounts for 7.62mm SGMB or PK machine guns on the sides of the troop compartment. The BTR-60P was fully amphibious, being propelled in the water by a single water jet. All eight wheels were driven, and the first four were used for steering, which was power assisted. A central tyre pressure regulation system, infra-red night-vision equipment, and a front-mounted 4,500kg capacity

BTR-60PB

winch were fitted. The maximum troop capacity was 16, though normally only 12 were carried.

The BTR-60PA (sometimes referred to as the BTR-60PK), which entered service in 1963, added overhead armour and NBC protection. The roof had a large rectangular hatch at the front, with pintle mounts for machine guns to the front and sides of this hatch. Three firing ports were fitted on either side of the troop compartment. Entry and exit were via roof hatches; there were no side doors or hatches.

The BTR-60PA1 added a small one-man machine gun turret to the BTR-60PA, identical to the one fitted to the BRDM-2. This turret mounted a 14.5mm KPVT machine gun and a co-axial 7.62mm PKT machine gun. Gun elevation and turret traverse were both manual. This was closely followed by the BTR-60PB, which added other improvements, such as roof-mounted periscopes for the driver and commander, vision blocks in the troop compartment, and side hatches for improved entry and exit from the troop compartment. The addition of the turret reduced troop capacity to 14, though normally only eight infantrymen were carried.

There were several command variants of the BTR-60. The BTR-60PBK was used by company commanders, and was a BTR-60PB with additional radios. The BTR-60PU was a command variant of the BTR-60P, with a tarpaulin, map boards, and extra radios. The BTR-60PAU was a command version of the BTR-60PA, with a 10m-high aerial for use when stationary, a "clothes rail" aerial, and a generator. The BTR-60PU-12 was also based on the BTR-60PA, and operated with air-defence units. The BTR-60 ACRV was a command and observation post vehicle, which served with towed artillery batteries and battalions.

Specifications: BTR-60PB

Crew: 2 + 14 passengers (usually only eight passengers were carried)
Combat weight: 10,300kg
Length: 7.56m
Width: 2.83m
Height: 2.31m
Ground clearance: 0.48m
Maximum road speed: 80km/hour
Maximum road range: 500km
Gradient: 60%
Vertical obstacle: 0.4m
Trench: 2m
Armour: 5-9mm

Armament:
1x 14.5mm KPVT machine gun (500 rounds)
1x 7.62mm PKT machine gun (2,000 rounds)

BTR-70

The BTR-70 entered production in 1972, though it was not seen in public until 1980. Its design was similar to the BTR-60PB, but with various improvements. The armour was slightly thicker, and the front of the vehicle was redesigned to provide more protection to the front wheels. The layout was the same as the BTR-60PB, and the same turret was fitted, but two small doors were added to the sides of the troop compartment for safer entry and exit. Internal stowage for an RPG-7 light anti-tank weapon and two AGS-17 automatic grenade launchers were included. The front winch had a capacity of 6,000kg, an increase over that fitted to the BTR-60PB. Like the BTR-60PB, the BTR-70 was fitted with a central tyre pressure regulation system, infra-red night-vision equipment, and NBC protection. The BTR-70 was fully amphibious, propelled in the water by a single water jet.

Combat experience in Afghanistan led to the introduction of an improved version, the BTR-70M. This had the same turret as the BTR-80, with a higher elevation for the weapons, and six smoke grenade launchers at the rear. This model also added brackets to the sides of the hull for additional armour, and two extra firing ports between the hull sides and roof to allow embarked infantry to engage targets at high angles. In Afghanistan, some vehicles were spotted with 30mm AGS-17 automatic grenade launchers mounted on the roof, behind the driver's and commander's hatches. This was in addition to the standard turret.

An NBC reconnaissance version, the BTR-70Kh, had extra equipment for detecting contamination and marking areas. A command variant, the BTR-70KShM, had extra radio equipment.

BTR-70

SPW-70CH

This was a variant developed for the East German army by the Soviet Union. It mounted a bank of 81mm smoke grenade launchers on the back of the turret, in a similar arrangement to the BTR-80.

SPECIFICATIONS: BTR-70

Crew: 2 + 9 passengers
Combat weight: 11,500kg
Length: 7.54m
Width: 2.8m
Height: 2.32m
Ground clearance: 0.48m
Maximum road speed: 80km/hour
Maximum road range: 450km
Gradient: 60%

Vertical obstacle: 0.5m
Trench: 2m
Armour: 5-10mm

ARMAMENT:
1x 14.5mm KPVT machine gun (500 rounds)
1x 7.62mm PKT machine gun (2,000 rounds)

BTR-80

The BTR-80 was a further progression of the BTR-60PB and BTR-70, and was largely similar to the earlier vehicles. Production began in 1984, and in 1988, units started to be delivered to the naval infantry to replace their BTR-60PBs. The BTR-80 replaced the twin petrol engines of the earlier vehicles with a single V8 diesel engine, which improved speed, range, and survivability.

The BTR-80 turret was an improvement on the earlier models. Elevation was increased from +30° to +60°, a new sight was fitted, and it had a bank of six smoke grenade dischargers at the rear. This new turret was designed to allow engagement of helicopters and targets on high ground. Compared to earlier vehicles, the BTR-80 was better able to withstand punishment. Experience in Afghanistan showed that anti-tank mines would usually only damage one wheel, and that the vehicle could continue to be driven on the other seven wheels.

The troop compartment had larger doors between the second and third axles, further improving ease of entry and exit for the vehicle's seven infantry. There were three firing ports in the side of the hull, angled forward. The front two ports were for use with the 7.62mm PK machine gun, while the others were for use with AKMS or AK-74 assault rifles. Each of the two roof hatches also had a firing port. The BTR-80 normally carried an AGS-17

BTR-80

automatic grenade launcher and a gripstock for a man-portable SAM system (SA-14 Gremlin, SA-16 Gimlet or SA-18 Grouse), with two missiles.

The BTR-80 had a front winch with a capacity of 6,000kg (which could be increased to 12,000kg with the aid of a pulley). It had a central tyre pressure regulation system, infra-red night-vision equipment, and NBC protection, including chemical and radiological reconnaissance devices. It was fully amphibious, propelled in the water by a single water jet.

SPECIFICATIONS: BTR-80

Crew: 2 + 10 passengers
Combat weight: 13,600kg
Length: 7.65m
Width: 2.9m
Height: 2.41m
Ground clearance: 0.48m

Maximum road speed: 90km/hour
Maximum road range: 600km
Gradient: 60%
Vertical obstacle: 0.5m
Trench: 2m
Armour: Proof against 12.7mm AP rounds

ARMAMENT:
1x 14.5mm KPVT machine gun (500 rounds)
1x 7.62mm PKT machine gun (2,000 rounds)

BTR-D

The BTR-D was based on a lengthened BMD-1 chassis, and was accepted for service in 1974 for use with the airborne forces. Like the BMD-1, it had a welded aluminium hull with front and side firing ports. The driver sat in the centre of the vehicle at the front, with an infantryman on either side of him operating the two 7.62mm PKT machine guns. A further ten infantrymen could be carried in the troop compartment to the rear, entering and exiting via a pair of rear doors. Four smoke grenade dischargers were fitted, two on each side of the hull. Some vehicles had a 30mm AGS-17 automatic grenade launcher fitted on a pintle mount. The BTR-D had NBC protection and was fully amphibious.

Two command variants were made. The BMD-KShM had a large "clothes rail" aerial around the superstructure, extra radios, no firing ports, and no smoke grenade dischargers. The BMD-1E was similar, but had a large telescopic aerial instead of the "clothes rail" aerial.

BTR-D prepared for parachute drop

SPECIFICATIONS: BTR-D

Crew: 1 + 12 passengers
Combat weight: 8,000kg
Length: 5.89m
Width: 2.63m
Height: 1.67m
Ground clearance: 0.1-0.45m
Maximum road speed: 60km/hour
Maximum road range: 500km
Armament: 2x 7.62mm PKT machine guns

ARMOUR:
Hull front upper: 15mm @ 78° [Effective: 72mm]
Hull front lower: 15mm @ 50° [Effective: 23mm]
Hull side: 10mm
Hull rear: 10mm

MT-LB

The MT-LB entered production in the early 1970s, and was used in various roles, including artillery prime mover and cargo carrier, as well as armoured personnel carrier.

The hull was made of welded steel armour, with the two-man crew seated at the front, engine immediately behind the crew, and troop/cargo compartment at the rear. There were twin doors at the rear of the vehicle. The driver sat to the left, with the commander (who also operated the small machine gun turret) to his right. The manually operated turret mounted a single 7.62mm PKT machine gun. Firing ports were fitted on each side of the rear compartment and in each of the rear doors.

The MT-LB was amphibious, propelled in the water by its tracks. It had NBC protection, a white/infra-red searchlight, and an infra-red periscope for the driver. It could carry up to 11 men or 6,500kg of cargo in the rear compartment, or tow a trailer or weapon weighing up to 6,500kg.

The SNAR-10 was an MT-LB with a Big Fred radar on a rotating mount at the rear of the vehicle. Initially thought by NATO to be an artillery radar location system, it was actually a battlefield surveillance radar. In 1982 the SNAR-10M was introduced. It was not amphibious, but retained the machine gun turret and NBC protection. In addition, it had extra communications equipment, an auxiliary power unit, a heater, and a navigation system.

The MT-LBV variant had wider tracks (565mm instead of the usual 350mm). The wider tracks reduced ground pressure from 0.46kg/cm2 to 0.28kg/cm2, and so this model was often used on snow and swampy ground. It was sometimes fitted with a 12.7mm NSVT machine gun in the turret instead of the usual 7.62mm PKT machine gun.

MT-LB

The MT-LB AT artillery tractor had ammunition stowage racks on the left side of the rear compartment. The ADZM was an engineer variant used in airborne brigades. This had a bulldozer blade, and an arm with a bucket was mounted on the roof. The MT-LBU was a command variant, with extra radios, a generator, and a navigation system. An ambulance variant had stretchers in the rear compartment.

The Poles made a variant fitted with the WAT turret (as fitted on the OT-64 and some OT-62 variants). This turret had a 14.5mm KPVT and a 7.62mm PKT machine gun.

SPECIFICATIONS: MT-LB

Crew: 2 + 11 passengers
Combat weight: 11,900kg
Maximum payload: 2,000kg
Maximum towed load: 6,500kg
Length: 6.45m

Width: 2.86m
Height: 1.87m
Ground clearance: 0.4m
Maximum road speed: 62km/hour
Maximum road range: 500km
Gradient: 60%
Vertical obstacle: 0.6m
Trench: 2.41m
Armament: 1x 7.62mm PKT machine gun (2,500 rounds)
Armour: 4-10mm

OT-810 (Czechoslovakia)

During the Second World War, the Skoda plant in Pilsen manufactured the German Sdkfz 251 half-tracked armoured personnel carrier. Production continued after the war ended, but was stopped when the communists took power. In the mid-1950s the Czech army was looking for an armoured personnel carrier to use instead of the Soviet BTR-152. A modified version of the Sdkfz 251, designed by Tatra, was selected. The modifications included an armoured roof and a new Tatra 120hp diesel engine to replace the original petrol engine.

The hull was made of welded steel, with the engine at the front. The commander and driver were seated behind the engine, in the centre of the vehicle, with the driver on the left. The commander was provided with a pintle-mounted 7.62mm machine gun. Both commander and driver had to access their positions via the troop compartment.

The troop compartment was at the rear, with a pair of doors at the back of the vehicle for entry and exit. Two roof hatches opened to either side of the hull. The OT-810 had no NBC capability, night-vision equipment, or amphibious capability. The

M59A mounted on OT-810

vehicle wasn't a great success, and was unpopular with the troops, earning the nickname "Hitler's Revenge".

The OT-810 was often used as a tow vehicle for the 82mm M59A recoilless gun. After the OT-64 had replaced the OT-810 in the APC role, OT-810s were modified to mount the M59A as a self-propelled gun system. In this variant, the M59A was mounted in the troop compartment, with armoured shields to the front and sides. These could be folded down when the gun was in use. The M59A had a traverse of 90°, when mounted in this way, an elevation of 25°, and a depression of 5°. The troop compartment's rear doors were replaced with a single hatch, which lowered to a horizontal position, giving more room for the gun crew.

The M59A could be removed and used from a ground mount with a traverse of 360°. HEAT and HE ammunition were carried, and there were sights for both indirect and direct fire. A spotting rifle was fitted to help with aiming in the direct fire role.

SPECIFICATIONS: OT-810

Crew: 2 + 10 passengers
Combat weight: 8,500kg
Length: 5.8m
Width: 2.1m
Height: 1.75m
Ground clearance: 0.3m
Maximum road speed: 53km/hour
Maximum road range: 320km
Gradient: 50%
Vertical obstacle: 0.26m
Trench: 1.98m
Armament: 1x 7.62mm machine gun

ARMOUR:
Hull front: 12mm
Hull side: 7mm

OT-62 (CZECHOSLOVAKIA/POLAND)

The OT-62 was jointly developed by Czechoslovakia and Poland, and was similar to the BTR-50P, the main physical difference being a pair of cylindrical bays projecting to the front. In comparison to the Soviet vehicle, the OT-62 had a more powerful engine, overhead armour, and NBC protection. It entered Czech service in 1964, and Polish service (where it was known as the TOPAS) in 1966. Both countries deployed the tracked OT-62 with tank divisions, while motor rifle divisions were equipped with the wheeled OT-64.

OT-62B. The recoilless gun is not fitted, but the mountings are visible

The OT-62 had an all-welded hull, with the crew compartment at the front and the engine at the rear. The driver sat in the middle, with a single-piece hatch cover fitted with an integral vision block. The commander sat in the left projecting bay, and was provided with a cupola that could be traversed by hand through a full 360°. Both projecting bays at the front of the vehicle were fitted with observation periscopes.

Access to the troop compartment was by a pair of large doors, one on each side of the vehicle. Each door had an observation/firing port, and each side had an additional port forward of the door. Two large rectangular hatches were fitted in the roof of the troop compartment.

The engine was behind the troop compartment, with access panels in the roof for maintenance. An automatic fire-suppression system was fitted in the engine compartment, which could be manually activated if required.

The OT-62 was fully amphibious, propelled in the water by a pair of water jets at the rear of the hull. Before entering the water, bilge pumps were switched on and a trim vane erected at the front. An over-pressure NBC system was fitted, and an infra-red driving light was mounted at the front right of the vehicle. The initial version, the OT-62A, was unarmed, although an M59A recoilless gun could be carried on, and fired from, the rear deck.

The OT-62B was only used by the Czech army, and was fitted with the same manually-operated turret as the OT-65A, mounted on top of the right bay. This had a 7.62mm M59T machine gun, with an 82mm T-21 recoilless gun mounted externally on the right side. An infra-red searchlight was mounted to the right of the recoilless gun. The T-21 could be aimed and fired from inside the turret, but could only be reloaded from outside. It had a maximum range of 2,500m, although the effective range was significantly less, at 300m to 450m. The 82mm HEAT projectile could penetrate up to 230mm of armour.

The TOPAS-2AP (sometimes referred to as the OT-62C) was only used by the Polish army. This mounted the same small turret as the OT-64C in the centre of the hull, reducing the space in the troop compartment. This turret was similar to the one fitted on the Soviet BTR-60PB and BRDM-2, mounting a 14.5mm KPVT and 7.62mm PKT machine gun. The TOPAS-2AP was often used to carry a pair of 82mm mortars and their four-man crews.

SPECIFICATIONS: OT-62B (TOPAS-2AP IN BRACKETS)

Crew: 2 + 18 passengers (2 + 12 passengers)
Combat weight: 15,000kg (16,390kg)
Length: 7.08m (7m)
Width: 3.14m (3.23m)
Height: 2.23m (2.73m)

Ground clearance: 0.37m (0.43m)
Maximum road speed: 58km/hour (60km/hour)
Maximum road range: 460km (570km)
Gradient: 65%
Vertical obstacle: 1.1m
Trench: 2.8m

Armament (OT-62B):
1x 7.62mm M59T machine gun (1,250 rounds)
1x 82mm T-21 recoilless gun (12 rounds)

Armament (TOPAS-2AP):
1x 14.5mm KPVT machine gun (500 rounds)
1x 7.62mm PKT machine gun (2,000 rounds)

Armour:
Hull front upper: 8mm @ 83° [Effective: 66mm]
Hull front lower: 10mm @ 53° [Effective: 17mm]
Hull side upper: 10mm
Hull side lower: 9mm
Hull rear upper: 7mm
Hull rear lower: 6mm @ 42° [Effective: 8mm]
Hull top: 7mm @ 86° [Effective: 100mm]
Belly: 6mm

OT-64/SKOT (Czechoslovakia/Poland)

Czechoslovakia and Poland began development of the OT-64 (SKOT in Poland) in 1959, and it entered service in 1964. The Czech company Tatra provided the chassis and automotive parts, many of which were the same as those used in the Tatra 813 series of lorries. FSC/Lubin of Poland provided the armoured body and weapon systems. It bore some resemblance to the Soviet BTR-60, though with notable differences.

OT-64C

The hull was welded steel, with the crew compartment at the front, the engine behind the crew, and the troop compartment at the rear. The driver sat on the left with the commander to his right, each with a side door and roof hatch. A searchlight was fitted to the roof between the hatches, and could be operated from inside the crew compartment.

Unlike the BTR-60, the OT-64 was powered by a single diesel engine. A pair of doors in the rear of the hull were the usual passenger entry/exit point, although there were also roof hatches, which could be locked in the vertical position if required. Firing ports were provided to the rear and sides, and the seats could be folded away to allow the vehicle to carry cargo instead of infantry.

Power steering was provided to the front four wheels, and all eight wheels had a tyre pressure regulation system. It was fully amphibious, with a pair of propellers at the rear of the hull providing propulsion in the water. A trim vane, which normally rested on the glacis, was erected before entering the water. An NBC protection system was also fitted, as well as a winch, and bilge pumps for use when swimming.

The original version was fully enclosed, with five roof hatches. Initially unarmed, it was later fitted with a 7.62mm machine gun on a pintle mount at the front of the troop compartment. Some models have been seen with a pair of AT-3 Sagger ATGMs mounted over the troop compartment.

The SKOT-2 was only used by Poland, and may have been a temporary measure pending delivery of the OT-64C. It had a square plinth with a 7.62mm or 12.7mm machine gun. The machine gun had a shield to provide the gunner with protection to the front.

The OT-64C (SKOT-2A) had an eight-sided plinth in the centre of the vehicle, and the five roof hatches over the troop compartment were reduced to four. A one-man, manually operated turret was mounted on the plinth. This turret was similar to that fitted on the Soviet BTR-60PB and BRDM-2, mounting a 14.5mm KPVT and 7.62mm PKT machine gun. Some vehicles had a pair of AT-3 Sagger missiles mounted on the turret, one on each side.

The SKOT-2AP was only used by Poland, and mounted a new turret with a curved top. It had the same armament as the OT-64C, but the weapons had an elevation of 89.5°, allowing them to be used against helicopters. Some turrets have been seen with a pair of AT-3 Sagger ATGMs fitted.

There were several command variants of the OT-64, with extra radios and aerials.

SPECIFICATIONS: OT-64C/SKOT-2A

Crew: 2 + 10 passengers
Combat weight: 14,500kg
Length: 7.44m
Width: 2.55m
Height: 2.71m
Ground clearance: 0.46m
Maximum road speed: 94km/hour
Maximum road range: 710km

Gradient: 60%
Vertical obstacle: 0.5m
Trench: 2m

Armament:
1x 14.5mm KPVT machine gun (500 rounds)
1x 7.62mm PKT machine gun (2,000 rounds)

Armour (max):
Hull: 10mm
Turret: 14mm

PSZH-IV (Hungary)

Initially, NATO mistakenly classified this vehicle as an amphibious scout car, and labelled it FÚG-66, then FÚG-70. Later, it was discovered to be an armoured personnel carrier. It was generally referred to in the West as the PSZH-IV, but the Hungarian designation was PSZH D-944.

The cross-country capability was not as good as the Soviet BTR series and Czech/Polish OT series, and it carried fewer passengers. Despite these shortcomings, it was adopted by the Hungarian army in preference to foreign imports.

The driver and commander sat at the front, each with a hatch and windscreen. The hatch covers were fitted with vision blocks for use when the hatches were closed. Each side of the vehicle had a two-piece door, four vision blocks, and two firing ports for the passengers. Six infantrymen could be carried in addition to the crew.

A small turret was fitted in the centre of the vehicle. It was similar to that on the BRDM-2, but not identical. The turret had a day periscope and a ventilator fan. The diesel engine was fitted behind the turret.

The PSZH-IV was fully amphibious. A trim board stowed on the glacis was erected before entering the water, where the vehicle was propelled by a pair of water jets at the rear of the hull. It was fitted with NBC protection, a powered winch, and a central tyre pressure regulation system. Night-vision equipment included infra-red driving lights and an infra-red searchlight mounted co-axially to the right of the main armament. Armament consisted of a 14.5mm KPVT machine gun with a 7.62mm PKT machine gun mounted co-axially.

Variants included a version without a turret, which was used for command, ambulance, and NBC reconnaissance. A second command version had a turret, but did not carry infantry. A turreted NBC reconnaissance version also existed, with similar equipment to the Soviet BRDM-2-RKha.

Specifications: PSZH-IV

Crew: 3 + 6 passengers
Combat weight: 7,600kg
Length: 5.7m
Width: 2.5m
Height: 2.31m
Ground clearance: 0.42m
Maximum road speed: 80km/hour
Maximum road range: 500km
Gradient: 60%
Vertical obstacle: 0.4m
Trench: 0.6m
Armour (max): 14mm

Armament:
1x 14.5mm KPVT machine gun (500 rounds)
1x 7.62mm PKT machine gun (2,000 rounds)

TAB-71 (ROMANIA)

The TAB-71 was a licence-built copy of the BTR-60PB, and so was very similar to the Soviet vehicle. The central tyre pressure regulation system, winch, amphibious capability, and NBC protection remained. The engines were replaced with more powerful 140hp versions, leading to an increase in speed. A large hatch was added to each side in the centre, above the second/third road wheels.

The TAB-71M replaced the original turret with a new, locally-designed one. This had the same armament of 14.5mm KPVT and co-axial 7.62mm PKT, but added a day gunsight on the left side, with a distinctive protective cage.

A mortar carrier variant, the TAB-71AR, had no turret, and carried an 82mm mortar, fired through the open roof hatches. This variant had a PKMS machine gun fitted at the rear of the vehicle, operated by opening a roof hatch.

Specifications: TAB-71

Crew: 3 + 8 passengers
Combat weight: 11,000kg
Length: 7.22m
Width: 2.83m
Height: 2.7m
Ground clearance: 0.47m
Maximum road speed: 95km/hour
Maximum road range: 500km
Gradient: 60%
Vertical obstacle: 0.4m
Trench: 2m

TAB-71M

ARMAMENT:
1x 14.5mm KPVT machine gun (500 rounds)
1x 7.62mm PKT machine gun (2,000 rounds)

ARMOUR:
Hull: 9mm max
Turret: 7mm max

TAB-77 (ROMANIA)

This was a Romanian-designed copy of the Soviet BTR-70, with some differences. Designed in the 1970s, production started in 1978. The TAB-77 had a pair of diesel engines in place of the BTR-70's petrol engines. Internal layout was similar to the Soviet vehicle, and it had the same turret as the TAB-71. The commander was provided with a roof-mounted searchlight that could be operated from inside the vehicle.

Like the BTR-70, it was fully amphibious. Before entering the water, a trim vane was erected at the front and bilge pumps were switched on. This could be done by the driver from his seat. A single water jet provided propulsion in the water.

The TAB-77 had NBC protection, infra-red night-vision equipment, automatic fire detection and suppression systems,

TAB-77

power steering, central tyre pressure regulation, and an engine preheater. A 5,500kg capacity winch was fitted at the front.

SPECIFICATIONS: TAB-77

Crew: 2 + 9 passengers
Combat weight: 13,350kg
Length: 7.42m
Width: 2.95m
Height: 2.32m
Ground clearance: 0.53m
Maximum road speed: 83km/hour
Maximum road range: 550km
Gradient: 60%
Vertical obstacle: 0.5m
Trench: 2m
Armour: 5-10mm

ARMAMENT:
1x 14.5mm KPVT machine gun (600 rounds)
1x 7.62mm PKT machine gun (2,500 rounds)

MLVM Mountaineers Combat Vehicle (Romania)

The MLVM was specifically designed to carry seven men and its crew of two in mountainous terrain. It could also be used to carry logistical stores such as ammunition. Construction was of welded steel, with armour sufficient to provide protection against small arms and shell splinters.

The driver sat at the front left, and was provided with a roof hatch and three day periscopes, one of which could be replaced with a night-vision device. The commander, sitting behind the driver, also had a roof hatch and three day periscopes. One of the commander's periscopes could be raised for forward observation, and he had an infra-red searchlight.

A turret, the same design as that on the TAB-71M, was fitted in the centre, with the troop compartment to its rear. Troop compartment entry and exit was through a pair of roof hatches or a door in the rear of the vehicle. One passenger would man the turret, with six in the troop compartment, sat facing outwards, each with a firing port and periscope. Two firing ports and periscopes were also fitted in the rear door. The MLVM was amphibious, propelled in the water by its tracks.

Specifications: MLVM

Crew: 2 + 7 passengers
Combat weight: 9,000kg
Length: 5.85m
Width: 2.71m
Height: 1.95m
Ground clearance: 0.38m
Maximum road speed: 48km/hour
Maximum road range: 700km

Gradient: 60%
Vertical obstacle: 0.6m
Trench: 1.5m
Armour: Proof against small arms and shell splinters

ARMAMENT:
1x 14.5mm KPVT machine gun (600 rounds)
1x 7.62mm PKT machine gun (2,500 rounds)

Anti-Tank Vehicles

With the introduction of anti-tank guided missiles in the 1950s, most Soviet anti-tank vehicles switched to missile armament, the notable exception being vehicles intended for the airborne forces. The introduction of the BMD provided the airborne forces with useful anti-tank firepower, and so development of gun-armed tank destroyers stopped altogether.

There were rumours of a tank destroyer designated the IT-130, based on a T-62 tank chassis and armed with an 130mm gun. This was "revealed" to the West by a defector, the former GRU agent known as Viktor Suvorov (real name Vladimir Rezun). It was claimed to mount a 130mm gun in an armoured superstructure on a T-62 chassis. The claim was eventually discovered to be completely fictitious, although Suvorov's motive remains unknown. He may have been trying to spread disinformation, or simply trying to please his investigators.

A design for a self-propelled 130mm gun, the ISU-130, did exist. Development of this vehicle, which was fitted with an adapted 130mm naval gun, started toward the end of the Second World War, and was abandoned after the war ended. There were several problems with the design, and it did not enter production.

SU-100

The SU-100 entered service in 1944, and remained in production until 1953 in the Soviet Union, and 1956 in Czechoslovakia. The welded hull housed the fighting compartment at the front, with the engine at the rear. The driver sat at the front left, and had a large hatch that opened upwards, with vision blocks for use when closed up. The gunner was positioned behind the driver, and had a hatch with an observation periscope, in addition to the gun sight. The loader was stationed at the rear of the fighting compartment, and the commander was seated to the right of the gun. He had a cupola with a periscope that could be turned through 360°.

Four long-range fuel tanks could be fitted, two on each side. The SU-100 had no night-vision equipment, NBC protection, or amphibious capability. Armament was a 100mm D-10S gun, developed from a naval gun, which was mounted to the right of the centre line. Elevation and traverse were manual, and it was not fitted with a fume extractor or muzzle brake.

A follow-on vehicle was developed, based on the T-44 chassis. This was armed with a 100mm D-10T gun, with the engine at the front and the fighting compartment at the rear. It did not enter production. A command variant, with armament removed, was produced in small numbers. This had space for map boards, seats for command staff, and additional radios.

SPECIFICATIONS: SU-100

Crew: 4
Combat weight: 31.6 tonnes
Length: 6.19m (9.45m including gun)
Width: 3.05m
Height: 2.24m

SU-100

Ground clearance: 0.4m
Maximum road speed: 55km/hour
Maximum road range: 300km
Gradient: 60%
Vertical obstacle: 0.73m
Trench: 2.5m
Armament: 1x 100mm D-10S gun (34 rounds)

ARMOUR:
Hull front upper: 78mm @ 50° [Effective: 121mm]
Hull front lower: 45mm @ 60° [Effective: 90mm]
Hull sides upper: 45mm @ 20° [Effective: 48mm]
Hull sides lower: 45mm
Hull top: 18-22mm
Belly: 18-22mm
Hull rear: 47mm @ 50° [Effective: 73mm]
Mantlet: 75mm

SU-122-54

Design of the SU-122-54 (sometimes erroneously referred to as the IT-122, which was another invention of Suvorov's) began in 1949, and it was accepted for service in 1954. The unusual "-54" suffix was added to the designation to avoid confusion with the wartime SU-122 self-propelled howitzer. It was only in production for two years (1955-1956), and fewer than 100 vehicles were built.

The SU-122-54 was based on a T-54 chassis, with a D-49 122mm gun mounted in a superstructure situated at the front, and equipped with a double-baffle muzzle brake and fume extractor. Two KPVT 14.5mm machine guns were fitted: one co-axial with the main armament, one mounted on the loader's hatch for use against aircraft.

Specifications: SU-122-54/IT-122

Crew: 5
Combat weight: 36 tonnes
Length: 6m (9.97m including gun)
Width: 3.27m
Height: 2.06m
Ground clearance: 0.43m
Maximum road speed: 48km/hour
Maximum road range: 400km
Gradient: 58%
Vertical obstacle: 0.73m
Trench: 2.7m

Armament:
1x 122mm D-49 gun (35 rounds)
2x 14.5mm KPVT MG (600 rounds)

Armour:
Front: 100mm @ 55° [Effective: 174mm]
Side: 80mm @ 17° [Effective: 84mm]
Top: 20mm
Belly: 20mm

ASU-57

The ASU-57 was specifically designed to be very light, for service with the airborne divisions. It entered service in 1950, initially carried under the wings in special aluminium containers. When larger transport aircraft were developed, it was carried inside, and parachuted from the rear door on a special pallet.

Initially made of steel, aluminium was later used, resulting in a significant decrease in weight. The engine and transmission were at the front of the vehicle, with the open-topped crew compartment at the rear. The driver and loader sat to the right of the gun. The commander/gunner sat to the left, with the fuel tank and ammunition behind him. More ammunition was held behind the loader's position. A tarpaulin was carried for use in inclement weather.

Armament consisted of a Ch-51 or Ch-51M 57mm gun. The Ch-51 was recognisable by the long, multi-slotted muzzle brake. The more common Ch-51M had a conventional double-baffle muzzle brake.

Specifications: ASU-57

Crew: 3
Combat weight: 3.4 tonnes
Length: 3.48m (with gun)
Width: 2.8m
Height: 1.18m

ASU-57 with Ch-51 gun

Maximum road speed: 45km/hour
Maximum road range: 250km
Armament: 1x 57mm Ch-51 or Ch-51M gun (30 rounds)
Armour: 6mm

ASU-85

Development of the ASU-85 started in the 1950s as a replacement for the ASU-57, and it entered production in 1960. The chassis was based on a heavily modified PT-76 chassis. The hull was all-welded, with the fighting compartment at the front and engine at the rear. The driver sat at the front of the vehicle on the right, with the commander behind him. The gunner and loader were both seated to the left of the main armament.

ASU-85

The main armament was a D-70 85mm gun with a co-axial 7.62mm SGMT machine gun. An infra-red searchlight was mounted over the main armament, moving in elevation and traverse with the gun. Later vehicles were fitted with a 12.7mm DShKM machine gun mounted on the roof, and some vehicles were fitted with smoke grenade dischargers at the rear of the hull, firing over the frontal arc.

The ASU-85 was air-portable, but because of the significant increase in weight compared to the ASU-57, could not be dropped by parachute. It had NBC protection for the crew, but was not amphibious. It was later replaced in service by the BMD-1.

Specifications: ASU-85

Crew: 4
Combat weight: 15.5 tonnes
Length: 6m (8.49m including gun)
Width: 2.8m
Height: 2.1m
Maximum road speed: 45km/hour
Maximum road range: 230km
Armour: 40-45mm

Armament:
1x 85mm D-70 gun (45 rounds)
1x 7.62mm SGMT MG (2,000 rounds)
1x 12.7mm DShKM MG (later vehicles)

2P26

The first Soviet anti-tank guided missile, the AT-1 Snapper, used manual command to line-of-sight guidance, with a wire link to transmit guidance commands to the missile. It was too large and heavy for a man-portable launcher, and so vehicular launchers were developed. The first of these, the 2P26, was a modified UAZ-69 light lorry and entered service in the late 1950s. It was sometimes referred to as the "Baby Carriage".

Four missiles were mounted on launch rails fitted behind the cab and covered with a canvas top. The launch rails pointed vertically upwards during transit, and were rotated to a near-horizontal position for firing. Two crew (driver and gunner) were seated in the cab. The gunner's seat faced to the rear, and both driver and gunner were provided with rear-facing sights. The guidance system could be deployed up to 30m away from the vehicle to allow remote firing.

2P26

Specifications: 2P26

Weight: 2.18 tonnes
Length: 3.85m
Width: 1.85m
Height: 2.03m
Maximum road speed: 90km/hour
Armament: 4x AT-1 missiles

Specifications: AT-1

Guidance: MCLOS (wire link)
Range: 500-2,000m
Length: 1.15m
Diameter: 136mm
Weight: 22.5kg
Warhead: 5.4kg HEAT
Penetration: 300mm

2P27

The 2P27 entered service in 1960, based on a BRDM-1 chassis. Three AT-1 missiles were mounted on retractable launch

2P27

rails. To fire, overhead covers were removed and placed on the side of the vehicle, a flap in the rear of the superstructure was opened, and the launch rails were raised. The guidance unit could be detached, allowing the gunner to be sited up to 50m away from the vehicle. The large size of the missile meant that on-board reloads could not be carried.

SPECIFICATIONS: BRDM-1

Crew: 5
Unloaded weight: 5,600kg
Length: 5.7m
Width: 2.25m
Height: 1.9m
Ground clearance: 0.315m
Maximum road speed: 80km/hour
Maximum road cruising range: 500km
Gradient: 60%

Vertical obstacle: 0.4m
Trench: 1.22m
Armament: 3x AT-1 missiles
Armour (max): 10mm

Specifications: AT-1

Guidance: MCLOS (wire link)
Range: 500-2,000m
Length: 1.15m
Diameter: 136mm
Weight: 22.5kg
Warhead: 5.4kg HEAT
Penetration: 300mm

2P32

In 1962, the 2P32 entered service. Like the 2P27, the 2P32 was based on the BRDM-1, but carried the AT-2 Swatter instead of the AT-1 Snapper. The smaller wingspan of the newer missile meant that four, rather than three, missiles were carried. As with the 2P27, no reload missiles were carried.

Specifications: BRDM-1

Crew: 5
Unloaded weight: 5,600kg
Length: 5.7m
Width: 2.25m
Height: 1.9m
Ground clearance: 0.315m
Maximum road speed: 80km/hour
Maximum road cruising range: 500km
Gradient: 60%

Vertical obstacle: 0.4m
Trench: 1.22m
Armament: 4x AT-2 missiles
Armour (max): 10mm

Specifications: AT-2

Guidance: MCLOS (radio link)
Range: 500-2,500m
Length: 1.16m
Diameter: 148mm
Weight: 27kg
Warhead: 5.4kg HEAT
Penetration: 500mm

9P110

In 1963, the 9P110 entered service, with six AT-3 Sagger anti-tank missiles mounted on a BRDM-1 chassis. It used a new mounting, which was raised as a whole to fire, without first removing the armoured cover. This significantly reduced the time required to prepare for firing.

The smaller size of the AT-3 missile allowed eight reload missiles to be carried inside the vehicle. The guidance unit could be removed from the vehicle and operated from up to 80m away, allowing the gunner to avoid return fire directed at the launch point.

Specifications: BRDM-1

Crew: 5
Unloaded weight: 5,600kg
Length: 5.7m
Width: 2.25m

Tanks and Combat Vehicles of the Warsaw Pact | 103

9P110

Height: 1.9m
Ground clearance: 0.315m
Maximum road speed: 80km/hour
Maximum road cruising range: 500km
Gradient: 60%
Vertical obstacle: 0.4m
Trench: 1.22m
Armament: 6x AT-3 missiles (plus eight reloads)
Armour (max): 10mm

Specifications: AT-3

Guidance: MCLOS (wire link)
Range: 500-3,000m
Length: 860mm
Diameter: 125mm

Weight: 10.9kg
Warhead: 2.6kg HEAT
Penetration: 200mm @ 60° (later warheads increase this to 520mm)

IT-1

The IT-1 was a missile-armed tank destroyer based on a T-62 chassis. It had a limited production run and was in service from 1968 to 1970. A low turret was fitted, which incorporated a pop-up launcher for the 3M7 Drakon anti-tank missile with 12 reload missiles in an autoloader. Three further missiles were carried, but had to be manually loaded. A 7.62mm PKT machine gun was mounted in the turret. The vehicle had a crew of three: driver, gunner, and commander.

The 3M7 system used SACLOS guidance, with a radio link to send guidance commands to the missile. Night-vision equipment was fitted, but was only useful up to a range of around 600m, severely limiting the useful range of the missile at night.

Specifications: IT-1 Vehicle

Crew: 3
Combat weight: 34.5 tonnes
Length: 6.63m
Width: 3.3m
Height: 2.2m
Ground clearance: 0.43m
Maximum road speed: 50km/hour
Maximum road range: 470km
Gradient: 60%
Vertical obstacle: 0.8m
Trench: 2.85m

IT-1

ARMAMENT:

1x 3M7 Drakon ATGM (plus 15 reloads)

1x 7.62mm PKT MG (2,000 rounds)

ARMOUR:

Hull front upper: 102mm @ 60° [Effective: 204mm]

Hull front lower: 102mm @ 54° [Effective: 174mm]

Hull side upper: 79mm

Hull side lower: 15mm

Hull rear: 46mm

Hull top: 31mm

Belly: 20mm

Turret front: 206mm

SPECIFICATIONS: 3M7 DRAKON

Guidance: SACLOS (radio link)

Range: 300-3,300m (300-600m at night)

Length: 1.24m

Diameter: 180mm
Weight: 54kg
Warhead: 5.8kg HEAT
Penetration: 250mm @ 60°

9P124

First seen in 1973, this was a BRDM-2 with the turret removed. Four AT-2 Swatter C missiles were carried on launch rails, attached to the underside of an armoured, retractable roof. The launch assembly was lowered into the vehicle for travelling, and raised for firing. The Swatter C used semi-automatic command to line-of-sight guidance, with an infra-red link to transmit guidance commands to the missile. Four reload missiles were carried within the vehicle.

SPECIFICATIONS: BRDM-2

Crew: 4
Combat weight: 7,000kg
Length: 5.75m
Width: 2.35m
Height: 2.31m
Ground clearance: 0.43m
Maximum road speed: 100km/hour
Maximum road range: 750km
Gradient: 60%
Vertical obstacle: 0.4m
Trench: 1.25m
Armament: 4x AT-2 missiles (plus four reloads)

ARMOUR:
Hull front upper: 5mm @ 80° [Effective: 29mm]
Hull front lower: 7mm @ 45° [Effective: 10mm]

Hull nose plate: 14mm @ 14° [Effective: 14mm]
Hull sides upper: 7mm @ 18° [Effective: 7.1mm]
Hull sides lower: 7mm
Hull rear: 7mm
Hull top: 7mm
Belly: 2-3mm

Specifications: AT-2C

Guidance: SACLOS (radio link)
Range: 500-4,000m
Length: 1.16m
Diameter: 148mm
Weight: 29kg
Warhead: 5.4kg HEAT
Penetration: 500mm

9P122

This was a modified BRDM-2, similar to the 9P124. It carried six AT-3 Sagger missiles on launch rails under an armoured, retractable roof. The launch assembly was normally lowered into the vehicle, and was raised for firing. The AT-3 used manual command to line-of-sight guidance.

As well as launching missiles from within the vehicle, they could be launched remotely, from up to 80m away, using a separate sight. Eight reload missiles were carried, and could be loaded while the launch platform was inside the vehicle.

A later version, the 9P133, replaced the original version of the AT-3 missile with the AT-3C, which used the simpler and more accurate semi-automatic command to line-of-sight guidance. The vehicle had a larger sight, and was identifiable by an extra small window on the front.

Specifications: BRDM-2

Crew: 4
Combat weight: 7,000kg
Length: 5.75m
Width: 2.35m
Height: 2.31m
Ground clearance: 0.43m
Maximum road speed: 100km/hour
Maximum road range: 750km
Gradient: 60%
Vertical obstacle: 0.4m
Trench: 1.25m
Armament: 6x AT-3 missiles (plus eight reloads)

Armour:
Hull front upper: 5mm @ 80° [Effective: 29mm]
Hull front lower: 7mm @ 45° [Effective: 10mm]
Hull nose plate: 14mm @ 14° [Effective: 14mm]
Hull sides upper: 7mm @ 18° [Effective: 7.1mm]
Hull sides lower: 7mm
Hull rear: 7mm
Hull top: 7mm
Belly: 2-3mm

Specifications: AT-3 (AT-3C in brackets)

Guidance: MCLOS (wire link) (SACLOS, wire link)
Range: 500-3,000m
Length: 860mm
Diameter: 125mm
Weight: 10.9kg (11.4kg)
Warhead: 2.6kg HEAT
Penetration: 200mm @ 60° (520mm)

9P148

Initially wrongly identified in the West as the BRDM-3, this was a BRDM-2 with the turret removed and replaced with a mounting for five AT-5 Spandrel missiles. The mounting folded down for travelling, but did not retract into the vehicle. Missiles were reloaded via a hatch behind the launcher.

The missile sight was located in the front right of the vehicle. Ten AT-5 reload missiles were carried within the hull. The launcher could mount and fire AT-4 Spigot missiles as well as AT-5 Spandrel, and it was occasionally spotted with AT-4 missiles in the outer two mounts. In this case, seven AT-5 and eight AT-4 reload missiles were carried within the hull.

Specifications: BRDM-2

Crew: 4
Combat weight: 7,000kg
Length: 5.75m
Width: 2.35m
Height: 2.31m
Ground clearance: 0.43m
Maximum road speed: 100km/hour
Maximum road range: 750km
Gradient: 60%
Vertical obstacle: 0.4m
Trench: 1.25m
Armament: 10x AT-5 missiles (plus ten reloads) or 3x AT-5 and 2x AT-4 missiles (plus seven AT-5 and eight AT-4 reloads)

Armour:
Hull front upper: 5mm @ 80° [Effective: 29mm]
Hull front lower: 7mm @ 45° [Effective: 10mm]
Hull nose plate: 14mm @ 14° [Effective: 14mm]

9P148

Hull sides upper: 7mm @ 18° [Effective: 7.1mm]
Hull sides lower: 7mm
Hull rear: 7mm
Hull top: 7mm
Belly: 2-3mm

Specifications: AT-4

Guidance: SACLOS (wire link)
Range: 70-2,000m
Length: 1.1m
Diameter: 120mm
Weight: 11.5kg
Warhead: HEAT
Penetration: 400mm @ 0°, 230mm @ 60°

Specifications: AT-5 (AT-5B in brackets)

Guidance: SACLOS (wire link)
Range: 75-4,000m

Length: 1.3m
Diameter: 135mm
Weight: 25.2kg (26.5kg)
Warhead: HEAT (Tandem HEAT)
Penetration: 600mm (750–800mm)

9P149

In 1990, it was announced that a new anti-tank vehicle, mounting an AT-6 Spiral launcher on an MT-LB chassis, had been deployed. The AT-6 used semi-automatic command to line-of-sight guidance, with a radio link to send guidance commands to the missile. The guidance system included ECCM (electronic counter-counter measures).

When the launcher was retracted, the vehicle was almost identical in appearance to a standard MT-LB, but the machine gun turret was replaced with a large sight at the front of the hull. The launcher, mounting a single missile, was retracted under armour for transport and loading, and raised for firing. A total of 12 missiles were carried in an autoloader. The system had a limited anti-aircraft capability, allowing it to engage attack helicopters.

The 9P149 retained the NBC protection and amphibious capability of the standard MT-LB. In the water, it was propelled by its tracks.

SPECIFICATIONS: MT-LB

Crew: 2 + 11 passengers
Combat weight: 11,900kg
Maximum payload: 2,000kg
Maximum towed load: 6,500kg
Length: 6.45m

9P149

Width: 2.86m
Height: 1.87m
Ground clearance: 0.4m
Maximum road speed: 62km/hour
Maximum road range: 500km
Gradient: 60%
Vertical obstacle: 0.6m
Trench: 2.41m
Armament: 1x AT-6 missile (plus twelve reloads)
Armour: 4-10mm

SPECIFICATIONS: AT-6

Guidance: SACLOS (radio link)
Range: 400-5,000m
Length: 1.83m
Diameter: 130mm
Weight: 48.5kg
Warhead: 5.3kg HEAT
Penetration: 560mm

Reconnaissance Vehicles

Although specialised reconnaissance vehicles are detailed in this chapter, it should be noted that the Warsaw Pact armies often fielded standard vehicles such as main battle tanks and IFVs alongside specialised vehicles in reconnaissance units.

BRDM-1

The BRDM-1 was accepted for service in 1957, and entered production in the same year. Initially it had an open-topped roof, but an enclosed roof was added in 1958 and this became the standard production model.

The hull was welded steel, with the engine at the front. The driver was seated on the left, with the commander to his right and the crew compartment behind them. There were two large hatches in the forward part of the roof. The BRDM-1 had four main wheels, all of which were driven. There were an additional four small wheels between the two main axles, which could be lowered by the driver for improved off-road and ditch-crossing performance. The vehicle was fully amphibious, propelled in the water by a single water jet. It did not have NBC protection, though it did have systems for detecting chemical warfare agents and nuclear contamination.

BRDM-1 with extra wheels lowered

Usual armament was a 7.62mm SGMB machine gun on a pintle mount at the front of the roof. Some vehicles were observed with a 12.7mm DShKM machine gun at the front, and a 7.62mm SGMB machine gun at the rear. There were two firing ports on each side of the hull, and two more at the rear.

The BRDM-1-RKhb NBC reconnaissance vehicle was a variant on the standard BRDM-1. This vehicle had NBC protection, and additional chemical sensors and nuclear contamination detectors. It also had a variety of alarm systems for warning nearby troops, including two rectangular racks containing marker poles with pennants.

Specifications: BRDM-1

Crew: 5
Unloaded weight: 5,600kg
Length: 5.7m
Width: 2.25m

Height: 1.9m
Ground clearance: 0.315m
Maximum road speed: 80km/hour
Maximum road cruising range: 500km
Gradient: 60%
Vertical obstacle: 0.4m
Trench: 1.22m
Armament: 1 × 7.62mm SGMB MG (1,250 rounds)
Armour (max): 10mm

BRDM-2

The BRDM-2 entered service during the 1960s. Based on the BRDM-1, it added a small turret and a more powerful engine, mounted at the rear instead of the front.

Like the BRDM-1, the armour was welded steel. The driver sat at the front left of the vehicle and the commander at the front right. There were roof hatches above the driver and commander for entry and exit. Immediately to the rear of these hatches was a small, manually operated, one-man turret. This had a 14.5mm KPVT machine gun with a co-axial 7.62mm PKT machine gun. A telescopic sight was provided for the main armament. Each side of the hull had a single firing port.

The BRDM-2 had four main wheels, all of which were driven. There were an additional four small wheels between the two main axles, which could be lowered by the driver for improved off-road and ditch-crossing performance. A central tyre pressure regulation system was fitted to further improve off-road performance.

The BRDM-2 was fitted with NBC protection, and was fully amphibious, propelled in the water by a single water jet at the rear of the hull. It had infra-red driving lights, an infra-red

BRDM-2s in convoy

searchlight, and a 4,000kg-capacity winch at the front of the hull.

The BRDM-2-RKha NBC reconnaissance vehicle was a variant on the standard BRDM-2. This vehicle had additional chemical sensors and nuclear contamination detectors. It also had a variety of alarm systems for warning nearby troops, including two rectangular racks containing marker poles with pennants. The later BRDM-2-RKhb replaced the 14.5mm KPVT with a second 7.62mm PKT, and had improved sensors.

SPECIFICATIONS: BRDM-2

Crew: 4
Combat weight: 7,000kg
Length: 5.75m
Width: 2.35m
Height: 2.31m
Ground clearance: 0.43m

Maximum road speed: 100km/hour
Maximum road range: 750km
Gradient: 60%
Vertical obstacle: 0.4m
Trench: 1.25m

ARMAMENT:
1x 14.5mm KPVT MG (500 rounds)
1x 7.62mm PKT MG (2,000 rounds)

ARMOUR:
Hull front upper: 5mm @ 80° [Effective: 29mm]
Hull front lower: 7mm @ 45° [Effective: 10mm]
Hull nose plate: 14mm @ 14° [Effective: 14mm]
Hull sides upper: 7mm @ 18° [Effective: 7.1mm]
Hull sides lower: 7mm
Hull rear: 7mm
Hull top: 7mm
Belly: 2-3mm
Turret front: 7mm @ 43° [Effective: 10mm]
Turret sides: 7mm @ 36° [Effective: 9mm]
Turret rear: 7mm @ 36° [Effective: 9mm]
Turret top: 7mm

BRM

The BRM was accepted for service in 1972. It was based on the BMP-1, but had a larger, two-man turret and two roof hatches to the rear instead of the BMP-1's four. It was armed with a 73mm 2A28 smoothbore gun and co-axial 7.62mm PKT machine gun. Unlike the BMP-1, there was no ATGM launcher or autoloader. Some vehicles had a bank of six smoke grenade launchers at the rear of the turret, firing over the turret to the front.

BRM

The BRM had a laser rangefinder and a Tall Mike ground surveillance radar. The radar was normally kept in the turret and was elevated above the turret roof when required. It had additional navigation and radio equipment, compared to the BMP-1. The BRM had a crew of six: the driver and navigator in the front hull, the commander and gunner in the turret, and a pair of observers in the rear hull.

Specifications: BRM

Crew: 6
Combat weight: 12,500kg
Length: 6.75m
Width: 2.97m
Height: 1.98m
Ground clearance: 0.43m
Maximum road speed: 70km/hour
Maximum road range: 500km

Gradient: 60%
Vertical obstacle: 0.8m
Trench: 2.2m
Armour (max): 10mm

Armament:
1x 73mm 2A28 gun (20 rounds)
1x 7.62mm PKT MG (2,000 rounds)

BRM-23 (Bulgaria)

The BRM-23 was a development of the BMP-23, modified for reconnaissance missions up to 100km ahead of the main force. It retained the armament of the IFV version, but only had three firing ports (two on the right, one on the left). It had a five-man crew: two in the front hull, two in the turret, and one in the rear.

It carried a range of specialised equipment for its reconnaissance role, including a handheld laser rangefinder with a range of 9km, and a handheld passive night-vision device. Both of these could be mounted on tripods for greater stability if required. A land navigation system, artillery aiming circle, man-portable mine detector, and radiation and chemical detectors were also carried, as well as extra radios. A large frame aerial was carried. When erected at the rear of the hull, it extended the range of the RM-130M radio to around 120km.

Like the BMP-23, it was fully amphibious, powered in the water by its tracks, and had NBC protection for the crew.

Specifications: BRM-23

Crew: 5
Combat weight: 14,800kg
Length: 7.23m
Width: 3.01m

Height: 2.53m

Ground clearance: 0.4m

Maximum road speed: 61.5km/hour

Maximum road range: 500km

Gradient: 60%

Vertical obstacle: 0.8m

Trench: 2.5m

ARMAMENT:

1x 23mm 2A14 cannon (600 rounds)

1x 7.62mm PKT MG (2,000 rounds)

1x AT-3 Sagger ATGM (1 + 3 missiles)

FÚG (HUNGARY)

The Hungarian FÚG served a similar purpose to the Soviet BRDM-1, and was visually similar. There were differences, however: the Hungarian vehicle's engine was at the rear, and it had two water jets for swimming instead of one. It entered service with the Hungarian army in 1964, and two years later entered service with the Czech and Polish armies. In Czech service it was known as the OT-65.

The hull was of welded-steel armour. The driver sat at the front left, with the commander to his right. Behind them was a troop compartment that could hold four soldiers. The only means of entry or exit was a roof hatch, which opened to either side. The hatch covers could be fixed vertically, providing some measure of protection when using the 7.62mm SGMB machine gun. Six firing ports were fitted: two on each side, and two in the rear.

The engine compartment was to the rear of the troop compartment. Like the BRDM-1, the FÚG had four small wheels that were normally retracted into the hull, but could be lowered by the driver to improve cross-country performance. The FÚG was fully amphibious. Before entering the water, a trim vane, normally kept under the nose, was erected and the bilge pumps switched on. In the water, the vehicle was propelled by a pair of water jets.

Standard equipment included infra-red driving lights, and some models had an infra-red searchlight and central tyre pressure regulation system. There was no NBC protection for the crew. Armament was a single pintle-mounted 7.62mm SGMB machine gun, operated by a crew member with the roof hatches open.

An NBC reconnaissance version, the D-442VS or FÚG-US, was used to mark contaminated areas. It had racks containing marker poles with pennants, to be fired into the ground.

The OT-65A was a Czech modification, fitted with the same manually-operated turret as the OT-62B armoured personnel carrier. This had a 7.62mm M59T machine gun, and an 82mm T-21 recoilless gun mounted externally on the right side. An infra-red searchlight was mounted to the right of the recoilless gun. The T-21 could be aimed and fired from inside the turret, but could only be reloaded from outside. It had a maximum range of 2,500m, although the effective range was significantly less, at 300m to 450m. The 82mm HEAT projectile could penetrate up to 230mm of armour.

SPECIFICATIONS: FÚG/OT-65 (OT-65A IN BRACKETS)

Crew: 2 + 4 dismounts
Combat weight: 7,000kg
Length: 5.79m
Width: 2.5m
Height: 1.91m (2.25m)
Ground clearance: 0.34m

Maximum road speed: 87km/hour
Maximum road range: 600km
Gradient: 60%
Vertical obstacle: 0.4m
Trench: 1.2m
Armour (max): 13mm

ARMAMENT (FÚG):
1x 7.62mm SGMB machine gun (1,250 rounds)

ARMAMENT (OT-65A):
1x 7.62mm M59T machine gun
1x 82mm T-21 recoilless gun

Self-Propelled Anti-Aircraft Weapons

Soviet army air defence was based on the principles of mass, mix, mobility, and integration. Sheer numbers provided mass; the variety of complementary weapon systems provided mix. The design of the systems emphasised mobility, and the weapons were integrated at every level, from platoon to front.

In 1944, the Soviet army trialled a 37mm V-47 AA gun mounted on an SU-76 chassis, designated ZSU-37. In 1945, they experimented with a naval twin 25mm gun on a similar vehicle, designated ZSU-25. These vehicles were produced in small numbers for trials, but neither was adopted for service. Both designs suffered from slow turret traverse, making them ineffective against low-flying aircraft.

BTR-40A & BTR-152A

These were modified BTR-40 and BTR-152 APCs which entered service in 1952. Each had a pair of 14.5mm KPV machine guns mounted over the troop compartment in a simple, manually operated turret. The turret had 360° traverse, 80° elevation, and 5° depression, but minimal armoured protection for the gunner. In addition to AA support, the BTR-40A and BTR-152A were used to provide general fire support against ground targets. The guns had an effective range of around 2,000m against ground targets, and 1,400m against airborne targets. The slow traverse speed of the turret and the ineffectiveness of the simple sights severely limited their usefulness as AA vehicles.

Further AA variants of the BTR-152 were developed. The BTR-152D had four 14.5mm KPV machine guns, and the BTR-152E, introduced in 1955, had the same twin KPV mount as the BTR-152A, but was based on the BTR-152V chassis.

SPECIFICATIONS: BTR-40A

Crew: 5 passengers
Combat weight: 5,300kg
Length: 5m
Width: 1.9m
Height: 2.5m
Ground clearance: 0.3m
Maximum road speed: 80km/hour
Maximum road range: 285km
Gradient: 60%
Vertical obstacle: 0.47m
Trench: 0.7m
Armament: 2x 14.5mm KPV machine gun (2,400 rounds)
Armour: 6-8mm

SPECIFICATIONS: BTR-152A

Crew: 4
Combat weight: 9,600kg
Length: 6.83m
Width: 2.32m
Height: 2.05m

Ground clearance: 0.3m
Maximum road speed: 65km/hour
Maximum road range: 780km
Gradient: 55%
Vertical obstacle: 0.6m
Trench: 0.69m
Armament: 2x 14.5mm KPV machine gun (2,000 rounds)

Armour:
Front: 13.5mm @ 35° [Effective: 16mm]
Side: 9mm @ 7° [Effective: 9mm]
Rear: 9mm
Belly: 4mm

ZSU-57-2

The ZSU-57-2 entered service in 1955. The hull was based on a lightened T-54 chassis, with much lighter armour and four road wheels rather the T-54's five. Two air-cooled 57mm S-68 guns were fitted in a large, boxy, open-topped turret. A tarpaulin cover was carried for protection against inclement weather.

The guns had optical sights (initially with no rangefinder, though a rangefinder was later added) and the turret had powered traverse and elevation. The sights were configured to allow use in a secondary role as a ground support vehicle. The guns had a maximum effective range of around 4,000m. The powered turret was a significant improvement over earlier vehicles, but the lack of radar limited the ZSU-57-2 to use in clear weather. It did not have NBC protection or amphibious capability.

ZSU-57-2

Specifications: ZSU-57-2

Crew: 6
Combat weight: 28.1 tonnes
Length: 6.22m
Width: 3.27m
Height: 2.75m
Maximum road speed: 50km/hour
Maximum road range: 420km
Gradient: 60%
Vertical obstacle: 0.8m
Trench: 2.7m
Armament: 2x 57mm S-68 guns (300 rounds)
Armour: 8-15mm

ZSU-23-4 Shilka

The ZSU-23-4 entered service in 1966, as a replacement for the much less effective ZSU-57-2. The chassis was based on a

ZSU-23-4 Shilka

modified ASU-85, and it had an enclosed turret holding four water-cooled 2A7 23mm guns (the gun mounting was designated AZP-23). Although the choice of a 23mm gun reduced the effective range, it had a much higher rate of fire, leading to a greater probability of a hit. The vehicle had NBC protection and infra-red night-vision equipment, but no amphibious capability.

The ZSU-23-4 had a Gun Dish radar for acquisition and tracking, connected to an analogue computer, allowing operation in all weather conditions. The radar could acquire targets at a range of up to 20km, and track targets at up to 18km. Optical sights were fitted for use as a backup and in heavy ECM environments.

The large number of electronic vacuum tubes in the fire-control computer generated a great deal of heat, which caused problems with cooling. In 1966, the ZSU-23-4V entered service, which had changes to the venting covers and removed the heat exchanger from the turret roof. In 1970, the ZSU-23-4V1 was introduced. This had an improved computer, and ventilation system cases at the front of the turret. The ZSU-23-4M, introduced in 1973, had further cooling improvements and enhanced ECCM. From 1977, vehicles were fitted with an improved IFF system and designated ZSU-23-4MZ. This IFF system was retrofitted to existing ZSU-23-4M systems.

SPECIFICATIONS: ZSU-23-4 SHILKA

Crew: 4
Combat weight: 19 tonnes
Length: 6.54m
Width: 3.13m
Height: 3.75m (2.6m with radar down)
Ground clearance: 0.35m
Maximum road speed: 50km/hour
Maximum road range: 450km
Gradient: 60%
Vertical obstacle: 1m
Trench: 2.4m
Armament: 4x 23mm 2A7 guns (2,000 rounds)

ARMOUR:
Hull: 15mm max
Turret: 9.4mm

2S6

The 2S6 entered limited service in 1982. Its layout was similar to the ZSU-23-4, with a large turret mounted in the centre of the hull and the engine at the rear. The 2S6 was armed with a pair of 2A38 30mm cannons (one on each side of the turret), and four SA-19 Grison missiles (two on each side of the turret). A target acquisition radar was fitted at the rear of the turret, and a

2S6M

tracking radar at the front. The guns were stabilised in both planes to allow firing on the move, but the missiles could only be fired when stationary. The vehicle was armoured to a level sufficient to provide protection from small arms and shell splinters.

In 1986, the main production system, the 2S6M, entered service. This increased the missile load from four to eight missiles (four on each side of the turret). The fire-control programmes were improved, and improved guns (2A38M) and missiles (Soviet designation 9M311M) were fitted.

Specifications: 2S6M

Crew: 4
Combat weight: 34 tonnes
Length: 7.93m
Width: 3.24m
Height: 4.01m (3.36m with radar stowed)

Maximum road speed: 65km/hour
Maximum road range: 500km
Vertical obstacle: 1m
Trench: 2m

ARMAMENT:
8x SA-19 Grison missiles (2S6: 4x SA-19 Grison missiles)
2x 30mm 2A38M cannon (1,904 rounds) (2S6: 2x 30mm 2A38 cannon)

SA-4 GANEF

The SA-4 Ganef (Krug) was the first self-propelled surface-to-air missile system deployed by the Soviet Union. It was built on a new tracked chassis, later used as the basis for the 2S3 self-propelled howitzer. The launch vehicle carried two missiles on an elevating turntable, but had no on-board fire control. The vehicle had NBC protection and infra-red driving lights, but was not amphibious.

The missile had a maximum range of 55km, a maximum altitude of 27.4km, and a 135kg HE warhead with terminal semi-active radar homing. Initial guidance came from the radar vehicle via radio link, although an optical backup could be used if required. A later version of the missile had a shorter minimum range but improved performance at low altitudes. Each battery usually had both versions of the missile, since they had complementary strengths and weaknesses.

The first version of the system entered service in 1965, with a modified version (Krug-A) entering full-scale production and service in 1967. Each battery had a Pat Hand radar, mounted on the same vehicle as the launch vehicle, for fire control and guidance. Spare missiles were carried on TZM transloader vehicles, based on Ural 375 lorries, with on-board cranes for

SA-4 Ganef

transferring missiles. Reloading the TEL vehicle took 10 to 15 minutes.

SPECIFICATIONS: SA-4 GANEF

Crew: 3-5
Combat weight: 28.2 tonnes
Length: 7.5m (9.46m including missiles)
Width: 3.2m
Height: 4.47m (including missiles)
Ground clearance: 0.44m
Maximum road speed: 35km/hour
Maximum road range: 780km
Gradient: 60%
Vertical obstacle: 1m
Armour: 15mm max

Number of missiles: 2
Missile diameter: 860mm
Warhead weight: 135kg
Missile length: SA-4A: 8.8m, SA-4B: 8.4m
Missile weight: 2,453kg
Missile range: SA-4A: 55km, SA-4B: 50km
Reload time: 10-15 minutes

SA-6 Gainful

After various difficulties in development, the SA-6 Gainful was accepted for service in 1967. It was the first Soviet SAM system designed to engage low-flying aircraft, and made extensive use of transistors and printed circuit boards instead of vacuum tubes. The launch and radar vehicles had hulls based on a modified ASU-85 chassis, similar to that used for the ZSU-23-4. Like the ZSU-23-4, the vehicles had infra-red night-vision equipment, NBC protection, and no amphibious capability.

The missile was unconventional in design, using an integral solid rocket engine that fell away once its fuel was expended, leaving a solid fuel ramjet to take over. This design offered a high maximum speed of Mach 2.5 and was very simple, with low unit and maintenance costs, although performance suffered at high altitudes.

The launch vehicle carried three missiles on an elevating launcher with 360° traverse. The radar vehicle carried a Straight Flush radar. Each battery had four launch vehicles and one radar vehicle. The battery was controlled from the radar vehicle, which was connected to the launch vehicles by cable or radio link.

SA-6 Gainful

SPECIFICATIONS: SA-6 GAINFUL

Crew: 3
Combat weight: 14 tonnes
Length: 6.8m

Width: 3.2m
Height: 3.45m
Ground clearance: 0.35m
Maximum road speed: 45km/hour
Maximum road range: 250km
Gradient: 60%
Vertical obstacle: 1m
Trench: 2.4m
Armour: 9mm max
Number of missiles: 3
Missile diameter: 335mm
Warhead weight: 59kg
Missile length: 5.8m
Missile weight: 599kg
Missile range: 24km
Reload time: 10 minutes

SA-8 Gecko

The **SA-8 Gecko** entered service in 1970, and was notable for being the first Soviet surface-to-air missile system to be fully self-contained, with the tracking radars mounted on the same vehicle as the missiles. The **TELAR** was based on an unarmoured BAZ-5937 chassis, and was amphibious and air-transportable. The missiles and radar were housed on a rotating mount at the centre of the vehicle. The Land Roll radar was in the centre of the mount, with a small antenna on each side. These small antennae were used to guide the missiles, allowing the vehicle to control two missiles simultaneously. A low-light television system was mounted above the Land Roll radar, and could be used to guide the missiles in a heavy ECM environment. Two missiles were mounted on rails on either side of the radar.

SA-8b Gecko Mod-0

In 1975, the SA-8b Gecko Mod-0 was introduced. This version was easily distinguished from the initial version, since it carried six missiles instead of four, housed in sealed containers. In 1980, another new version (SA-8b Gecko Mod-1) added an IFF antenna and improved missiles, with increased range and maximum height.

A dedicated reload vehicle was developed on the same chassis, and carried 18 missiles in a cargo compartment covered by a tarpaulin. A crane was fitted to facilitate reloading, which took around five minutes. An SA-8 battery had four TELAR vehicles and two reload vehicles.

Specifications: SA-8b Gecko Mod-0

Crew: 5
Combat weight: 17.5 tonnes
Length: 9.14m
Width: 2.8m

Height: 4.2m
Ground clearance: 0.4m
Maximum road speed: 80km/hour
Maximum road range: 500km
Number of missiles: 6
Missile diameter: 210mm
Warhead weight: 20kg
Missile length: 3.16m
Missile weight: 126kg
Missile range: 10km
Reload time: 10 minutes

SA-9 Gaskin

The SA-9 Gaskin entered service in 1968, and was based on a BRDM-2 chassis with the retractable belly wheels removed. The turret was replaced with a mounting for four 9M31M Strela-1 missiles. The missiles were normally folded down flat to the hull roof for transport, then raised for firing. An improved missile (SA-9B Gaskin Mod-0) was introduced in 1970.

The vehicle was amphibious, using the same water-jet propulsion system as the BRDM-2, and had NBC protection. There was a crew of three: driver, gunner, and commander. The driver and commander were supplied with periscopes and infrared night-vision equipment.

Each SA-9 battery normally had a single SA-9 Mod-A vehicle, mounting a Flat Box A passive radar detection system in addition to the missiles. It should be noted that this was a passive system, which simply detected radar emissions from approaching aircraft to provide a bearing. The gunner would traverse the launch mounting to the appropriate bearing, then acquire the target visually.

The SA-9 was normally deployed in tandem with the ZSU-23-4 anti-aircraft gun, so that the two systems complemented one another. Missiles were fired in pairs to increase the chance of a hit, and used infra-red, heat-seeking sensors to home in on their target. The SA-9 vehicle itself did not normally carry reload missiles. In foreign service, however, they were sometimes seen with a missile attached to each side of the hull.

Specifications: SA-9 Gaskin

Crew: 4
Combat weight: 7,000kg
Length: 5.75m
Width: 2.35m
Height: 2.31m
Ground clearance: 0.43m
Maximum road speed: 100km/hour
Maximum road range: 750km
Gradient: 60%
Vertical obstacle: 0.4m
Trench: 1.25m
Number of missiles: 4
Missile diameter: 120mm
Warhead weight: 2.6kg
Missile length: 1.8m
Missile weight: 32kg
Missile range: 6.5km (Mod-0: 8km)
Reload time: 5 minutes

Armour:
Hull front upper: 5mm @ 80° [Effective: 29mm]
Hull front lower: 7mm @ 45° [Effective: 10mm]
Hull nose plate: 14mm @ 14° [Effective: 14mm]

Hull sides upper: 7mm @ 18° [Effective: 7.1mm]
Hull sides lower: 7mm
Hull rear: 7mm
Hull top: 7mm
Belly: 2-3mm

SA-10 Grumble

After a protracted development period, the SA-10A Grumble became operational in 1980. The initial version was designed for deployment at fixed sites. The launcher was a trailer, towed by a KrAZ-260V 6x6 tractor unit and positioned on concrete pads for firing, stabilised by four hydraulic jacks.

A mobile system, designated SA-10B Grumble Mod-1 by NATO, was deployed in 1985. It was based on a MAZ-7910 8x8 chassis, with four missiles, engagement radar, and a fire-control system. The missiles were stored in cylinders, which were kept horizontal during transit. Before firing, four hydraulic jacks were lowered and the missiles were raised to 90°. Time needed to prepare for firing was around five minutes. There were two variants of the TEL: the 5P85S had control logic and datalink hardware, while the 5P85D had no control hardware, and was controlled by a 5P85S. A typical battery would consist of one 5P85S TEL, two 5P85D TELs, and one 5N63S mobile Flap Lid B radar.

Two versions of the missile were developed. The first (5V55K) entered service in 1980, then the improved 5V55R entered service in 1984. The 5V55K used command guidance and had a maximum range of 47km. The 5V55R used semi-automatic radar homing, had almost double the range (90km), and an increased warhead size.

SA-10 Grumble battery

Specifications: SA-10 Grumble

Length: 12.1m
Width: 3.05m
Maximum road speed: 60km/hour
Range: 850km
Number of missiles: 4
Missile diameter: 450mm
Warhead weight: 5V55K: 100kg, 5V55R: 133kg
Missile length: 7m
Missile weight: 5V55K: 1,450kg, 5V55R: 1,664kg
Missile range: 5V55K: 47km, 5V55R: 90km

SA-11 Gadfly

Development of a system to replace the SA-6, which was to become the 9K37 Buk (known to NATO as the SA-11 Gadfly),

SA-11 Gadfly

began in the early 1970s, and was accepted for service in 1980. An SA-11 battery consisted of two launch vehicles and one reload vehicle. The target acquisition radar was at battalion level, but each launch vehicle had an on-board fire control radar. It took a battery around five minutes to prepare for action after moving, and five minutes to prepare for movement.

The launch vehicle was based on a tracked chassis and had NBC protection. A traversing mount was fitted on the hull, with a Fire Dome radar at the front and an elevating launcher for four missiles at the rear. The reload vehicle was similar, but had a crane in place of the radar. The reload vehicle could launch missiles, but would have to rely on a nearby launch vehicle's radar for guidance. The missiles had a maximum speed of Mach 3, a maximum range of 30km, and a maximum height of 14km. Semi-active radar homing guidance was used, although an electro-optical guidance system could be used in heavy ECM environments, with commands sent to the missile via a radio link.

An improved version of the SA-11, the 9K37M1 Buk-M1 was accepted for service in 1983. This had improved radar performance, kill probability, and ECM resistance. A new threat-classification system was fitted, which analysed radar return signals to classify targets without IFF.

SPECIFICATIONS: SA-11 GADFLY

Ground clearance: 0.45m
Maximum road speed: 65km/hour
Maximum road range: 500km
Number of missiles: 4
Missile diameter: 400mm
Warhead weight: 70kg
Missile length: 5.55m
Missile weight: 690kg
Missile range: 30km

SA-12 GLADIATOR

The SA-12 Gladiator replaced the SA-4 Ganef, and was designed to provide protection against cruise missiles as well as aircraft. The missile had the same design roots as the SA-10 Grumble, but was mounted on a tracked TELAR based on the MT-T chassis, with four missiles and a guidance radar. A separate Grill Pan radar was used for tracking. The reload vehicle was very similar to the TELAR vehicle, but had a crane instead of a radar. It could launch missiles, but needed a TELAR vehicle to control them.

SPECIFICATIONS: SA-12 GLADIATOR

Length: 8.71m
Width: 3.28m

SA-12 Gladiator

Maximum road speed: 65km/hour
Maximum road range: 500km
Gradient: 60%
Vertical obstacle: 0.65m
Trench: 2.5m
Number of missiles: 4
Warhead weight: 150kg
Missile weight: 420kg
Missile range: 75km

SA-13 GOPHER

After some problems in development, the SA-13 Gopher was approved for service in 1976. The SA-13 was based on an MT-LB, but without the machine gun turret. A launcher fitted over the cargo compartment carried four 9K35 Strela-10 missiles and was folded down flat to the roof when in transit. A parabolic antenna was fixed in the centre of the missiles, for the range-only

SA-13 Gopher

Hat Box radar. This radar was used to ensure that a target was within range before launching missiles. A Flat Box B passive radar detection system was fitted to most vehicles, but not to the battery commander's vehicle. Eight reload missiles were carried within the vehicle.

The Strela-10 infra-red, heat-seeking missile offered several improvements over the SA-9's Strela-1. It had an improved, cooled seeker head, which could home in on an aircraft from any angle, not only onto the jet exhaust. The SA-13 launcher could fire the older Strela-1 missile as well as the Strela-10. The Strela-10 travelled at just under Mach 2 to a maximum range of 5km and maximum height of 3.5km. In 1981 an improved missile was introduced, which had a heavier warhead and improved ECCM, proximity fuse, and engine.

The SA-13 had NBC protection and was fully amphibious, propelled in the water by its tracks.

Specifications: SA-13 Gopher

Crew: 2 + 11 passengers
Combat weight: 11,900kg
Maximum payload: 2,000kg
Maximum towed load: 6,500kg
Length: 6.45m
Width: 2.86m
Height: 1.87m
Ground clearance: 0.4m
Maximum road speed: 62km/hour
Maximum road range: 500km
Gradient: 60%
Vertical obstacle: 0.6m
Trench: 2.41m
Armour: 4-10mm
Armament: 4x 9K35 Strela-10 missiles (plus eight reloads)
Number of missiles: 4
Missile diameter: 123mm
Warhead weight: 5kg
Missile length: 2.2m
Missile weight: 41kg
Missile range: 5km
Reload time: 3 minutes

BTR-ZD

The BTR-ZD was a standard BTR-D airborne APC. However, the BTR-ZD carried two surface-to-air missile teams equipped with SA-7, SA-14, or SA-16. It also had a ZU-23-2 twin 23mm AA gun, which could be towed behind the vehicle or mounted on top of the troop compartment. Ramps were carried to assist with loading and unloading the guns onto the vehicle. The ZU-23-2

BTR-ZD

had simple optical sights, and full 360° traverse, whether mounted on the vehicle or used separately. Like the BTR-D, the BTR-ZD had NBC protection and amphibious capability.

SPECIFICATIONS: BTR-ZD

Combat weight: 8,000kg
Length: 5.89m
Width: 2.63m
Height: 1.67m
Ground clearance: 0.1-0.45m
Maximum road speed: 60km/hour
Maximum road range: 500km

ARMAMENT:
1x ZU-23-2 AA gun
2x SAM launchers (SA-7, SA-14 or SA-16)

ARMOUR:
Hull front upper: 15mm @ 78° [Effective: 72mm]
Hull front lower: 15mm @ 50° [Effective: 23mm]
Hull side: 10mm
Hull rear: 10mm

M53/59 (CZECHOSLOVAKIA)

When the Czech army was looking for an APC in the mid-1950s, Praga put forward an armoured version of its V3S 6x6 lorry. The design lost out to a Tatra design based on the German Second World War Sdkfz 251, but it was used as the basis for a self-propelled anti-aircraft gun. Entering service in the late 1950s, it mounted a modified version of the M53 twin 30mm anti-aircraft gun at the rear. The guns could, and often were, dismounted for use on the ground.

The vehicle had a welded hull with the engine at the front, crew compartment in the centre, and armament at the rear. The driver sat on the left, with the commander to his right. They had a windscreen to their front, which was fitted with an armoured cover with a vision slit. Each had a side door with vision slit, and the top section of the doors could be folded down. The commander also had a clear dome on the roof to for full 360° observation. The loaders were seated behind the driver and commander, facing backward, each with a vision slit to the side. A two-piece hatch cover at the rear folded down, forming a platform for the loaders when in action.

The two 30mm cannons had full 360° traverse, could be elevated to 85°, and depressed to -10°. The crew compartment limited depression over the frontal arc to +2°, and a steel plate prevented the guns hitting the commander's dome. Elevation, depression, and traverse were all hydraulic, and manual controls

M53/59

were provided as a backup. The gunner was seated to the left of the guns with armour protection to the front, side, and rear, although the position was open topped. Originally the barrels had multi-baffle muzzle brakes, but these were later replaced by conical flash hiders. Barrels could be quickly changed, with spares kept at regimental level.

The cannons were fully automatic, with a cyclic rate of fire of 450-500 rounds per minute each, and a practical rate of fire of 150 rounds per minute each. Note that the towed version of the guns had a lower rate of fire, because they did not have magazines, whereas the M53-59 guns were fed from 50-round vertical magazines. Maximum horizontal range was 9,700m, maximum vertical range was 6,300m, and effective anti-aircraft range was around 3,000m.

API and HEI projectiles were available. Three magazines were carried on either side of the gun platform, with more fastened to the floor in the rear of the crew compartment. The vehicle was limited to use in clear weather, had no NBC protection, night-vision equipment, amphibious capability, or central tyre pressure regulation system.

SPECIFICATIONS: M53/59

Crew: 5
Combat weight: 10.3 tonnes
Length: 6.92m
Width: 2.35m
Height: 2.95m (2.56m without magazines)
Maximum road speed: 60km/hour
Maximum road range: 500km
Gradient: 60%
Vertical obstacle: 0.46m
Trench: 0.69m
Armament: 2x 30mm M53 guns (800 rounds)
Armour: 10mm max

RIVER CROSSING

During the Cold War, the Soviet army studied the disposition of rivers in Western Europe. It concluded that they would have to cross water obstacles up to 100m wide every 35 to 60km. Every 100 to 150km, they would encounter a water obstacle between 100m and 300m wide. Every 250 to 300km, they would encounter one that was wider still. In a war in Western Europe, the Soviet army expected to advance an average of 100km per day, leading to a significant number of river crossings. NATO would obviously try to destroy bridges to slow the advance. Therefore, the Warsaw Pact armies put a great deal of emphasis on their ability to cross water obstacles quickly and efficiently. A range of equipment was created to bridge gaps or ferry vehicles over rivers. River reconnaissance systems were developed to quickly measure water depth and river width. Some of these were mounted on sleds that were towed behind boats or amphibious vehicles. Many light armoured vehicles could swim. Main battle tanks carried snorkels that allowed them to wade through water up to five metres deep.

Most river crossings would have been assault crossings from the march, at sites that were only lightly defended, if at all. Reconnaissance patrols, equipped with specialised equipment, would find suitable sites. These would be up to platoon size, and operated up to 50km ahead of the main body. When a crossing site had been selected, a forward detachment would secure the site. This detachment would be two to three hours ahead of the main body, and would avoid enemy contact. A typical forward detachment would consist of a motor rifle battalion with an attached tank company and artillery battalion. Amphibians, ferries, air defence, anti-tank, and chemical defence units would also be attached. Heliborne, or occasionally airborne, troops could also be used in this role.

If the crossing site was defended, the attack would be carried out with significant artillery and air support. River crossings got priority for air support, and were considered particularly vulnerable to enemy air attack. Air defence assets would be deployed close to the crossing site, and would cross the river as soon as feasible to extend their coverage.

The crossing itself would be carried out by APCs or IFVs swimming across the river, supported by tank and artillery fire from the near shore. A few tanks may have crossed in the first wave, but most would provide fire from the near bank and cross later. Artillery and anti-tank units would cross immediately after the infantry to provide support in holding the bridgehead. Tanks would cross using ferries, bridges, or by snorkelling.

SNORKELLING

The ability to wade, or snorkel, through water up to 5m deep was a standard feature in Soviet main battle tanks. It seems likely that ferries or bridges were the preferred method of crossing water obstacles. That said, a 1971 British army intelligence report stated that the Soviet army considered snorkelling "a practical operation of war". Every tank crew was fully trained in it. Training took place on purpose-built sites with good facilities. Emphasis was placed on ensuring the crew were confident in their ability to snorkel well and safely.

Training was split into two phases. The first phase, lasting up to two months, concentrated on preparing the crews to operate tanks under water. Training covered swimming, diving, and carrying out procedures underwater whilst wearing escape masks. There was a good deal of safety training, which helped with crew confidence and morale. Rescue operations were practised on simulators. Crews were not allowed to move onto the second phase until they had passed this first phase.

In the second phase of training, the crew put their skills to the test. A five-metre deep lake was used to practice driving underwater. Initially, drivers would drive 90m underwater, progressing to 150m as their skills improved. At least some sites also had facilities for blind driving, with the driver guided only by the tank's gyro compass. After passing this second phase of training, crews would join their units.

Sealing and preparing a tank for snorkelling could take as little as 15 minutes. Older tanks took longer, up to half an hour. This would be done in a concealed area 3 to 5km from the river. When the tanks got to within 1 to 2km of the river, snorkels would be fitted. Tanks crossed at slow speed, in a column formation, with a 30m gap between vehicles. Drivers would not change gear or stop while in the water. Once across, the tank would have to stop while the crew removed the waterproofing. Until this was done, the turret could not be traversed or the gun fired. If a tank stalled in the river, the crew would flood the vehicle, then escape through the hatches.

An alternative method used winches to pull unmanned tanks across. A pair of armoured recovery vehicles would set up on the far bank with a pulley block and anchoring unit. Up to three tanks could be pulled across the river simultaneously. Using this method, a 10-tank company could cross a 200m-wide river in 35 minutes, assuming the tanks had already been sealed. The crews would cross separately, either in amphibious vehicles such as APCs, or on boats.

Snorkelling was not to be carried out under fire, and in some cases the banks would make it impossible. The entry bank had to have a slope of less than 25°, the exit bank one of less than 15°, and the current no more than three metres per second. In winter, drifting ice could damage the snorkel. The river bottom had to be reasonably firm, and free of boulders and craters.

Swimming

Many lighter AFVs were amphibious, and could swim across water obstacles. All APCs from the BTR-50 onwards, and all IFVs, were fully amphibious. The BRDM series of reconnaissance vehicles, and even some self-propelled artillery and AA vehicles, could swim. Many were propelled in the water by their wheels or tracks, although some used water jets to achieve better performance in the water.

Water obstacles would only be crossed under fire as a last resort. In these cases, a great deal of artillery would be called upon to support the operation. If at all possible, helicopter troops would be landed on the far bank, and attack simultaneously with the crossing. Tanks would stay on the near bank to provide covering fire, while amphibious armoured vehicles swam across. Once a bridgehead was established, tanks and other vehicles

BTR-80 Swimming

would snorkel or be ferried across. These would then continue the advance, while engineers used pontoons to make a permanent bridge crossing.

VEHICLE-LAUNCHED BRIDGES

Soviet estimates found that two-thirds of the river obstacles they would encounter in Europe were less than 20m wide. This led to the development of vehicle-launched bridges capable of quickly crossing these narrow gaps. The Polish army developed a tracked bridge, which was pushed into place by a tank. Small numbers of a T-34-based bridging tank were delivered to the Soviet army in 1957. This was soon superseded by the MTU-54, sometimes referred to as the MTU or MTU-1.

MTU-54

In 1958, the MTU-54 was introduced, based on a T-54 chassis. This mounted a simple 12.3m bridge, carried horizontally. Unlike later vehicles, the bridge was not folded for transit. To launch, a chain-drive mechanism moved the bridge forward, before it was lowered into place. This method had the advantage of keeping the silhouette low during launch and recovery operations. The MTU-54 could bridge an 11m gap, and had a load capacity of 50 tonnes. Launch time was three to five minutes, and recovery could take place from either end of the bridge.

It was fitted with a DShKM machine gun for defence, mounted in the centre of the vehicle. This had to be removed before launching the bridge. Later vehicles were fitted with a deep-wading snorkel, NBC protection, and automatic fire-suppression system.

SPECIFICATIONS: MTU-54

Crew: 2
Weight: 34 tonnes (including bridge)
Length: 12.3m (including bridge)
Width: 3.27m (including bridge)
Height: 2.87m (including bridge)
Ground clearance: 0.43m
Maximum road speed: 48km/hour
Maximum road range: 400km
Gradient: 60%
Vertical obstacle: 0.8m
Armament: 1x12.7mm DShKM MG

MTU-54

ARMOUR:
Hull glacis: 100mm @ 60° [Effective: 200mm]
Hull sides: 70mm
Hull top: 30mm
Hull rear: 60mm
Belly: 20mm

MT-34 (CZECHOSLOVAKIA)

Introduced in 1960, the Czech MT-34 mounted a scissor bridge on a T-34-85 chassis, with a boxy superstructure holding the cable winches and hydraulic units. A contemporary of the Soviet MTU-54, the bridge was much shorter than the Soviet design when in transit, making it less cumbersome. It was much easier to spot when launching, however, since the bridge was raised to vertical before being unfolded into place. It had a bow mounting for a 7.62mm DTM machine gun, but the machine gun was not usually fitted. The system served with various Warsaw Pact armies, in addition to the Czech army.

Specifications: MT-34

Crew: 3
Weight: 32 tonnes (including bridge)
Length: 8.5m (including bridge)
Width: 3.2m (including bridge)
Height: 3.7m (including bridge)
Ground clearance: 0.4m
Maximum road speed: 55km/hour
Maximum road range: 300km
Gradient: 45%
Vertical obstacle: 0.73m

Armour:
Hull glacis: 45mm @ 60° [Effective: 90mm]
Hull sides (upper): 45mm @ 40° [Effective: 59mm]
Hull sides (lower): 45mm
Hull top: 18-22mm
Hull rear: 45mm @ 50° [Effective: 70mm]
Belly: 18-22mm

MTU-20

From 1967, the MTU-20, based on a T-55 chassis, became the primary Soviet tank-launched bridge. In order to allow a longer span length whilst maintaining a low launch silhouette, the ends of the bridge folded back on top when in transit. When launching the bridge, a stabiliser at the front was lowered. The ends of the bridge were then unfolded and the bridge rolled forward, before being lowered into place. The MTU-20 had a

MTU-20

span length of 20m, with a load capacity of 60 tonnes. Launching the bridge took five minutes, recovery from either end took between five and seven minutes. Both launching and recovery could be carried out while the crew remained inside the vehicle. It was fitted with a deep-wading snorkel, NBC protection, and an automatic fire-suppression system.

SPECIFICATIONS: MTU-20

Crew: 2
Weight: 37 tonnes (including bridge)
Length: 11.64m (including bridge)
Width: 3.3m (including bridge)
Height: 3.4m (including bridge)
Ground clearance: 0.43m
Maximum road speed: 50km/hour
Maximum road range: 500km

Gradient: 40%
Vertical obstacle: 0.8m

Armour:
Hull glacis: 100mm @ 60° [Effective: 200mm]
Hull sides: 70mm @ 40° [Effective: 91mm]
Hull top: 30mm
Hull rear: 60mm
Belly: 20mm

BLG-60 (Poland/DDR)

The non-Soviet Warsaw Pact armies showed a preference for the more common scissor bridge design. Poland and East Germany jointly developed the BLG-60, which mounted a 50-tonne, 21.6m scissor bridge on a T-55 chassis. The bridge was launched by being lifted up to the vertical, then unfolded and simultaneously lowered over the gap. This design gave a quicker launch time than the Soviet designs, at the expense of a very high silhouette during launch. The BLG-60 was fitted with NBC protection and a deep-wading snorkel. An improved version, the BLG-67, was introduced in the late 1970s.

Specifications: BLG-60

Crew: 2-3
Weight: 37 tonnes (including bridge)
Length: 10.57m (including bridge)
Width: 3.48m (including bridge)
Height: 3.4m (including bridge)
Ground clearance: 0.43m
Maximum road speed: 50km/hour
Maximum road range: 500km

Gradient: 58%
Vertical obstacle: 0.8m

ARMOUR:
Hull glacis: 100mm @ 60° [Effective: 200mm]
Hull sides: 7mm @ 40° [Effective: 9mm]
Hull top: 30mm
Hull rear: 60mm
Belly: 20mm

BRIDGE:
Weight: 6 tonnes
Length extended: 21.6m
Width: 3.2m
Load capacity: 50 tonnes

MT-55A (CZECHOSLOVAKIA)

Like the earlier MT-34, the MT-55A mounted a scissor bridge, but was based on a T-55 chassis. A front spade stopped the vehicle being tipped over by the weight of the bridge. Launch time was two to three minutes, recovery time five to six minutes. Both tasks could be carried out from inside the vehicle. It could span an obstacle of up to 18m, and load capacity was 50 tonnes. A gap-measuring device and inclinometer were fitted, to help with finding a suitable site for the bridge. Other equipment included infra-red night-vision equipment, a snorkel, an automatic fire extinguisher, and NBC protection. Unusually, the Soviet army adopted the MT-55A, albeit in small numbers.

Initially, the scissor bridge carried by the MT-55A had circular holes in the sides of the bridge. Later models had solid sides. Multiple bridges could be combined to span larger gaps.

MT-55A (later model bridge)

SPECIFICATIONS: MT-55A

Crew: 2
Weight: 36 tonnes (including bridge)
Length: 10.05m (including bridge)
Width: 3.3m (including bridge)
Height: 3.5m (including bridge)
Ground clearance: 0.43m
Maximum road speed: 35km/hour
Maximum road range: 500km
Gradient: 30%
Vertical obstacle: 0.7m

ARMOUR:

Hull glacis: 100mm @ 60° [Effective: 200mm]

Hull sides: 70mm

Hull top: 30mm

Hull rear: 60mm

Belly: 20mm

BRIDGE:

Weight: 6.5 tonnes

Length extended: 18m

Length folded: 9.6m

Width: 3.3m

Track width: 1.15m (each)

Load capacity: 50 tonnes

MTU-72

In 1974, a new bridge layer entered service: the MTU-72. These were made from existing T-72 tanks with the turret removed, and a bridge-launching mechanism fitted instead. The bridge was of cantilever design, similar to that on the MTU-20, but made of an aluminium alloy. The 20m bridge had a load capacity of 50 tonnes and could span a gap of up to 18m. A second bridge could be launched from the first one to span a gap of up to 35m. Launching the bridge took three minutes, recovery eight minutes. Both launching and recovery could be carried out while the crew remained inside the vehicle.

A blade was fitted to the front of the hull. Primarily intended for stabilising the vehicle during launching and recovery, it could also be used as a bulldozer blade. A light machine gun, deep wading-snorkel, NBC protection system, fire-suppression system, and thermal smoke generation unit were also fitted.

MTU-72

SPECIFICATIONS: MTU-72

Crew: 2
Weight: 40 tonnes (including bridge)
Length: 11.64m (including bridge)
Width: 3.46m (including bridge)
Height: 3.38m (including bridge)
Ground clearance: 0.49m
Maximum road speed: 60km/hour
Maximum road range: 500km
Gradient: 60%
Vertical obstacle: 0.85m
Armament: 1x 7.62mm PKMS MG

BRIDGE:
Weight: 6.4 tonnes
Length extended: 20m
Length folded: 9.42m
Width: 3.3m
Load capacity: 50 tonnes

KMM

The Warsaw Pact made use of unarmoured bridge layers, based on lorries, as well as armoured variants based on tank chassis. The first of these was the KMM lorry-mounted bridge, which had a 12-tonne load capacity. A full system comprised five sections, each mounted on a ZIL-157 6x6 2.5-tonne chassis. Each lorry carried a single straight 7m bridge span. Four spans had integral trestle legs; the fifth span, which would connect to the far bank, had no legs.

To launch, the trackway was spread to its full width and the trestle legs were adjusted to ensure that the bridge would be level once placed. The vehicle reversed to the gap, and the bridge was raised to the vertical, before being lowered down into the final position. Further vehicles repeated the process, adding spans until the gap was completely bridged. A single span could be launched in about 15 minutes, and bridge a 9.5m gap. A full five spans took 45 to 60 minutes, and would bridge 34m. Recovery could take place from either end, in roughly the same time as it took to launch.

SPECIFICATIONS: KMM

Crew: 1+2
Weight: 8.8 tonnes (including bridge)
Length: 8.3m (including bridge)
Width: 3.15m (including bridge)
Height: 3.36m (including bridge)
Ground clearance: 0.31m
Maximum road speed: 40km/hour
Maximum road range: 430km
Gradient: 28%

BRIDGE:
Weight: 1,420kg
Length: 7m
Width: 3.95m
Load capacity: 15 tonnes

TMM

The KMM was replaced by the much improved TMM system, which entered service in 1964. A full set consisted of four 10.5m scissor spans carried on modified KrAZ-214 6x6 7-tonne lorries. Three spans had trestle legs with adjustments to allow for different depths. The fourth span had no legs, since it connected to the far bank. A later version, the TMM-3, used KrAZ-255B 6x6 7.5-tonne lorries, and featured improvements in the bridge-laying mechanism. The two versions could be readily identified by the position of the spare tyre. It was to the rear of the cab on the TMM, and on top of the cab on the TMM-3.

Before launching, the trestle legs were adjusted to the correct height and the trackways spread to their full width. The lorry reversed to the launch position, and a hydraulic girder raised the

TMM-3

folded span to the vertical. A cable and winch system straightened the span, and then lowered it into place. The trestle legs dropped into place as the span was lowered. Once in position, the cables were removed, the launching girder returned to the transit position, and the lorry drove away.

The standard four units could cross a 40m obstacle, although extra units could be added to bridge wider gaps. The bridge had a load capacity of 60 tonnes. An average crew would take 45 to 60 minutes to lay a four-section bridge. Recovery took the same time, and could be performed from either end.

In each division, some TMMs would be kept in reserve, and used to replace tank-launched bridges. The armoured bridge-layers would then re-join the advance unit.

The time to launch both KMM and TMM bridges could be halved with a well-trained crew. Both types could be laid underwater to reduce the possibility of detection. The difficulty of laying an underwater bridge increased the time taken by about 50%.

Specifications: TMM

Crew: 1+2
Weight: 19.5 tonnes (including bridge)
Length: 9.3m (including bridge)
Width: 3.2m (including bridge)
Height: 3.15m (including bridge)
Ground clearance: 0.36m
Maximum road speed: 55km/hour
Maximum road range: 530km

Bridge:
Weight: 7 tonnes
Length: 10.5m
Width: 3.8m
Load capacity: 60 tonnes

AM-50 (Czechoslovakia)

Czechoslovakia developed their own lorry-mounted scissors bridge, mounted on the rear of a Tatra 813 8x8 lorry. Launched in a similar manner to the Soviet TMM, the trestles on the AM-50 were adjusted hydraulically rather than manually. The bridge had a full width roadway, 4m wide and 13.5m long, with 50 tonne load capacity.

SMT-1 (Poland)

The SMT-1 was a lorry-mounted bridge developed in Poland. Organised in units of four, each vehicle carried a straight 11m span on a Star 660 6x6 2.5-tonne lorry. Unlike the Soviet vehicles, the bridge was launched over the front of the cab, rather than over the rear. The trackways were of a lightweight design

SMT-1 laying a multi-span bridge

and fixed, so that they did not need to be spread before launching.

Placing a span took three to five minutes, and was controlled from inside the cab. SMT spans were sometimes used as single-span bridges or as ramps onto pontoon bridges. Extra spans could be carried on a single-axle trailer.

SPECIFICATIONS: SMT-1

Crew: 1+2
Weight: 9.6 tonnes (including bridge)
Length: 11.97m (including bridge)
Width: 3.3m (including bridge)
Height: 3.15m (including bridge)
Ground clearance: 0.27m
Maximum road speed: 50km/hour
Maximum road range: 500km

BRIDGE:
Weight: 2.3 tonnes
Length: 11m
Width: 3m
Load capacity: 40 tonnes

Pontoon Bridges

LPP

The LPP light pontoon bridge was developed as a replacement for the Second World War-era DLP pontoon bridge. A full set consisted of 24 bow sections and 12 centre sections, each one carried on a GAZ-63 4x4 2-tonne lorry.

Pontoons were launched by gravity. Each pontoon had a turntable on top, holding the track and superstructure. Once in the water, the turntable was turned through ninety degrees and the superstructure assembled. Depending on the load to be carried, pontoon sections could be joined together or used singly.

An LPP bridge could be configured to carry loads of 12, 24, or 40 tonnes. The capacity was determined by the configuration of

LPP pontoon

pontoon elements. For a 12-tonne bridge, each support was a single pontoon. For a 24-tonne bridge, two pontoons were used for each support. Three pontoons per support would be required for a 40-tonne load. Assembly time was 50 to 60 minutes. LPP pontoons could also be configured as 24-tonne or 40-tonne-capacity ferries.

TMP

The TMP heavy pontoon bridge entered service in the Second World War, but only went into volume production after the war. It was the standard Soviet heavy pontoon bridge until it was replaced by the TPP. The pontoons were carried on ZIL-151 6x6 2.5-tonne lorries, which would back into the water, launching the pontoons by gravity. In the water, the pontoons were joined together. A complete set had 36 bow and 36 centre sections.

A full TMP set could create a 109m-long 70-tonne bridge, a 228m-long 50-tonne bridge, or a 518m-long 16-tonne bridge. Alternatively, TMP pontoons could be configured as 16-tonne, 30-tonne, or 50-tonne rafts, which would be powered by outboard motors or pushed by bridging boats.

TPP

The TPP was the heavy counterpart to the LPP, also developed as a replacement for a Second World War-era pontoon bridge, in this case the TMP. Like the LPP, each pontoon had a turntable holding the track and superstructure, which was turned through ninety degrees once launched. This allowed a TPP bridge to be constructed much more quickly than the older TMP.

A complete TPP set included 48 bow and 48 centre pontoons, eight trestles, four flotation drums, and twelve BMK-150 boats. In Soviet service, these were carried on 116 ZIL-151 or ZIL-157 6x6 2.5-tonne lorries. Other Warsaw Pact countries used locally-built lorries as transport vehicles.

A full TPP set could create a 205m-long 70-tonne bridge, a 265m-long 50-tonne bridge, or a 335m-long 16-tonne bridge. A working party of 384 men would take between two and three hours to build the bridge. Alternatively, TPP pontoons could be configured as 50-tonne ferries.

PMP

Introduced in 1962, the PMP marked a significant improvement in folding bridge design. The design concepts were adopted and further improved upon by the US army, resulting in the Ribbon Bridge. Each pontoon was made up of four sections,

PMP pontoon

folded in an accordion style when in transit, and with an integrated roadway. Initially carried on KrAZ-214 6x6 7-tonne lorries, they were later carried on more powerful KrAZ-255B 6x6 7.5-tonne lorries. In Czech service, they were carried on Tatra 813 8x8 8-tonne lorries, some of which were fitted with bulldozer blades to help with preparing river banks.

To launch a pontoon, the travel locks were released. The lorry then reversed up to the river bank, and braked sharply. Momentum carried the pontoon over a series of rollers, off the back of the lorry, and on into the river. The pontoon started to unfold automatically. It was fully unfolded, and a set of six locking devices used to make it fully rigid. The pontoons were connected together at the near shore, then swung into position. To recover a pontoon, the lorry reversed to the edge of the river. A winch and jib built into the lorry would be set up, and used to winch the pontoon back onto the lorry bed. The winch simultaneously re-folded the pontoon as it pulled it out of the water and onto the lorry. The pontoon was secured, and the lorry driven away. A full bridge took 50 minutes to assemble, while ferries took 8 to 20 minutes to assemble, depending on size. If the river was too shallow at the edges to accommodate the pontoons, TMM bridges could be used to connect the PMP bridge to the shore.

A standard PMP bridge was 227m long, with a load capacity of 60 tonnes, but the design was very flexible and offered other options. Extra hinges allowed the pontoons to be split lengthways. By doing this, and including full-size pontoons at regular intervals, a 389m, 20-tonne bridge could be built. Pontoons could also be used to create ferries of various sizes, with loads from 20 tonnes to 170 tonnes. A complete PMP pontoon set consisted of 32 river pontoons, four shore pontoons, and 12 bridging boats (BMK-T, BMK-130, BMK-130M, BMK-150, or BMK-150M).

PVD-20

The PVD-20 was an air-portable pontoon bridge designed for use by airborne forces. It could be dropped by parachute or carried by helicopter. A full set was made up of ten units. Each unit included two NDL-20 boats and trackways, made of duralumin to save weight. They were carried in ten GAZ-63 4x4 2-tonne or six ZIL-157 6x6 2.5-tonne lorries.

The PVD-20 could be used to build an 88m-long, 6-tonne bridge, or a 64m-long, 8-tonne bridge, in 50 minutes. Alternatively, ten 4-tonne rafts could be built in 15 minutes, six 6-tonne rafts in 20 minutes, or four 8-tonne rafts in 25 minutes.

Any of these configurations were sufficient to support the 3.4-tonne ASU-57 air-portable tank destroyer.

TZI

The TZI was a pontoon footbridge, first used during the Second World War. It consisted of floats made of rubberised fabric, filled with straw or hay, and with wooden boards and metal posts. The TZI was primarily used as a single-lane footbridge, but it could be built as a double-lane bridge to allow crew-served weapons to cross. A full set could be carried in a pair of light lorries.

A single-lane bridge was 56m long and could be constructed in 10 to 18 minutes. A double-lane bridge could cross a 28m obstacle, and took 14 to 22 minutes to construct. Sets of four or seven floats could also be combined into rafts, taking four or ten minutes respectively.

PPS

The PPS was a heavy girder pontoon bridge, with each pontoon built up from four sections (one bow, two central, one stern). The stern section included a power unit. Each section was carried on a ZIL-151 6x6 2.5-tonne lorry. An assembled pontoon was 23m long, and supported a 6m-wide full-width roadway. The maximum capacity of the bridge was 60 tonnes.

DPP-40

The DPP-40 was an air-portable pontoon bridge designed for use by airborne forces. As such, it was designed to be dropped by parachute. Development started in the late 1950s, and it was in service by the early 1970s. A full set consisted of 32 pontoons, each carried on a GAZ-66 4x4 2-tonne lorry, with 16 outboard motors and an extra GAZ-66 to carry auxiliary equipment.

Each pontoon consisted of a sealed metal box in the centre, with a pair of inflatable sides. In transit, the inflatable sections were folded on top of the centre piece. To launch, the vehicle reversed to the water's edge, then used a winch to unfold the sides and an air pump to inflate them. The assembled pontoon was then dropped into the water. If required, the sides could be inflated on the water, using a hose connected to the vehicle. Pontoons are connected together in such a way that the centre pieces form the roadway for the bridge.

A full DPP-40 bridge was 128m long, with a capacity of 40 tonnes. Alternatively, the pontoons could be formed into eight 40-tonne or sixteen 20-tonne ferries. When used as ferries, the outboard motors provided propulsion. Any of these configurations were able to support a BMD airborne fighting vehicle or ASU-85 air-portable tank destroyer.

LPB (DDR)

The LPB was a light pontoon bridge introduced in the 1950s, based on the Soviet Second World War DLP design. The pontoons had sheet steel hulls instead of the original's plywood, which improved stability and durability. A full set included 40 bow and 20 centre pontoons.

A set could bridge a 162m gap with a 10-tonne bridge, a 109m gap with a 16-tonne bridge, or a 58m gap with a 30-tonne bridge. Rafts with carrying capacities of 6, 10, or 30 tonnes could be created from the components, or pontoons could be assembled into assault boats.

PP-64 pontoon

PP-64 (POLAND)

The Polish PP-64 was inspired by the Soviet PMP folding pontoon bridge. Design work started in 1964, with the first production units delivered in 1966. Although inspired by the PMP, it was by no means a copy. The PP-64 had a different design which allowed for faster construction, but a lower load capacity for the standard bridge (40 tonnes compared to the PMP's 60 tonnes). A full PP-64 set included 48 river pontoons, six shore pontoons, twelve ramps, and six KH-200 bridging boats. A special connecting piece to join a PP-64 to a Soviet PMP was also included as standard.

A PP-64 set could bridge a 186m gap with a 40-tonne bridge, or a 97m gap with an 80 tonne bridge. On faster-flowing rivers, a second type of 40-tonne bridge configuration could be used to span up to 145m. In transit, pontoons were folded lengthways in an inverted V shape. To launch, the lorry (a Star 660 6x6 2.5-tonne) reversed up to the river edge. The pontoon was unfolded on the lorry, then launched into the water.

As well as bridges, PP-64 pontoons could be used to create a set of six ferries, each 14.8m long and 12.8m wide, with a 40-tonne load capacity. Alternatively, two large ferries could be constructed, each 37m long and 12.5m wide.

LMS (Czechoslovakia)

The LMS was a Czech light pontoon bridge, made out of aluminium. The bow pontoon was open, while the centre pontoon was fully enclosed. Once in the water the pontoons were assembled and bolted together, and then the trackway was added. The trackway could be full width, or more commonly, a dual-track type.

The bridge had a load capacity of 20 tonnes, and could be assembled in 40 minutes. The LMS could also be built as 10-tonne, 15-tonne, 20-tonne or 24-tonne rafts. Rafts were propelled in the water by an outboard motor, up to a maximum speed of 11km/hour. A complete set included 48 bow and 24 centre sections, carried on Praga V3S 6x6 3-tonne lorries.

SMS (Czechoslovakia)

The SMS was another Czech design, similar to the LMS, but larger and heavier. Classified by the Czech army as a medium pontoon bridge, it would be considered a heavy bridge by the US army. Built of steel, each full pontoon consisted of a single centre and two bow sections. Each pontoon was carried on a Praga V3S

6x6 3-tonne lorry. Decking and balking for three pontoons were carried on a single Tatra 111 6x6 10-tonne lorry.

Each bow pontoon had a winch and a removable deck, which were often not fitted. The centre pontoon had a fixed deck. Unlike other designs, pontoons had to be removed from their transport vehicles by crane, leading to a long construction time. A complete set included 72 bow and 36 centre sections.

SMS pontoon bridges could be built in 20-tonne, 40-tonne, or 60-tonne configurations. All took around 200 minutes to construct. Alternatively, the pontoons could be used to create rafts with capacities of 20, 40, or 60 tonnes. These were significantly quicker to construct, taking only 30 to 40 minutes.

PR-60 (Romania)

The PR-60 was developed as a replacement for the Soviet Second World War-era TMP, and could be used as a raft as well as a bridge. It did not use a folding design like the PMP, leading to a significantly longer construction time. Pontoons were carried on Bucegi SR-114 4x4 4-tonne lorries, and launched by gravity. Each lorry could carry two river pontoons, one on top of the other, or a single shore pontoon. The lorry had no recovery capacity, and so pontoons were recovered by crane. A complete PR-60 set had 56 river pontoons and four shore pontoons. A full set could make a 143m, 40-tonne bridge or an 80m, 60-tonne bridge.

Amphibians and Ferries

K-61

The K-61 tracked amphibious ferry was introduced in 1950, a direct result of wartime experience with American DUKW amphibious lorries supplied through the lend-lease program. It remained in Soviet service until the late 1960s. It was fully tracked, and based on a light AFV chassis, but was not armoured. The K-61 could carry eight wounded on stretchers or 40 fully armed infantry. Alternatively, it could carry up to five tonnes of equipment, a single lorry of up to 2.5 tonnes, or an artillery piece.

K-61

Loading was via ramps at the rear. Vehicles could be driven on, and a winch was provided for loading heavy equipment such as artillery pieces. It was driven through the water by a pair of propellers, at a speed of up to 10km/hour.

GSP

The GSP heavy amphibious ferry was introduced in 1959. A single ferry was made up of two distinct units, one left and one right. The two units were mirror images of each other, and not interchangeable. Before entering the water, a trim vane was erected at the front of the hull. The two units then entered the water separately and joined up in the water. Once linked, the pontoons, which were inverted while in transit, were swung upright, and the trackways deployed. It was important that the pontoons were both unfolded together, to avoid overbalancing the whole. Assembly time was 6 to 10 minutes.

The ferry had hydraulically operated ramps at each end, allowing vehicles to be driven on at one end and off at the other. Load capacity was 52 tonnes, enough to carry a main battle tank. It was reported that in good conditions, a tank could fire its main armament whilst on the ferry.

The vehicle itself was tracked, with a suspension similar to the PT-76 light tank. It had infra-red driving lights, although these were only used on land. The hull and pontoon were lightweight steel filled with plastic foam. The foam increased buoyancy and reduced vulnerability to enemy fire, allowing buoyancy to be retained even if the hull was holed. Propulsion in the water was provided by four propellers (two per vehicle), mounted in tunnels under the hull. Maximum speed in the water was 8km/hour.

SPECIFICATIONS: GSP VEHICLE UNIT

Crew: 3
Weight: 17 tonnes
Length: 12m
Width: 3.24m

GSP vehicle unit (left)

Height: 3.2m
Ground clearance: 0.35m
Maximum road speed: 40km/hour
Maximum road range: 300km
Gradient: 45%
Vertical obstacle: 0.8m

SPECIFICATIONS: GSP FULL FERRY

Weight: 34 tonnes
Length: 12m
Width: 12.63m
Draught (unloaded): 0.97m
Draught (loaded): 1.5m
Maximum water speed (unloaded): 10.8km/hour
Maximum water speed (loaded): 7.7km/hour
Load capacity: 52 tonnes

PTS

The PTS was introduced in 1966, as a replacement for the K-61. Larger than its predecessor, with a more powerful engine, it could carry up to 5 tonnes on land and 15 tonnes on water. Alternatively, it could carry up to 70 seated troops or 12 stretcher cases. The cargo area was open, but a tarpaulin was provided for protection from the elements.

PTS-M

The crew were seated in a cab at the front, and provided with full NBC protection. The engine was under the cargo compartment, and the vehicle was propelled in the water by two propellers in tunnels. A pair of rudders at the rear of the hull were used to steer. Before entering the water, the bilge pumps were switched on, and a trim vane erected at the front.

A boat-shaped trailer, designated PKP, was developed for use with the PTS. This had two small pontoons that folded onto the top when travelling, and were rotated through 180° and locked into place before entering the water. The trailer could be towed at speeds of up to 30km/hour when not loaded, down to 25km/hour when loaded. The trailer was not a success, as it was found to be unusable in anything other than very calm waters.

Rear ramps were used to load cargo, with a winch for loading heavy non-motorised loads. An infra-red searchlight and infra-red driving lights were fitted. A later version, with several minor improvements, was designated PTS-M.

PMM-2

Initially known to NATO as the ABS(T), the PMM-2 was introduced in 1974 as a replacement for the GSP ferry, and possibly the PMP pontoon bridge. It was based on a BAZ-5937 chassis, with two aluminium folded pontoons mounted on top, with entrance ramps. As the vehicle entered the water, the pontoons were hydraulically unfolded to either side. The vehicle itself formed a centre section. It was propelled in the water by water jets.

As a ferry, units could be used individually (40 tonne capacity), in pairs (80 tonne capacity), or in threes (120 tonne capacity). A single vehicle could be used as a bridge, to span gaps of up to 17m. Up to ten vehicles could be combined to span larger gaps, with no need for bridging boats.

PTS-2

The PTS-2, introduced in 1985, was an improved and modernised version of the PTS-M. It had a new suspension,

PTS-2

derived from the MT-T artillery tractor. The cab was larger than that on the older vehicle, and had NBC protection. The cargo space was larger, and it could carry up to 12 tonnes of cargo. As with the PTS-M, it had a pair of propellers for propulsion on the water, although a new engine meant that it was faster on both land and water.

Bridging Boats

Soviet bridging boats were designed to be resilient to damage. They used compartments to limit flooding, and could stay afloat even if one or two compartments were holed and took on water. All designs were fitted with bilge pumps to remove any water taken on. The bilge pumps would be switched on prior to entering the water.

BMK-70 AND BMK-90

The steel-hulled BMK-70 dated from the Second World War, where it saw extensive service. It was normally carried on a trailer and towed behind a lorry.

The BMK-90 was developed in the 1950s as a replacement for the BMK-70. It had a corrugated steel hull, with a more powerful engine. Two wheels simplified launching and recovery of the boat, and could be removed or folded up alongside the hull when in the water. The later BMK-90M used duralumin instead of steel, and had a redesigned propeller shaft.

SPECIFICATIONS: BMK-70

Crew: 2
Weight: 2,450kg (without fuel)
Length: 7.83m
Beam: 2.1m
Depth: 1.5m
Draught: 0.64m
Maximum speed: 20.5km/hour (unloaded)
Towing power (forward): 681kg

SPECIFICATIONS: BMK-90 (BMK-90M IN BRACKETS)

Crew: 2
Weight: 2,450kg (without fuel)
Length: 7.83m
Beam: 2.1m
Depth: 1.5m
Draught: 0.53m (0.52m)
Maximum speed: 20.5km/hour (unloaded)
Maximum speed: 8km/hour (loaded)

Endurance: 14 hours
Towing power (forward): 1,100kg
Towing power (reverse): 1,400kg

BMK-130

Developed for use with the PMP pontoon bridge, the BMK-130 also gradually replaced the BMK-90. It was usually towed by a ZIL-131 6x6 3.5-tonne or ZIL-157 6x6 2.5-tonne lorry. A pair of integrated wheels negated the need for a separate trailer. These wheels were swung forward to the side of the hull when in the water. The boat had a steel hull and a single propeller driven by a two-stroke, 100hp diesel engine. It could achieve speeds of up to 19km/hour in the water.

As well as its use with pontoon bridges and for river reconnaissance, the BMK-130 was used to carry infantry reconnaissance teams across water obstacles. Introduced in 1960, it was followed by an improved version, the BMK-130M, in 1965. This had recesses in the hull for the wheels to fold into, reducing drag and the chance of wheel damage when in the water.

SPECIFICATIONS: BMK-130M

Crew: 2
Weight: 3,450kg
Length: 7.85m
Beam: 2.1m
Depth: 1.5m
Draught: 0.62m
Maximum speed: 21km/hour
Endurance: 12 hours
Towing power (forward): 1,450kg
Towing power (reverse): 800 tonnes

BMK-150

The BMK-150 was normally towed by a ZIL-131 6x6 3.5-tonne or ZIL-157 6x6 2.5-tonne lorry. The hull was made of aluminium, making it significantly lighter than the BMK-130. It had two screws, controlled by a pair of engines. A pair of integrated wheels meant that no trailer was required, simplifying launching. Once in the water, the wheels were folded back, and lay outside the hull. A petrol engine drove the boat at speeds of up to 22km/hour on the water. Unlike the BMK-130, it had a windscreen and a cover for protection against inclement weather. A seating area in the back allowed the boat to be used as a ferry for infantry.

The later BMK-150M had improved performance, and added wells in the hull to accommodate the wheels when they were folded back.

SPECIFICATIONS: BMK-150

Crew: 2
Weight: 2,500kg
Length: 8.2m
Beam: 2.55m
Depth: 2m
Draught: 0.66m
Maximum speed: 22km/hour
Endurance: 7 hours
Towing power (forward): 1,500kg

SPECIFICATIONS: BMK-150M

Crew: 2
Weight: 3,800kg
Length: 7.4m
Beam: 2.55m
Draught: 0.75m
Maximum speed: 22km/hour
Endurance: 6 hours

BMK-T

The BMK-T was introduced to replace the earlier BMK boats. Unlike earlier designs, it did not have integrated wheels. Instead, it was carried on the back of a KrAZ-214 6x6 7-tonne or KrAZ-255V 6x6 7.5-tonne lorry. It had a fully enclosed crew cabin and engine compartment, allowing it to operate in rough water. A large area at the back could be used to transport up to 25 fully equipped infantrymen.

Steering was done by turning the two propellers, rather than using rudders, making the boat very manoeuvrable. The propellers would automatically lift out of the water if an obstacle was encountered. The 180hp diesel engine powered the boat at speeds of up to 17km/hour. The boat could be remotely controlled at a distance of up to 30m. A powerful bilge pump was fitted, which could be used as a hose to extinguish fires or wash down pontoons, as well as evacuating water from the boat itself.

The boat was launched by gravity, often with the engine already running. Recovery was affected using a winch mounted on the lorry, pulling the boat over runners onto the rear bed. When travelling, the propellers were swung onto the top of the boat.

BMK-T on a KrAZ-260 lorry

SPECIFICATIONS: BMK-T

Crew: 2
Weight: 6 tonnes
Length: 8.6m
Beam: 2.7m
Depth: 2.2m
Draught: 0.75m
Maximum speed: 17km/hour
Endurance: 15-17 hours
Towing power (forward): 2,000kg
Towing power (reverse): 750 tonnes

BB-120 (DDR)

The BB-120 was essentially an East German copy of the Soviet BMK-90. The BB-120 differed in having no hand rails on the sides and a spray rail at the rear. It had a three-bladed propeller and a standard rudder. On land, it was carried on a four-wheel flatbed trailer.

SPECIFICATIONS: BB-120

Crew: 2
Weight: 3,500kg (without fuel)
Length: 7.85m
Beam: 2.1m
Depth: 1.5m
Draught: 0.55m
Maximum speed: 22km/hour
Towing power (forward): 1,200kg
Towing power (reverse): 700kg

KH-200 (POLAND)

Development of the KH-200 started in the late 1960s, and it was approved for production in 1971. The hull was made of steel, with a cabin for the crew toward the front. Behind the cabin was a large open area, which could accommodate up to 15 troops, allowing the KH-200 to be used as a troop transport.

KH-200 being towed by a Ural-375 lorry

The engine drove a single propeller, with a top speed of 25km/hour. The KH-200 was used with the PP-64 pontoon bridge, and was transported on a two-axle trailer.

Specifications: KH-200

Crew: 2-3
Weight: 3,865kg
Length: 8.14m
Beam: 2.3m
Draught: 0.72m
Maximum speed: 25km/hour
Endurance: 12 hours
Towing power (forward): 2,500kg
Towing power (reverse): 1,200kg

Mo-108, Mo-111, Mo-930 (Czechoslovakia)

Czechoslovakia produced three bridging boats during the Cold War. The Mo-108 and Mo-111 were modifications of a German Second World War design, introduced in the 1950s. The only difference between the two was the engine. The Mo-111's engine was larger and more powerful, giving it a better performance. Both boats had three rudders and a single screw in a metal ring guard known as a Kort nozzle. They were transported on two-wheeled trailers, designated MP-4.

The later Mo-930 used the same engine as the Tatra 813 8x8 8-tonne lorry. Like the earlier boats, it had a single propeller and was transported on a two-wheel trailer. It was larger and heavier than the Mo-111, but had a more powerful engine, giving a similar performance.

SPECIFICATIONS: MO-111

Crew: 2
Weight: 3,200kg
Length: 7.5m
Beam: 2.2m
Depth: 1.2m
Draught: 0.85m
Maximum speed: 24km/hour

SPECIFICATIONS: MO-930

Crew: 2
Weight: 4 tonnes
Length: 7.68m
Beam: 2.2m
Draught: 0.85m
Maximum speed: 20km/hour
Endurance: 7 hours
Towing power (forward): 2,275kg
Towing power (reverse): 1,200kg

LINE OF COMMUNICATION BRIDGES

As well as bridging systems for use close to the front lines, considerable effort was put into the issue of bridges further behind the lines. During the Second World War, Soviet engineers built large bridges from scratch, using timber. After the war, pre-fabricated wooden bridges were developed. These required timber supports, but were still faster to construct. Supporting machinery, such as mobile cranes and specialised laying machines, were also developed.

The Warsaw Pact nations also used heavy barges to construct bridges. These would be lined up, either end to end or side to side, so that it was possible for a vehicle to drive over the barges from one bank to the other. The end-to-end arrangement was most common, though some barges were fitted with supports to allow a roadway to be fitted when lined up side to side. The barges could also be used to support tracks to create a railway bridge. These barge bridges were slow to construct, and blocked normal river traffic, so dedicated bridges and ferries were preferred where possible.

In the late 1980s, an underwater pontoon bridge set was introduced. The pontoons were similar to those used by the PMP bridge, and the bridge was constructed in a similar manner. When the bridge was complete, the pontoons were flooded, so that the bridge lay just under the water, making it difficult to spot.

PVM, LVM, TVM Suspension Bridges

These three bridges were developed primarily for use in mountainous areas. They were usually transported by pack animals, but could be carried on lorries if the terrain permitted.

The PVM was a foot bridge, and could be built as a single 120m bridge or two 60m bridges. In both cases, the bridge was 0.7m wide. An 18-man team took two hours to construct a single long bridge, or three hours to construct two shorter bridges. The set weighed a total of 4,360kg and could be carried by 46 pack animals.

The LVM set built 2m-wide bridges, one of 80m length or two of 40m length. They would take a team of 27 men two or four hours to build. The complete set weighed 13.5 tonnes and was transported on 160 pack animals. The completed bridge had a load capacity of 2 tonnes, but the axle load of any vehicle using it had to be no more than 635kg. The TVM was similar, but with a length of 60m and a load capacity of 10 tonnes.

MARM

The MARM light sectional bridge was used to cross dry gaps or rivers, and was often used as a road overpass to ease congestion at busy junctions. Each span was 6m long and included a set of adjustable-height folding trestles. The spans were put into place with a lorry-mounted crane, and the trestles braced. Spans were transported in pairs on semi-trailers towed by ZIL-130V tractor units. The MARM had a load capacity of 50 tonnes. A 118m bridge would take around eight hours to construct.

SARM

The SARM medium sectional deck truss bridge was made up of sections bolted together, with a roadway of steel deck panels. It could be built with a 4.2m-wide single roadway, having a capacity of 40 tonnes, or a 7.2m-wide dual roadway of 20 tonnes capacity. Each individual span could be 18.6m, 25.6m, or 32.6m long. Existing piers were used whenever possible.

Components were carried on single-axle semi-trailers towed by MAZ-504 or ZIL-130V tractor units. No individual pieces weighed more than 4.4 tonnes, so a 5-tonne crane was sufficient for construction. A 200m bridge would take 24 to 30 hours to construct.

BARM

This was a heavy pre-fabricated road bridge. It had a 60-tonne load, but could take special loads of up to 90 tonnes. Each span could be up to 52.5m long, and a set included two spans, an

8.84m-high pier, and installation and ancillary equipment. It took 24 hours to construct.

NZhM-56

The NZhM-56 was developed as a replacement for the wartime SP-19 bridge. The earlier bridge could carry road or rail traffic, but the NZhM-56 could carry both simultaneously.

A pontoon bridge, the NZhM-56 pontoons were in three sections: bow, centre, and stern. Each section was carried on a ZIL-131 6x6 3.5-tonne or ZIL-157 6x6 2.5-tonne lorry, with a trailer to accommodate the length of the pontoon section. Originally launched by crane, a later development allowed the pontoons to be launched by gravity. Once in the water, the sections were joined up, superstructure added, and the pontoons were pushed into position by boats.

NZhM-56 pontoon

The two-level superstructure included a roadway on the lower level and a railway on the upper level. The railway could be built to Soviet gauge (1.524m track) or European gauge (1.435m track). The roadway had a wooden deck on I-beam stringers with a capacity of 40 tonnes.

RMM-4

The RMM-4 portable fixed bridge was developed in the late 1940s. It could be used to repair destroyed bridges or, with the addition of supports, could be used to construct longer bridges. A complete set included 24 intermediate and eight end sections, carried on 12 GAZ-63 4x4 2-tonne lorries. The bridge had a wooden deck and two to four steel trusses, depending on the required length and capacity. Once assembled, the section would be pushed into place, and ramps would be added to complete the bridge. An RMM-4 set could create a 16-tonne bridge of 34m length, a 30-tonne bridge of 25m length, or a 60-tonne bridge of 16m length.

REM-500

The REM-500 was a sectional railway bridge, which could also function as a road bridge if a wooden floor was added. It consisted of 12.51m-long spans with integrated trestles. Each span weighed 10.7 tonnes, and the trestles could be adjusted from 3m to 12.7m. The railway track could be built to Soviet gauge (1.524m track) or European gauge (1.435m track). It was constructed a span at a time, using an overhead gantry (the SRK-2D) that travelled along the bridge as it was built. Trains had to slow to 30km/hour when crossing the bridge, with a maximum axle load of 20 tonnes.

SP-19 Self-Propelled Pontoon Bridge

A combination road and railway bridge introduced in 1939, the SP-19 saw use throughout the Second World War, and was replaced by the NZhM-56. Although it could be used to carry road or railway traffic, it could only carry one or the other, unlike the NZhM-56, which could carry both simultaneously.

An individual pontoon had a capacity of 22 tonnes. When formed into a ferry, the ferry had a capacity of 100 tonnes. A bridge could have a capacity of up to 180 tonnes, or sacrifice capacity for length, allowing a maximum length of 1,140m with a capacity of 30 tonnes.

TMS (Czechoslovakia)

The TMS was a heavy truss panel bridge. It was a double-truss, single-storey bridge, with a capacity of 100 tonnes and a span of 45m.

MS-1 (Czechoslovakia)

Sometimes referred to as the SM-60, the MS-1 was a single-storey heavy panel bridge with a 4m-wide roadway and a 60-tonne load capacity. Each span could be up to 21m long, and trestles could be used to make a multi-span bridge. The trestles had large baseplates to minimise ground pressure, and could be adjusted for heights of 1.5m to 7m. Cranes were required to construct the bridge, which was carried on Tatra 111 6x6 10-tonne lorries.

DMS-65 (POLAND)

The DMS-65 could be seen as an improved version of the venerable British Bailey bridge. It was usually built as a road bridge, but could also be built as a railway bridge. It had five basic elements, and could be constructed by manpower alone, or with the aid of cranes. Single or multi-span bridges could be built. The roadway consisted of metal sheets that could be optionally covered with crushed stone. The bridge was normally carried on Star 66 6x6 2.5-tonne lorries.

ESB-16 (DDR)

The ESB-16 railway-road bridge had both civilian and military variants, and could take European and Soviet-gauge railway track. Each span was 16m long, with a 4m-wide roadway, and made up of hollow box girders with cross-pieces. Nine trestles were provided, which could be adjusted to heights from 1.65m to 11.5m in 1cm intervals. The trestles had large, 7m2 rectangular bases. An SRK-50 crane was normally used to construct the bridge, though smaller cranes could be used if necessary.

SBG-66 (DDR)

Another bridge intended for both civilian and military use, the SBG-66 could be built on pontoons or fixed supports. It could be built as a road or railway bridge, and with fixed supports could be built as a jetty or overpass. It had a load capacity of 80 tonnes, and could have a single 4m-wide roadway or a 7m-wide, two-lane roadway. The pontoons were 32.5m long, 8.2m wide, and positioned by boats.

SB-30 AND SB-45 (DDR)

The SB-30 road bridge was designed to be compatible with existing bridging, but faster to construct and easier to maintain. SB-30 spans were 30m long with a load capacity of 60 tonnes, a single roadway width of 4.2m or double roadway width of 7.75m. Individual elements were made of corrosion-resistant steel, 7.5m long and 10 tonnes in weight.

Tests revealed that for wheeled vehicles, including tank transporters, the spans could be lengthened to 45m. The use of longer spans resulted in significantly reduced construction times, since fewer supports were needed. This resulted in a new version, the SB-45, which could have spans 30m, 37.5m, or 45m long. Load capacities were 80 tonnes, 60 tonnes, and 40 tonnes respectively. With a double-lane bridge used as a single lane, loads of up to 86 tonnes could cross 45m spans. If the spans were reduced to 22.5m it could carry railway traffic.

Mine Warfare

The Soviet army considered mines to be an important part of both offensive and defensive warfare. There are no precise figures for the number of mines deployed in Afghanistan, but it is estimated to be in the millions. It is known that when the Soviets withdrew, they handed over records of 613 minefields to the Afghan army.

Minelaying

The traditional method of laying mines by hand was time-consuming, labour-intensive, and vulnerable. The Soviet army therefore developed equipment that allowed vehicles to lay mines quickly. Initially, these were simple chutes that could be attached to the side of a lorry or APC. Mines would drop down the chute by gravity, to lay on the surface, possibly to be buried by a follow-on team. These evolved into the more advanced PMR-2 and PMR-3 remotely-delivered mines (also known as scatterable mines). These could be deployed by helicopter, aircraft, artillery (tube or rocket), or missile.

Remotely-delivered mines were used in large quantities in Afghanistan. They were used to interdict mujahideen lines of communication and supply, and to block escape routes during attacks. Multiple-launch rocket systems were generally favoured for delivering mines, since they could cover a large area in a short time.

Helicopter Minelaying Equipment

Warsaw Pact armies deployed minelaying chutes on Mi-4 and Mi-8 helicopters. The Mi-4 could carry 200 mines, while the Mi-8 could carry 400. Both could lay mines on the surface at a rate of four per minute. The introduction of the very small PFM-1 "butterfly" mine allowed over 7,000 mines to be carried by a single helicopter. Very many of these mines were dispensed by helicopter in Afghanistan.

GMZ and GMZ-2

The **GMZ** tracked minelayer entered service in the mid-late 1960s. It is based on the SU-100P chassis, a prototype tank destroyer that never entered full production. It was fitted with infra-red driving lights, an NBC protection system, and could generate smoke by injecting diesel fuel into the exhaust. It had a 14.5mm KPVT heavy machine gun for self-defence.

Preparing the mines would take 15 to 40 minutes. Once this was done, the vehicle would be driven at a speed of up to 16km/hour if the mines were to be laid on top of the ground. If the mines were to be buried, it would drive at about 3km/hour. Mines would be fed onto trays on top of the vehicle. If the mines were to be buried, a plough would lift the ground. The mines would be automatically placed on the ground or inside the ploughed trough.

The GMZ-2 was an improved model. It had a more powerful engine, and allowed for different fuse types to be fitted to the mines.

GMZ-2

Specifications: GMZ

Crew: 4
Weight: 25 tonnes
Length: 9.1m (travelling)
Length: 10.3m (operating)
Width: 3.1m
Height: 2.5m
Maximum road speed: 50km/hour
Gradient: 60%
Vertical obstacle: 10.3m
Operating speed: 4-10km/hour (surface mines)
Operating speed: 2-3km/hour (buried mines)
Minelaying rate: 8 mines/minute (surface mines)
Minelaying rate: 4 mines/minute (buried mines)
Mine spacing: 4-5.5m
Reload time: 12-15 minutes

GMZ-3

Unlike the earlier vehicles in the series, the GMZ-3 was based on the SA-4 chassis. The driver and vehicle commander were seated at the front, with the engine to their right. A land-navigation system was fitted, and the driver had infra-red night vision, allowing minelaying operations to be conducted at night. The commander also had infra-red night vision equipment, and operated the PKT machine gun. Smoke dischargers were fitted on the side of the superstructure, at the rear. Unlike the earlier models, it could not generate smoke by injecting diesel into the exhaust.

GMZ-3, showing the mine-laying mechanism

The mine stowage and laying equipment was at the rear of the vehicle. 208 mines were carried, loaded into the vehicle through a pair of large roof hatches. When laying mines, they were fed into two chutes, one on each side. The laying system could bury mines up to 12cm deep in soil or 50cm deep in snow. When laying mines on the surface, they were laid at a rate of up to eight per minute at a speed of 6 to 16km/hour. When laying buried mines, the rate was halved, and the maximum speed reduced to 6km/hour.

SPECIFICATIONS: GMZ-3

Crew: 3
Weight: 28.5 tonnes
Length: 8.62m (travelling)
Width: 3.25m
Height: 2.7m (travelling)
Ground clearance: 0.45m
Maximum road speed: 60km/hour
Maximum road range: 500km
Gradient: 58%
Vertical obstacle: 0.7m
Operating speed: 6-16km/hour (surface mines)
Operating speed: 6km/hour (buried mines)
Minelaying rate: 8 mines/minute (surface mines)
Minelaying rate: 4 mines/minute (buried mines)
Mine spacing: 5-10m
Reload time: 15-20 minutes
Armament: 7.62mm PKT MG

PMR-2, PMR-3, AND PMZ-4

The PMR-2 was a two-wheel trailer with a pair of chutes. The chutes were wide at the top, where mines were loaded. Mines rolled down a conveyor to the laying mechanism. In the PMR-2, mines were laid on the surface, and could be buried by a follow-on team if required.

The PMR-3 had a single chute, but added a plough which allowed mines to be laid on the surface or buried up to 30 to

PMR-3

40cm deep in soft soil. The PMZ-4 was identical, but the capacity was increased from 120 to 200 mines.

All three were usually towed behind a BTR-152, but could also be towed behind an unarmoured lorry or a BTR-60 armoured personnel carrier. Capacity was increased when towed behind a lorry, up to 350 mines when towed by a Ural-375 6x6 4.5-tonne lorry.

SPECIFICATIONS: PMR-3

Crew: 4 or 5
Length: 3.25m
Width: 2m
Height: 2.5m
Operating speed: 4-10km/hour (surface mines)
Operating speed: 2-3km/hour (buried mines)
Minelaying rate: 10-12 mines/minute

Mine spacing: 4-5.5m
Reload time: 10-12 minutes

UMZ

Adopted in the late 1970s, the UMZ scatterable minelayer consisted of six rotating launcher units mounted on the back of a ZIL-131 6x6 3.5-tonne lorry. Each launcher unit had 30 firing tubes. Mines were fitted into cylindrical cassettes, which were then loaded into the firing tubes. Depending on the type of mine, up to 64 mines could be fitted into each cassette, giving a total of up to 11,520 mines.

Mines were fired to a distance of 30 to 60m from the UMZ, with the vehicle driving at up to 40 km/hour. Minefields of varying widths and depths could be laid, depending on the elevation of the launcher units and speed of the vehicle. The UMZ had a crew of two, and reloading would take 1.5 to 2.5 hours, depending on the type of mines being loaded. With six men, reloading time was reduced to 40 to 60 minutes.

MLG-60 (DDR)

The East German MLG-60 was similar to the Soviet PMR-3. However, where the PMR-3 included a seat for the operator, with the MLG-60 the operator was seated inside the towing vehicle. The MLG-60 also added a large twin follow-up scraper on the rear of the trailer. Mines could be laid on the surface or buried, with spacing between 4m and 6m. It was normally towed by a 6x6 lorry or BTR-152 APC. A slightly improved model, the MLG-60M, was introduced later.

SPECIFICATIONS: MLG-60

Crew: 2
Weight: 800kg
Length: 4.9m (travelling)
Length: 5.9m (operating)
Width: 1.87m
Height: 1.95m (travelling)
Height: 2.1m (operating)
Operating speed: 3-5km/hour

Mine Detection

Various Warsaw Pact armies experimented with the use of helicopter-mounted mine detectors. The detection assembly would be slung under a helicopter, which would fly over a suspected minefield. Once the presence of a minefield, and its extent, had been determined, breaching operations could be carried out.

In addition to mine detectors, the Soviet army made extensive use of mine-sniffer dogs in Afghanistan. They were particularly useful for detecting non-metallic mines. Although they gave good service, they would have been of less use in a highly mobile campaign such as was expected in Western Europe.

VIM-625 and VIM-695 Portable Mine Detectors

Developed during the Second World War, these had a rubber-insulated search head, a search handle, a tuning box, a battery box, and headphones. The battery box, carried in a backpack, contained a 2.8V and a 60V battery. The complete equipment weighed 13kg and could be operated for 10 hours.

VIM-203M Metallic Mine Detector

Developed during the Second World War, the VIM-203M worked on the beat frequency oscillation principle. Two models were used, one with a circular search coil and separate tuning box, the other with a square search coil and a tuning box mounted on the rear of the coil. The former model was heavier (13.5kg), with a higher battery voltage and operating time of 30 hours.

UMIV-1 Portable Mine Detector

Introduced after the Second World War, the UMIV-1 had a rectangular detector at the end of a cylindrical metal handle. A backpack contained the control box and headset. The handle was made up of four pieces, two of which were detachable. It could detect metallic objects at depths of up to 450mm.

Specifications: UMIV-1

Weight: 6.6kg
Detector head size: 220x146mm
Detection range: 450mm
Handle length: 660-1300mm

IMP Portable Mine Detector

The IMP had a cylindrical detector at the end of a four-piece aluminium handle, headphones, and a tuning box combined with battery pack. For working in confined spaces, some pieces of the handle could be removed. With all four handles fitted, the handle was 1.58m long. The detector had two transmitting antennae and one receiving antenna in a Bakelite case. Detection range was up to 460mm.

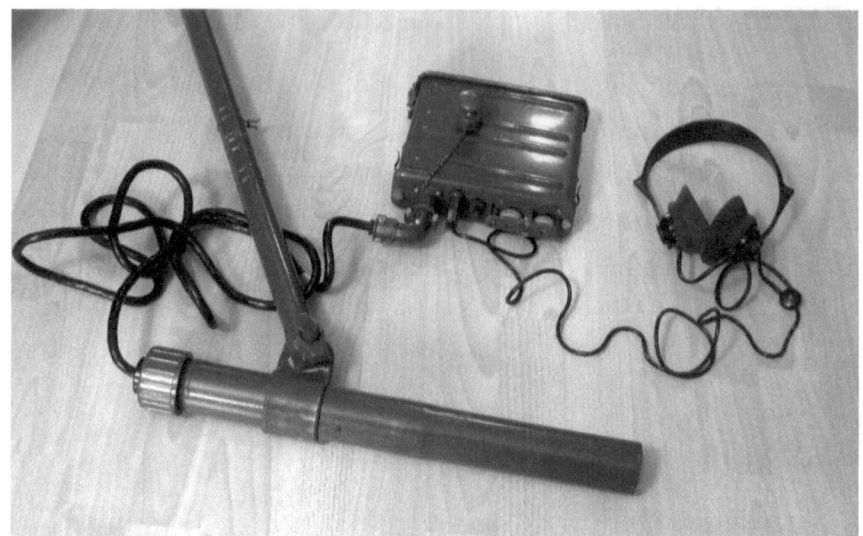

IMP mine detector

The IMP could detect metal mines and plastic mines with some metal components. When disassembled, the IMP was carried in a lightweight, rectangular metal box. It could be used underwater up to a depth of 1m.

SPECIFICATIONS: IMP

Weight: 9.7kg
Detection range: 460mm
Detector head diameter: 38mm
Detector head length: 417mm

DIM VEHICLE-MOUNTED MINE DETECTOR

This mine detector was normally fitted to a GAZ-69 or UAZ-469 4x4 light vehicle. In Afghanistan, the unarmoured vehicles were found to be vulnerable to sniper fire, so they were fitted to T-62 tanks instead. The DIM consisted of a non-magnetic sensing head mounted on a frame. The frame had a pair of rubber-tyred wheels behind the sensing head, which ran along the road surface when in use. When in transit, the assembly was rotated back to rest on top of the vehicle.

When in use, the vehicle was driven at up to 10km/hour, and would detect mines at a depth of up to 250mm. When a mine was detected, an alarm sounded and the vehicle's brakes were automatically applied. The operator could then adjust the search coils to determine the exact location of the mine.

VISF Model 1946 Portable Mine Detector (Bulgaria)

An improved version of the Soviet VIM-203M. It had a rectangular search head assembly with the amplifier box mounted on it. The search handle was made up of four wooden pieces, and could be adjusted with extension pieces. The tone regulator was mounted on the top section of the search handle, and a cast iron battery box was attached at the end of the same section. It was a good deal lighter than the Soviet model (6.2kg), doubled the detection range.

M62 Portable Mine Detector (Bulgaria)

This handheld mine detector could detect metallic mines or plastic mines with metal components. The rectangular detector head was mounted on a search handle, which contained the power source and operating controls. It could detect a 300mm-diameter metallic object at a 500mm distance. It weighed 2.5kg.

M-10 and M-11 Portable Mine Detectors (Czechoslovakia)

These two handheld mine detectors were very similar, but with different search head designs. Both operated on the beat frequency oscillation principle. The M-10 had two detachable, 300mm-diameter plates, while the M-11 had a single plate, with the same effective area. The handle was made up of four jointed sections, each 500mm long. A canvas pack contained the tuning box and batteries. Both weighed 12kg, and were carried in a canvas backpack.

MSG 64 Portable Mine Detector (DDR)

This handheld mine detector had an oval detector assembly and three-piece search handle. The handle contained the tuning box, tone regulator, and batteries. It could detect a 50mm-diameter metallic object at a 180mm distance. It could be disassembled for carrying in a camouflaged waterproof canvas case. The angle of the waterproof detector head was adjustable. It weighed 4.4kg.

Specifications: MSG 64

Weight: 4.4kg
Detection range: 180mm
Handle length: 2.4mm
Detector head weight: 2.35kg

Mine Clearance

The Warsaw Pact armies made extensive use of mine rollers and ploughs in the early part of the Cold War. These were very heavy, requiring cranes for fitting and removal. The KM-61 crane, fitted on a KrAZ-214 6x6 7-tonne lorry, was developed for this task. It had a maximum capacity of 3.2 tonnes and a reach of 2m.

Although vehicles with mine rollers and mine ploughs were a huge improvement over foot troops with mine detectors, they presented a tempting target. Minefields would normally be covered by anti-tank weapons, which would focus on mine-clearing vehicles. In the 1970s, NATO introduced new mine systems such as the US FASCAM system. This enabled NATO commanders to lay remote minefields rapidly, markedly increasing the mine threat. Experiments with explosive-breaching systems, which would allow minefields to be cleared much more quickly, had already begun in the 1960s. The MTK was the first operational system to result from these experiments.

PT-54, PT-54M, AND PT-55 MINE ROLLERS

Introduced during the 1950s, the PT-54 replaced the Second World War-era PT-3 mine rollers. The PT-54 used smaller rollers than the PT-3, in an improved mounting. The PT-54, PT-54M, and PT-55 all worked in the same way. All three consisted of sets of rollers with serrated edges, positioned in front of the host tank's tracks. These rollers would detonate any mines, and also cut a 100mm-wide furrow, marking the safe track for other tanks to follow. A weighted chain between the rollers detonated tilt-rod fused mines before the hull of the tank passed over them.

The PT-54 had six rollers in each set. This was reduced to five per set in the PT-54M, and four per set in the PT-55. Reducing the number of rollers meant that the cleared lane was narrower, but the tank could move faster whilst clearing. All three required a crane to fit, which took around 10 to 15 minutes. Removal time was three to five minutes. A set of rollers had to be replaced after 10 anti-tank mines had been swept. Since the area between the tracks was not swept, three tanks would usually operate in a wedge pattern.

Czechoslovakia used their own version of the Soviet mine rollers. The Czech designs were similar, but with larger rollers, a different design of serrated edge, and a frame instead of a chain to detonate tilt-rod fused mines.

SPECIFICATIONS: PT-54

Weight: 8.8 tonnes
Lane width: 1.3m
Operating speed: 6-10km/hour
Attachment time: 10-15 minutes

SPECIFICATIONS: PT-54M

Weight: 7 tonnes
Lane width: 0.89m
Attachment time: 10-25 minutes

SPECIFICATIONS: PT-55

Weight: 6.7 tonnes
Lane width: 1.7m
Operating speed: 8-12km/hour
Attachment time: 10-15 minutes

KMT-4 MINE PLOUGH

The Warsaw Pact armies found that mine rollers had some significant disadvantages. They were heavy, and significantly reduced the host tank's mobility, especially over rough ground.

The extra weight reduced the life of the tank's transmission and power plant. In addition, advances in fuse design meant that mines would not always be detonated by rollers. The KMT-4 mine plough was introduced in the 1960s to address these issues.

The KMT-4 was the first plough design used by the Warsaw Pact armies. It had a 600mm-wide cutting device in front of each track, with five teeth mounted at an angle. In transit, the blades were kept above ground, allowing the tank to travel at full speed. When in use, the blades were lowered to the ground by a hydraulic ram, and the tank would move at a maximum speed of 12km/hour. As the tank moved forward, the plough would dig up any buried mines and deposit them to the side of the tank's path.

The KMT-4M, which had improvements to the blade attachment system, was introduced in the late 1960s.

KMT-5 Mine Plough and Rollers

The KMT-5 was introduced in the mid-1960s. It combined a KMT-4 mine plough with two sets of three rollers. The individual rollers were thicker than those on the PT-55, and cleared roughly the same width. It was only possible to use both plough and rollers on good, flat ground. Usually one or the other would be used, depending on ground conditions. When used together, the plough was fitted behind the rollers, so that it would clear mines that were not detonated by the rollers. Despite having both rollers and ploughs, the weight was not a great deal more than that of the PT-55, and less than that of the earlier PT-54. The device took 30 to 45 minutes to attach, and could be operated at a speed of 12 to 18km/hour, depending on ground conditions.

An improved version, the KMT-5M, was introduced in the late 1960s. This added a lane-marking plough and the PSK marking system, which used a luminescent substance and flares to mark the cleared lane. Romania made their own copy of the KMT-5M, designated the D-5M.

SPECIFICATIONS: KMT-5

Weight: 7.5 tonnes
Lane width: 0.81m

KMT-6 Mine Plough

Introduced in the late 1960s, the KMT-6 was an improved version of the KMT-4M. Originally developed for use with the T-64 tank, it was also used with the T-72 and T-80. Each plough cleared a path 750mm wide, with a gap of 1.9m.

KMT-7 Mine Plough and Rollers

The KMT-7 was similar to the earlier KMT-5, but with some improvements, and mountings suitable for use with the T-64, T-72, and T-80 tanks. The frames for the rollers allowed more vertical movement, reducing the effect of a blast on the rollers. The KMT-7 could clear two tracks of 1.65m width at a speed of 6-12km/hour. As with earlier systems, fitting required a crane, but the tank driver could disconnect the system using explosive squibs. This allowed the tank to drive away and continue as a combat vehicle.

KMT-8 Mine Plough

Similar to the KMT-7, this was intended for use with all Soviet main battle tanks, and the IMR-2 combat engineer vehicle.

Pneumatic cylinders raised and lowered the ploughs. Once lowered, sensors kept the ploughs at the optimum depth, and each plough could clear a path 600mm wide. The plough units were connected by a metal rod to detonate tilt-rod fused mines.

Installation took around 90 minutes, and once fitted, the tank's performance was not affected. A single set could plough for up to 30km, at speeds of up to 15km/hour, before requiring repair.

SPECIFICATIONS: KMT-8

Weight: 1.2 tonnes
Lane width: 0.6m
Operating speed: 15km/hour
Attachment time: 90 minutes

KMT-10 Mine Plough

Unlike the other mine ploughs described in this section, the KMT-10 was not used with tanks. Rather, it was developed for use with the BMP-1 and BMP-2 infantry fighting vehicles. This necessitated it being much smaller and lighter than the other ploughs.

As with the tank ploughs, rods were fitted between the ploughs to detonate tilt-rod fused mines. Since the BMP's armour was thin, an extra plate of armour was provided to be fitted to the lower front, to provide protection from detonating mines. The BMP could travel at a speed of 6 to 15km/hour while clearing mines. Each cleared lane was 300mm wide, with a gap of 2.4m between lanes.

MTK Armoured Mine-Clearing Vehicle

The MTK was the first result of the experiments with rocket-breaching mine systems, begun in the 1960s. Based on the BTR-50PK armoured personnel carrier, it carried a UR-67 rocket launcher system. The rocket was attached to a 170m length of UZR-3 high-explosive triple line charge. The vehicle was driven to the edge of a minefield, the rocket's launcher at the rear of the hull was elevated, and the rocket fired. The rocket pulled the line charge across the minefield. The crew then used a line towed behind the line charge to position the charges for maximum effect. Once it was in place, the charge was detonated, clearing any mines in the vicinity.

MTK-2 Armoured Mine-Clearing Vehicle

The MTK-2 entered service in the early 1980s, based on the 2S1 self-propelled howitzer chassis. A low superstructure housed three UR-77 rockets and their launch ramps. Before firing, the launch ramps and the upper part of the superstructure were raised hydraulically. Each rocket towed a pair of 93m-long UZ-67 or UZP-77 high-explosive line charge. The UZ-67 could be used over ranges of 200 to 350m, while the UZP-77 could be used over ranges of 200 to 500m.

A cable connected the line charges to the vehicle. After firing, the vehicle would manoeuvre to position the line charges for greatest effect before detonating the charges. The charges would clear a path 6 to 8m wide and 75 to 80m (UZ-67) or 80 to 90m (UZP-77) long. The whole operation would take three to five minutes, without any need for the crew to exit the vehicle. The MTK-2 had NBC protection for the crew of two, and was amphibious.

Specifications: MTK-2

Crew: 2
Weight: 15.5 tonnes
Length: 7.26m
Width: 2.85m
Height: 3.91m
Maximum road speed: 61.5km/hour

ITB-2, SPZ-2, and SPZ-4

The ITB-2 was a rocket-launched anchor and cable, launched across a minefield. The cable was then used to draw a linear explosive charge across the minefield, usually using a winch. Once the charge was in position, it was detonated to clear a path.

The SPZ-2 used a metal-framed anchor to winch a cable with explosive charge across the area to be cleared, at a speed of up to 200m/hour. Single, double, and triple charges were available, and would clear a path up to 500m long and 6m wide.

The SPZ-4 was a double or triple charge, used with tanks. It could be pushed onto the minefield at a rate of up to 100m/hour. If the tank had a mine-clearing plough or roller, it could be towed behind the tank, to clear the gap between the paths cleared by the plough or roller.

BDT

The BDT was a mine-clearing charge in a 305mm-long, 50mm-diameter light metal tube. It contained three linear charges connected in parallel to form a triple charge, but could be disassembled to form single or double charges. Charges were connected end to end, to create a charge of the desired length, up to about 500m. A squad of men would take 60 to 90 minutes to create a 500m-long charge.

Once the charge had been made up to the required length, the detonator was added. A roller was then fitted to the front, to allow the charge to be pushed into place. A shield was also added, to prevent enemy fire causing a premature detonation. The charge would be assembled to the rear, then towed to the minefield and pushed into place by an armoured vehicle, at a speed of up to 10km/hour. Once in place, the charge was detonated, to clear a 6m-wide path.

UZ-1 and UZ-2 Bangalore Torpedoes

Bangalore torpedoes were used to clear paths through minefields and barbed wire. The UZ-1 was a metal tube, 1m long and 53mm in diameter, with 5.3kg of explosive. The UZ-2 was 2m long, 52mm in diameter, with 3.3kg of explosive. Both types were intended to be connected in series to the required length.

Once assembled, the torpedo would be pushed onto the minefield or into the barbed wire, then detonated to clear a path around 3m wide. Special collars were provided which would allow the torpedoes to be connected as double or triple charges, to clear a wider path. A metal shield was sometimes fitted to the front of the complete charge to prevent enemy small-arms fire causing a premature explosion.

PW-LWD (Poland)

Like the MTK, this was a system based around the UR-67 rocket launcher and UZR-3 line charge. It consisted of two bathtub-shaped containers, each containing a rocket and 110m of line charge. The container roofs were raised to allow the rockets to be fired. Once the rocket had towed the line charge over the minefield, the charge was detonated. The charge would clear a path 4m wide and up to 110m long.

The equipment was carried on a T-55A or T-72 tank, or an IWT combat engineer vehicle. When fitted to a tank, a standard mine plough and lane-marking equipment were also fitted.

SPECIFICATIONS: PW-LWD

Weight: 920kg (line charge)
Weight: 230kg (launcher)
Length: 110m (line charge)
Length: 2.82m (launcher)
Width: 15.5m (launcher)
Height: 0.68m (launcher)

TANK-MOUNTED ROLLERS AND PLOUGHS (CZECHOSLOVAKIA)

The Czech army used tank-mounted mine-clearing rollers and ploughs rather than Soviet designs. The roller system had three to five rollers of varying thicknesses mounted on an arm in front of each track, in a similar way to the Soviet systems. The Czech designs were larger, with a different type of serrated edge. A frame was mounted between and in front of the rollers to detonate tilt-rod fused mines.

The plough equipment was similar to the Soviet equivalents, though larger. Like the rollers, it had a frame for detonating tilt-rod fused mines.

Trailer-based system (Czechoslovakia)

The Czech army developed a system very similar to the Polish PW-LWD, but mounted the containers on an armoured, four-wheel trailer. This was usually towed behind an OT-64 8x8 APC, and was used in the same way as the Polish system.

Armoured Engineer Vehicles

IMR Combat Engineer Vehicle

Developed from a prototype built in 1969, the IMR was based on the T-55 chassis. The turret was replaced by a hydraulic crane with full 360° traverse. The crane jib was telescopic, and when in transit, was turned to the rear and seated on a cradle. The cradle folded down against the hull when the crane was in use.

The crane was normally fitted with a pair of pincer grabs, but a small bucket was also provided, stowed above the left rear track when not in use. The operator was seated in an armoured cupola, and a searchlight on the crane allowed for use at night.

A hydraulic bulldozer blade was fitted to the front hull. This blade could be used in the straight or V configuration, but could not be used in the angle configuration. An unditching beam was fitted at the rear of the hull.

The Polish army used a variant, designated IWT. It was basically the same vehicle, but could be fitted with a PW-LWD mine-clearing line charge system.

Specifications: IMR

Crew: 2
Weight: 37.5 tonnes
Length: 10.6m
Width: 3.27m
Height: 3.37m
Ground clearance: 0.43m
Maximum road speed: 48km/hour
Maximum road range: 400km
Gradient: 60%
Vertical obstacle: 0.8m

Armour:
Hull front: 100mm @ 60° [Effective: 200mm]
Hull sides: 70mm
Hull top: 30mm
Hull rear: 60mm
Belly: 20mm

IMR-2 Combat Engineer Vehicle

The IMR-2 replaced the IMR, and was based on a T-72 chassis. The turret was replaced by an armoured superstructure with armoured windows. A telescopic arm was fitted to the superstructure, with 360° traverse, 8.15m reach, and a lift capacity of 2 tonnes. This was normally fitted with a gripper-type manipulator, but could also be fitted with a bucket or shovel.

A set of KMT-8 mine ploughs were carried, and later models had a mine-clearing line charge system. A hydraulically operated bulldozer blade was fitted at the front, and folded upwards when not in use.

In 1982, the IMR-2M1 was introduced, which sacrificed the mine-clearing line charge in favour of greater protection for the hydraulic system. A new version, the IMR-2M2, was introduced in 1990. This had an improved manipulator for the telescopic arm.

All models had night-vision equipment for the driver and commander, NBC protection, and fire detection/suppression systems. They could all create smoke by injecting diesel fuel into the exhaust manifold.

SPECIFICATIONS: IMR-2

Crew: 2
Weight: 44.3 tonnes
Length: 9.55m
Width: 4.35m
Height: 3.68m
Ground clearance: 0.46m
Maximum road speed: 59km/hour
Maximum road range: 500km

IRM ENGINEER RECONNAISSANCE VEHICLE

Originally identified in the West as the IPR amphibious engineer vehicle, the IRM was based on the BMP-2's automotive components. It was intended to facilitate specialised engineering reconnaissance over a wide variety of terrain and climate conditions. It could be carried by cargo aircraft, assault ship, or hovercraft.

Although it used BMP-2 automotive components, the IRM had seven road wheels on each side, rather than the BMP-2's six, and five return rollers. It was fully amphibious, with a trim vane for use in the water, and was propelled in the water by a pair of propellers. It could also carry a 10m snorkel, to allow it to operate fully submerged.

The vehicle was divided into three internal compartments: the driver's compartment at the front, a fighting compartment in the centre, and the engine compartment at the rear. The crew compartments had NBC protection. The vehicle also had a bilge pump, a fire-extinguishing system, and could generate smoke by injecting diesel into the exhaust.

The basic crew consisted of driver and commander, both seated near the front, and each had a hatch in the roof. The commander also had a small turret, mounting a 7.62mm PKT machine gun and an infra-red searchlight. The vehicle normally carried one or two engineers, or up to four if required, for dismounted operations. The engineers also had roof hatches, and there was an emergency escape hatch at the bottom of the hull.

A variety of specialised engineering reconnaissance equipment was carried. This included a TNA-3 inertial navigation system, a mine detection system, and a sensor for determining the load-bearing capability of terrain. Equipment for reconnaissance of river crossing sites and beaches was fitted, including an artificial horizon and an inclinometer. An echo sounder and hydro-acoustic transducers were used to determine water depth and firmness of river beds. Day and night-vision devices were carried, along with an engineer reconnaissance periscope and a range finder. Portable equipment was carried for use by dismounted engineers. This included mine detectors, devices to measure the thickness of ice, and load-bearing measuring instruments.

For mine detection, a pair of arms were fitted which could be extended in front of the tracks. These had mine detectors, which

IRM

used a hydraulic terrain-following mechanism to keep a fixed distance above the ground. The vehicle stopped automatically if a mine was detected or if a detector struck an obstacle. The mine would then have to be removed manually.

The IRM was fitted with an innovative system to allow it to recover itself from difficult terrain. Two banks of rockets were fitted on the rear roof, which could be activated with the crew remaining inside the vehicle. These rockets would provide tractive force of 312kg each, to help the vehicle extract itself.

SPECIFICATIONS: IRM

Crew: up to 6
Weight: 17.2 tonnes
Length: 8.22m
Width: 3.15m
Height: 2.4m

Maximum road speed: 52km/hour
Maximum road range: 500km
Gradient: 36%
Vertical obstacle: 0.65m
Armament: 1x 7.62mm PKT MG

ADZM Engineer Vehicle

The ADZM was a combat engineer variant of the MT-LB. Only slightly modified from the standard vehicle, it was used by airborne brigades. It carried a plough blade, which was fitted on the hull side or roof for transit. Two hydraulic arm assemblies were added to the rear, to which the plough could be manually attached. There were no attachments to the front, so the blade could only be used to the rear. An arm with a bucket was mounted on the roof. Combat engineer equipment was carried inside the vehicle.

MT-LB Engineer Vehicles

The East German army used MT-LBs for combat engineering, but this version did not have a plough blade. It did have a rectangular box on the hull roof for engineering equipment. A Czech design named Zabot mounted a large bulldozer blade at the rear. This design never got past the prototype stage.

The Polish army used an engineer variant of the MT-LB which had been designed and produced in Poland. Intended primarily for engineering reconnaissance, it was fitted with a WAT turret (as fitted on the OT-64 and some OT-62 variants). This turret had a 14.5mm KPVT and a 7.62mm PKT machine gun. Eight smoke grenade dischargers were mounted on the hull sides, near the rear, four per side. These were mounted such that four fired forward, and four to the rear. The vehicle had a crew of two, and could carry up to six additional engineers. It was amphibious and had NBC protection.

Recovery and Repair Vehicles

The Soviet army had no armoured recovery vehicles during the Second World War. This was in marked contrast to the German army, which had developed specialised recovery vehicles and tactics for their use. Toward the end of the war, the Soviet army started to experiment with armoured recovery vehicles.

Some Western sources have identified an armoured recovery vehicle based on the "IT-130" tank destroyer. The IT-130 was said to mount a 130mm gun on a vehicle based on the T-62 tank. Little was known about this vehicle, although photographs were occasionally published. Since the IT-130 was later proved to be fictitious, it seems that the ARV variant did not actually exist.

T-34 ARVs

The Soviet army's initial experiments with ARVs were conversions of existing armoured vehicles with little or no specialised equipment. There was no standard design, but they were usually a T-34 with the turret removed. Shortly after the war, a standardised vehicle, the T-34-T, was produced. Like the wartime vehicles, this had no specialised equipment, being a T-34 with the turret opening plated over and a commander's cupola added. Units often added civilian winches and cranes to improve the vehicle's usefulness.

IS-T

As ISU assault guns started to be withdrawn from Soviet service in the late 1950s, some were used as the basis for heavy recovery vehicles. The initial examples simply had their guns removed, but most were rebuilt in one of two versions. One version had winches, a rear entrenching spade, and a stowage box over the rear hull. The other version had a simple, large A-frame crane fitted to the front, which was swung back to lay along the hull roof when not in use.

BTS-1

A number of armoured recovery vehicles were built based on the T-54 and T-55 chassis, and designated BTS (medium armoured tower) in the Soviet Union. The first, the BTS-1, was basically a turretless T-54, much like the earlier T-34-T. The driver sat at the front on the left, with the commander to his right. Other crew members sat in the rear cargo area, which also held a snorkel for deep wading. Tow bars of various lengths were carried, as was an unditching beam, carried on the right of the hull.

BTS-2

The BTS-2 was based on the BTS-1, but added a winch in the hull, and a container for tools and equipment. A 2-tonne capacity tripod jib crane was fitted, and a large entrenching spade was added to the rear. This spade could be used to anchor the vehicle when the winch was in use.

BTS-3

Introduced in the 1960s, the BTS-3 was based on a T-55 hull. It had a bulldozer blade at the front and a 20-tonne capacity crane on the right side of the hull. This crane had a telescopic jib, and was traversed to the rear, resting along the hull, when not in use.

T-54 (A) AND T-54 (B) (DDR)

Developed by the East German army, these differed from the T-54-T by not having a spade at the rear. They did have push-pull bars, welding and cutting equipment, and a dismountable 1-tonne crane. They were fitted with detectors to warn of radiation or chemical contamination, and had fittings for PT-54 or PT-55 mine rollers.

The T-54 (B) added brackets at the rear for securing tow ropes, and a protective plate on the front hull glacis.

BREM-64

Shortly after the introduction of the T-64 MBT, a new ARV was introduced, based on the new chassis. The turret was replaced by an armoured superstructure, which included a raised cupola for the commander. A 2.5-tonne capacity folding-jib crane was fitted on the superstructure, toward the left. Unlike the earlier T-54/55-based ARVs, the BREM-64 had two winches. The primary winch had a capacity of 25 tonnes, and a front-mounted bulldozer blade was used to anchor the vehicle when it was in use. The secondary winch had a capacity of 2.5 tonnes. As well as anchoring the vehicle, the bulldozer blade could be used to clear obstacles and prepare sites.

An auxiliary power unit was carried, which could be used to power dismounted power tools and welding equipment. The BREM-64 carried a 12.7mm NSVT machine gun, primarily for air defence, and had a crew of three: driver, gunner, and fitter.

BREM-1

Introduced in 1984, the BREM-1 was an ARV based on the T-72 MBT chassis. It had a crew of three (driver, commander, and mechanic), all of whom were provided with day and night-vision equipment. It had a top road speed of 60km/hour, a road range of 700km, and an off-road range of 500km. Towing another tank significantly reduced the range, to just 220km on roads. Like the main battle tank, it had long-range fuel drums at the rear of the vehicle, which could be jettisoned if needed. An unditching beam was mounted underneath the external fuel drums. A large-diameter snorkel was carried on the rear right of the vehicle, which could be used for deep wading at depths of up to 5m.

A crane was fitted on the left side of the vehicle. This had a lift capacity of 19 tonnes when extended up to 2m, or 3 tonnes at the maximum extension of 4.4m. The crane was powered hydraulically, normally using power from the vehicle's main engine to run the pump. If the main engine was not running, the vehicle batteries could power the crane via an electrical pump. The crane was controlled from an elevated position, with a full set of controls. The crane turntable could be locked, and the vehicle could travel over level ground with a load suspended from the crane. When in transit, the crane was folded down along the side of the vehicle and secured in place with a clamp.

A full set of electric welding equipment, including a working position, was carried in a hermetically-sealed panel over the left

BREM-1

track. Special tools were carried in portable containers on a load platform. This load platform was located at the centre of the roof, and was 1.7m long and 1.4m wide. It had removable side panels, and could carry a load of up to 1.5 tonnes.

The BREM-1 had two winches, a plough, a bulldozer blade, and towing equipment. The mechanical main winch had a 200m cable and a basic capacity of 25 tonnes. Snatch blocks could be used to increase this capacity to 100 tonnes. The winch was normally used at the front, with the bulldozer blade to anchor the vehicle, but it could also be used to the rear for self-recovery.

The bulldozer blade was 3.1m wide and hydraulically driven, using controls at the driver's station. A BREM-1 could use this blade to create an MBT firing position in 12 to 20 minutes, depending on the state of the soil.

For towing, the vehicle had a pair of 1.68m towing rods, with internal shock absorbers, and a pair of 5.5m tow lines. Loads of up to 50 tonnes could be towed for prolonged periods, at the cost of greatly increased fuel consumption.

Other equipment included a 30-tonne capacity hydraulic jack, R-123U radio, tank telephone system, navigation system, and NBC protection. Armour protection was the same as the T-72 MBT, although the only armament was a 12.7mm NSVT machine gun with 840 rounds of ammunition. Four smoke-grenade dischargers were sometimes fitted, and all vehicles could create a smokescreen by injecting diesel fuel into the exhaust manifold.

Specifications: BREM-1

Crew: 3
Weight: 41 tonnes
Length: 7.98m
Width: 3.46m
Height: 2.43m
Ground clearance: 0.46m
Maximum road speed: 60km/hour
Maximum road range: 700km
Gradient: 60%
Vertical obstacle: 0.85m
Armament: 1x 12.7mm NSVT MG (840 rounds)

BREM-2

The BREM-2 was an ARV based on the BMP-1 IFV. The turret was removed and replaced by an armoured plate. A swivelling jib crane was fitted on the hull roof, with a 1.5-tonne capacity (sufficient to lift a BMP power unit). A stowage platform with a capacity of 1.5 tonnes was fitted to the rear of the roof. A variety of recovery equipment, including a welding kit, was stowed around the hull roof and sides.

BREM-2

The interior was rearranged to carry a four-man crew, 6.5 tonne winch, and five folding seats for passengers. It had an NBC protection system, six smoke-grenade launchers, and a 7.62mm PKT machine gun.

SPECIFICATIONS: BREM-2

Crew: 4+5
Weight: 14 tonnes
Length: 7.68m
Width: 3.16m
Height: 2.27m
Maximum road speed: 65km/hour
Maximum road range: 550km
Armament: 1x 7.62mm PKT MG (1,000 rounds)

BREhM-D

The BREhM-D was an ARV based on the chassis of the BTR-D airborne armoured personnel carrier. Specialised equipment included a hydraulic crane, recovery winch, and bulldozer blade (which doubled as a spade to stabilise the vehicle). Towing equipment and a welding kit were also carried.

The crane boom was stowed in a frame on the upper hull when not in use. This crane had a traverse of 150° and reach of 2m. Lift capacity was at least 1.5 tonnes, depending on the number of cable runs used. Cable runs were rigged to the top of the hull. The crane was operated from the commander's position, using power from the vehicle hydraulic system. A hand pump could be used when the engine was not running.

The hydraulic winch had a capacity of 3.5 tonnes, using the main cable. Additional cable runs could be used to increase this to 10.5 tonnes. Like the crane, the winch was controlled from the commander's station. When performing heavy recovery tasks, the bulldozer blade would be manually lowered and used as an anchoring spade. The winch cable was 100m long, and fed through heavy rubber rollers that kept it free of mud and snow.

A pair of telescopic tow bars, fitted with shock absorbers, were carried on the rear of the hull. Folding seats were provided for up to four passengers. A 7.62mm PKT machine gun was fitted in the bow, and the vehicle had smoke-grenade dischargers and NBC protection.

SPECIFICATIONS: BREhM-D

Crew: 3+4
Weight: 8 tonnes
Length: 5.89m

Width: 2.63m
Height: 1.82m
Maximum road speed: 61km/hour
Maximum road range: 500km
Gradient: 60%
Armament: 1x 7.62mm PKT MG (1,000 rounds)

BTR-50PK(B)

Since many light armoured vehicles in the Warsaw Pact armies were amphibious, there was a requirement for an amphibious recovery vehicle. The BTR-50PK(B) was developed to fulfil this need. Like the original BTR-50P upon which it was based, it was fully amphibious, and propelled in the water by a pair of water jets. These provided enough power to tow an amphibious AFV through the water.

Recovery equipment included tow couplings at the rear, towing cables, and quick-release and standard shackles. Because of its amphibious recovery role, it carried life belts and life jackets. A set of RG-UF life-saving equipment was carried, but only for use in emergency, and only if no properly qualified divers were available. The crew consisted of commander and driver, although there was provision for up to four other personnel. Up to eight rescued personnel could be accommodated during recovery operations.

MTP-1 (Bulgaria)

This was a variant of the MT-LBus (often referred to as the ACRV in the West), which was built in Bulgaria under licence. It was used for recovering damaged vehicles, changing components, and preparing positions. Virtually identical to the MT-LBus, it had the same turret as the standard MT-LB, although some

MTP-1

mounted a 12.7mm machine gun in place of the standard 7.62mm PKT.

A crane was mounted in a small turret on the roof, providing the operator with all-round armour protection. The crane extended to 5m, with a capacity of 2 tonnes when fully extended, rising to 3 tonnes when extended no further than 3.4m.

An entrenching blade was mounted at the rear of the vehicle on hydraulic arms, and could prepare a position for a vehicle in around two hours. A rear-mounted winch had a capacity of 30 tonnes when the blade was used to anchor the vehicle, or 10 tonnes with the blade raised.

The MTP-1 had NBC protection and was fully amphibious, propelled in the water by its tracks.

AD-090 Wheeled Recovery Vehicle (Czechoslovakia)

The AD-090 was based on a Tatra 138 6x6 lorry chassis, with a rear-mounted hydraulically-operated 9-tonne capacity crane, and 8-tonne capacity winch. It was normally used in conjunction with a 10-tonne capacity towing axle.

SPECIFICATIONS: AD-090

Weight: 15.9 tonnes
Length: 9.25m
Width: 2.45m
Height: 3.08m (travelling)
Maximum road speed: 60km/hour

VT-34 (CZECHOSLOVAKIA)

The Czech army developed a T-34-based ARV, designated VT-34, borrowing heavily from concepts found in the wartime German Bergepanther. It had a box-shaped superstructure at the rear, a winch, and an entrenching spade that could be used to anchor the vehicle. The VT-34 saw service with the Czech and Polish armies.

VT-34

VT-55A (CZECHOSLOVAKIA)

The VT-55A was a Czech armoured recovery vehicle based on a T-55 hull. A hydraulic crane was fitted on the right of the hull, with a capacity of 1.5 tonnes. The rear of the hull roof held a 2m

VT-55A

x 1.6m platform, which could carry loads of up to 3 tonnes. Two winches were fitted. The primary winch was driven mechanically by the vehicle's engine, and had a capacity of 44 tonnes. The secondary winch was hydraulically operated, with a capacity of 800kg.

Several tow bars and a 4.2m tow cable were carried. Welding equipment, a workbench, and a vice were fitted above one of the tracks, and could be pulled out for use. A spade was fitted at the rear, and could also be used as a bulldozer blade. Fittings for mine-clearing rollers were mounted at the front.

A 7.62mm machine gun was fitted in a small turret, with 360° traverse and sufficient elevation for use against aerial targets. The vehicle had a crew of four, NBC protection, infra-red night-vision equipment, and a snorkel for deep wading.

Specifications: VT-55A

Crew: 3.14
Weight: 36.5 tonnes
Length: 8.3m
Width: 3.4m
Height: 2.52m
Ground clearance: 0.43m
Maximum road speed: 50km/hour
Maximum road range: 270km
Gradient: 32%
Armament: 1x 7.62mm MG

VT-72B (Czechoslovakia)

The VT-72B was developed by Czechoslovakia. Like the Soviet BREM-1, it was based on a T-72 chassis, but differed in several ways from the Soviet vehicle. It was intended to tow stricken vehicles to a safe place, where repairs could be effected. It had a crew of two (driver and commander), although an extra three could be accommodated in the armoured superstructure.

The main recovery winch was hydrostatic, with 200m of cable and a traction force of 300kN when used with the provided pulley system. A secondary 10kN winch had 400m of cable. A front bulldozer blade could be used as an anchor when recovering heavy loads. The blade could also clear obstacles and debris or create emplacements for vehicles.

A hydraulic crane was fitted on the right front of the hull, on a small turntable with full 360° traverse. The crane had a lift capacity of 19 tonnes and a reach of 7.6m. A platform at the rear of the vehicle, measuring 1.4m x 1.4m, could carry loads of up to

4 tonnes. Tools and welding equipment were included for carrying out repairs to recovered vehicles.

A 12.7mm NSV machine gun was fitted, primarily for air defence. Extra fuel could be carried in drums or jerry cans, fitted on racks at the rear.

VPV (Czechoslovakia)

The VPV was an armoured recovery vehicle based on a Czech-built BMP chassis, and was similar to the Soviet BREM-2. The turret was replaced with a cable drum, and a traversable 5-tonne crane was fitted at the rear of the hull roof. The crane could extend to a maximum length of 4.5m. A winch was fitted, which had a tractive force of 125kN, though this could be increased by the use of pulleys. A hydraulically-operated spade was fitted to anchor the vehicle when the winch was in use. A welding set and cutting devices were carried, and both crew members would be trained welders. Like the BMP, the VPV was fully amphibious, propelled in the water by its tracks.

SU-76 Armoured Workshop Vehicle (DDR)

This was a Soviet SU-76, extensively modified to meet the East German army's requirement for a fully-tracked armoured repair vehicle. The gun and ammunition racks were removed, overhead armour added, and a stowage area added between the driver and superstructure.

The driver is seated in the front centre, with the working area at the rear, with a single door for access. The engine is to the right of the driver, with the fuel and batteries to his left. In place of the original two engines were replaced with a single engine of East German design. Equipment included a bench, drill press, generator, lathe, small forge, vice and welding kit. There was no winch for recovery operations, but it was used for repairing components.

SPECIFICATIONS: SU-76 ARMOURED WORKSHOP VEHICLE

Crew: 4
Weight: 11.2 tonnes
Length: 5m (travelling)
Width: 2.74m (travelling)
Height: 2.1m (travelling)
Ground clearance: 0.3m
Maximum road speed: 45km/hour
Maximum road range: 360km
Gradient: 47%
Vertical obstacle: 0.65m

ARMOUR:
Glacis plate: 25mm @ 30° [Effective: 29mm]
Superstructure front: 25mm @ 27° [Effective: 28mm]
Superstructure sides: 12mm @ 17° [Effective: 13mm]
Hull sides: 16mm
Hull top: 10mm
Rear: 15mm
Belly: 10mm

WPT-TOPAS (POLAND)

This Polish vehicle was based on the Czech OT-62A APC, which itself was similar to the Soviet BTR-50. In Polish service, the WPT-TOPAS was designated a "technical support vehicle". The East German army also used it, designating it a "recovery, maintenance, and repair vehicle".

The hull was of welded steel armour, with a crew compartment at the front. The engine and transmission were to the rear. The driver was sat at the front centre, with a semi-circular bay to either side of him, and the commander in the bay his left. The bay to his right had an armoured mounting for a 7.62mm machine gun, with full 360° traverse.

The vehicle was fully amphibious, propelled in the water by a pair of water jets at up to 10.8km/hour. Before entering the water, a trim board was erected and bilge pumps switched on. It also had an NBC protection system and infra-red night-vision equipment.

Engineering equipment included a 2.5-tonne winch with 600m of cable and a 1-tonne capacity hand-operated crane that could be mounted at various points. Spare parts, welding equipment, tools, and a four-man tent were also carried.

Specifications: WPT-TOPAS

Crew: 5
Weight: 15 tonnes
Length: 7m
Width: 3.14m
Height: 2.72m
Ground clearance: 0.41m
Maximum road speed: 60km/hour
Maximum road range: 500km
Gradient: 55%
Vertical obstacle: 1.1m
Armament: 1x 7.62mm PK MG

Armour:
Hull front: 11mm
Hull sides: 14mm
Hull top: 10mm
Hull rear: 10mm
Belly: 10mm

WZT-1 (Poland)

In the late 1960s, Poland started work on its own ARV, the WZT-1. Production started in 1970, using a T-54 chassis, and based on the Soviet T-54-T. It had a 25-tonne powered winch, with pulleys to increase the capacity to 50 tonnes. An auxiliary winch, towing equipment, and 1.5-tonne capacity crane were also fitted. A large spade was provided, which could anchor the vehicle when the winch was in use. It had night-vision equipment, NBC protection for the crew, and could produce smoke by injecting diesel into the exhaust. A 12.7mm DShK heavy machine gun was carried.

WZT-2 (Poland)

The WZT-2 was similar to the earlier WZT-1, but based on the T-55 chassis. In service in the Polish army from 1973, it was also supplied to India, Iraq, and Yugoslavia. It had a hydraulically operated crane, winch, bulldozer blade, and welding equipment. The bulldozer blade could be used to prepare fighting positions. The vehicle could also be used as an emergency ambulance, able to carry up to three stretcher cases. Other equipment included a deep-wading snorkel and NBC protection, and it could create smoke by injecting diesel into the exhaust. A 12.7mm DShK heavy machine gun was fitted for local defence.

WZT-3 (POLAND)

With the introduction of the T-72 tank, a new ARV was required, and the obvious design decision for the Poles was to base it on Polish-made T-72M hulls. Tests and trials were carried out from 1986 to 1988, following which it was accepted into service with the Polish army.

Up to four crew could be carried, although only the driver and commander were required. Both sat at the front, the driver on the left, with the commander to his right. Both had night-vision devices, and the commander had a cupola mounting a 12.7mm NSV machine gun. A crew hatch was fitted in the centre of the superstructure roof, with a load-carrying platform to the rear. This platform measured 1.91m x 2.16m, with 0.62m-high sides, and had a load capacity of 3.5 tonnes.

A bulldozer blade was fitted at the front, which could be used for anchoring the vehicle as well as excavating. A TD-50 crane was fitted on a small turntable at the front left of the superstructure. This had a lift capacity of 15 tonnes, a reach of 5.8m, and a maximum hook height of 8.6m. The main winch was mechanical, with a pulling capacity of 840kN with tackle, and 200m of cable. A secondary hydraulic winch was also provided. This had a pulling capacity of 20kN, and 400m of cable.

A snorkel allowed the vehicle to wade through water obstacles at a depth of up to 5m, and extra fuel drums could be fitted to the rear.

WZT-3

SPECIFICATIONS: WZT-3

Crew: up to 4
Weight: 42 tonnes
Length: 8.3m
Width: 3.6m
Height: 2.17m
Ground clearance: 0.43m
Maximum road speed: 60km/hour
Maximum road range: 650km
Vertical obstacle: 0.7m
Armament: 1x 12.7mm NSV MG

Earth-Moving Equipment

The Warsaw Pact armies placed a good deal of emphasis on digging shelters. As with other areas, speed was important. Specialised machines were developed to excavate and dig earth far faster than could be achieved with manpower.

As well as the specialised vehicles described in this section, fittings for entrenching blades were mounted on the bow of T-54 and T-55 tanks. The bulldozer blades were designated BTU and BTU-55, and either blade could be fitted to either model of tank. The later BTU-55 was lighter (1.4 tonnes rather than the BTU's 2.3 tonnes), had better performance, and could be fitted and removed more quickly. The T-64, T-72, and T-80 tanks had entrenching blades fitted as standard, which were stowed under the front lower hull when not in use.

BAT Digger

The BAT (also referred to as the BAT-1) was based on the AT-T artillery tractor. It had a large bulldozer blade at the front, which was lifted above the vehicle when in transit. A 20-tonne winch was also fitted. The original version used an electro-pneumatic system to lift the bulldozer blade, while the later BAT-M lifted the blade hydraulically. The BAT-M also added a 2-tonne capacity jib crane with 360° traverse and 70° elevation.

BAT-M

The BAT's primary roles were the speedy construction of roads, approaches to bridges and crossing sites, and filling in obstructions such as ditches. It was also used for felling trees, removing stumps and boulders, and digging emplacements. Attachments were available to convert the basic demolition blade to a V-blade, bulldozer, or angle dozer.

SPECIFICATIONS: BAT

Weight: 25.3 tonnes
Length: 10m
Width: 4.78m
Height: 2.95m
Maximum road speed: 35km/hour
Maximum road range: 700km
Vertical obstacle: 1m
Working speed: 1.5-10km/hour

Specifications: BAT-M

Weight: 27.5 tonnes
Length: 7m (travelling)
Width: 4.85m
Maximum road speed: 35km/hour
Maximum road range: 550km
Vertical obstacle: 1m
Working speed: 1.5-10km/hour

BAT-2 Digger

The BAT-2 was based on the MT-T tracked carrier chassis, which in turn used suspension and running gear components from the T-64 tank. It had the same bulldozer blade as the earlier BAT-M, but the hydraulic system was more powerful. A different system was used to raise the blade vertically when it was not in use.

An armoured cab at the front could carry the crew of two, and there was a compartment to the rear for an eight-man combat engineer squad. There was space for combat engineering stores behind the cab.

A crane was mounted on top of the vehicle. This had a lift capacity of 2 tonnes and a boom outreach of 7.3m. Alongside the crane was a 25-tonne capacity winch with 100m of cable.

The BAT-2 could create graded tracks over normal terrain at a rate of 6.8km/hour, and at up to 8.15km/hour in snow. Terrain with trees of up to 300mm diameter could be cleared at a rate of 2.3km/hour. The bulldozer blade had a clearing capacity of 350-450m3/hour when route-clearing or creating earth barriers, 200-250m3/hour when digging ditches. Solid or frozen ground could be loosened down to a depth of 500mm.

Specifications: BAT-2

Crew: 2+8
Weight: 39.7 tonnes
Length: 9.64m (travelling)
Width: 4.2m
Height: 3.69m
Ground clearance: 0.43m
Maximum road speed: 60km/hour
Maximum road range: 500km

BTM and BTM-TMG Digger and Ditcher

These vehicles were based on the AT-T artillery tractor chassis. The BTM was introduced in 1958, and had a civilian bucket excavator. This mounted 10 to 12 buckets on a rotary frame, which was lifted onto the rear of the vehicle for transit. Before use, it was lowered to the ground at the rear of the vehicle. The BTM-TMG, introduced in 1968, had reinforced buckets to allow operation in frozen ground. This version normally mounted 8 to 10 buckets on the frame.

Specifications: BTM

Crew: 2
Weight: 26.5 tonnes
Length: 7.35m (travelling)
Width: 3.2m
Height: 4.3m (travelling)
Maximum road speed: 35km/hour
Maximum road range: 500km

BTM

SPECIFICATIONS: BTM-TMG

Crew: 2
Weight: 30 tonnes
Length: 7.6m (travelling)
Width: 3.2m
Height: 4.3m (travelling)
Maximum road speed: 36km/hour
Maximum road range: 400km

PZM AND PZM-2 DIGGER AND DITCHER

The PZM was based on the T-150K four-wheel tractor, while the PZM-2 was based on the newer T-155 tractor. Both had a front-mounted bulldozer blade. These vehicles mounted buckets in an arrangement akin to a conveyor belt, driven from the main engine. The transmission had to be disconnected when the excavator was in use. A front-mounted hydro-mechanical winch

PZM-2

was used to pull the vehicle forward when digging. The digger was raised and lowered manually.

Specifications: PZM

Crew: 2
Weight: 13.2 tonnes
Length: 7m (travelling)
Width: 2.52m
Height: 3.75m (travelling)
Maximum road speed: 45km/hour
Maximum road range: 500km

MDK-2 and MDK-3 Excavator

The MDK-2, introduced in 1965, was based on an AT-T artillery tractor chassis. It mounted a large rotary digger at the

MDK-2

rear to excavate earth, and a hydraulically-operated bulldozer blade at the front. When in transit, the digger was mounted horizontally behind the cab. It was swung around to a vertical position at the rear of the vehicle for operation. The improved MDK-2M was largely similar, but had a faster working speed. The later MDK-3 was based on the MT-T tractor chassis, with an armoured cab. The MDK series were used to dig trenches, vehicle positions, and gun pits.

SPECIFICATIONS: MDK-2 (MDK-2M IN BRACKETS)

Crew: 2
Weight: 27 tonnes (28 tonnes)
Length: 8m (travelling)
Width: 4m (travelling) (3.4m)
Height: 3.95m (travelling)

Maximum road speed: 35km/hour
Vertical obstacle: 1m (0.65m)

SPECIFICATIONS: MDK-3

Crew: 2
Weight: 40 tonnes
Length: 10m (travelling)
Width: 3.2m (travelling)
Height: 4m (travelling)
Maximum road speed: 50km/hour
Maximum road range: 500km

E-305V SINGLE-BUCKET CRANE SHOVEL

Mounted on a KrAZ-214 6x6 7-tonne lorry, this could be used for digging, or as a crane. The shovel had a capacity of 0.3m3 and could dig 50 to 60m3 per hour. As a crane, it had a lift capacity of 5 tonnes.

DOK BULLDOZER (CZECHOSLOVAKIA)

The DOK fitted a bulldozer blade at the front of a four-wheeled, articulated chassis, with a rear-mounted engine. An electric winch was fitted to the rear of the cab. A multi-purpose bucket was normally fitted, although a snowplough was also available. The cab was hermetically sealed with a filtered ventilation system, providing NBC protection for the operator.

There were three variants: the DOK-L had a universal shovel; the DOK-R had a V-shaped blade that could form a straight blade. The DOK-M was a variant of the DOK-L, with a saw tooth edge and central ridge added to the shovel. The DOK-M also had hydraulic steering, improved brakes, and improved hydraulics.

The DOK saw service in the Czech and East German armies.

SPECIFICATIONS: DOK

Crew: 1
Weight: 28 tonnes
Length: 10.53m (travelling)
Width: 3.15m (travelling)
Height: 3.15m (travelling)
Ground clearance: 0.45m
Maximum road speed: 50km/hour
Maximum cross-country range: 250km
Towed load: 65 tonnes

Artillery Vehicles

The Soviet Union developed several specialised vehicles for artillery command and control, and some fully tracked artillery prime movers, although artillery was more commonly towed by lorries, which would usually have all-wheel drive.

MT-LBu5

Often referred to in the West as the Artillery Command and Reconnaissance Vehicle (ACRV), this family of vehicles were developed alongside the 2S1 and 2S3 self-propelled howitzers. Variants were later developed for a range of specialised roles to support other arms. Based on the MT-LB, it shared a number of automotive components with both that vehicle and the 2S1.

The hull was of welded steel armour, thick enough to provide the crew with protection from small arms and shell splinters. The commander and driver were seated at the front, and each had a roof hatch that could be locked in the vertical position, and a large window with an armoured shutter. The driver had three periscopes, the commander one swivelling periscope. The engine was mounted behind the driver and commander. It had a torsion bar suspension with seven rubber-tyred road wheels on each side and the drive sprocket at the front.

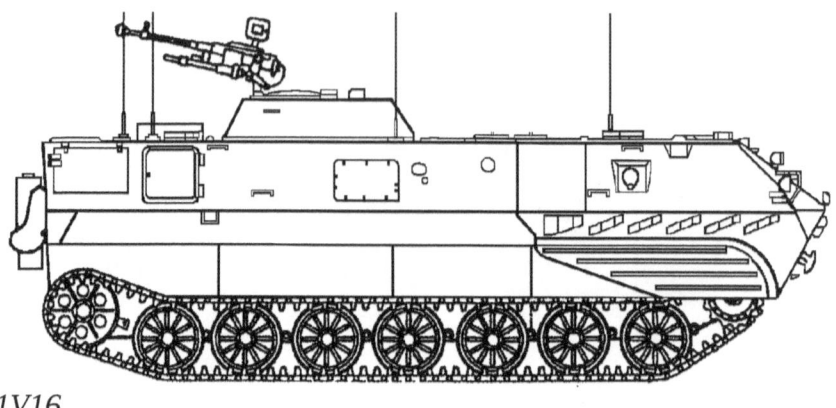

1V16

A single door was fitted at the rear, with a vision device and firing port. Roof hatches varied according to the role the vehicle was intended for. Seating was provided for seven, but the crew varied according to role, with all except the driver and commander in the rear. An auxiliary power unit was fitted, the vehicle had overpressure NBC protection, and was fully amphibious, propelled in the water by its tracks at a speed of up to 4.5km/hour. To prepare for swimming, the bilge pump was switched on, the trim vane erected, shrouds fitted to the hull side at the front, and the front road wheels were covered.

Each 2S1 or 2S3 battery had two vehicles, for the battery commander and deputy commander. The battery commander's vehicle would serve as an observation post for the commander, and the deputy commander's vehicle would serve as the battery fire direction centre. The battalion command platoon had a vehicle for the battalion commander, and one for the deputy commander, which would serve as the battalion fire direction centre.

Four variants with minor differences were used by 2S1 and 2S3 batteries. Known as the 1V12 series, they were designated 1V13 (battery fire direction centre), 1V14 (battery command vehicle), 1V15 (battalion command vehicle), and 1V16 (battalion fire direction centre). The 1V13 had a crew of six, and was fitted with a one-person cupola with vision equipment and a 12.7mm DShKM machine gun. The 1V14 had a crew of six, was fitted with whip antennas, and carried a dismountable range finder. The 1V15 had a crew of seven and was fitted with a 10m telescopic antenna, stowed horizontally on the upper left hull when in transit. The 1V16 had the same antenna as the 1V15, but was also fitted with an electronic field artillery computer.

SPECIFICATIONS: MT-LBUS

Combat weight: 15.5 tonnes
Length: 7.48m
Width: 2.85m
Height: 2.43m
Ground clearance: 0.4m
Maximum road speed: 62km/hour
Maximum road range: 500km
Gradient: 77%
Vertical obstacle: 0.7m

Armour:
Turret: 20mm
Hull: 15mm

PRP-3

This vehicle, also known as BMP-SON, was based on a BMP-1 hull. It entered service in the early 1970s and was used with 2S1 and 2S3 units. The original turret was replaced with a larger two-man turret, fitted with two single-piece hatch covers opening forward. Each hatch had periscopes and a large optical device in front of the hatch. The vehicle had a crew of five, and the only armament was a 7.62mm PKT machine gun in the turret.

An antenna for the Small Fred battlefield surveillance radar was mounted on the rear of the turret, which was folded forward to the horizontal when not in operation. The Small Fred radar had a detection range of 20km and tracking range of 7km. There was a circular hatch and telescopic aerial on the left of the turret, toward the rear. A 90mm launcher for illumination rounds was fitted on the rear deck. Twenty illumination rounds were carried, which could be fired at ranges of 100m to 3,000m. Night vision devices and a laser rangefinder were also fitted.

PRP-4

This was a further development of the PRP-3, which entered service in the 1980s with units equipped with 2S1 and 2S3 self-propelled guns. It was designed to carry out reconnaissance of both stationary and moving targets, including low-flying helicopters, under all weather conditions, at day and at night.

Like the PRP-3, the hull was similar to that of the BMP-1, but with a larger, two-man turret, mounting a single 7.62mm PKT machine gun and optical devices. An antenna for an IRL-133-1 radar was fitted to the rear of the turret, and was folded down when not in use. The radar could detect and track MBT-sized targets at a range of 8-10km. A thermal imaging system was fitted on the left side of the turret, and an IR night vision device was fitted on the right side, along with a laser rangefinder. A man-portable laser rangefinder was carried inside the vehicle for use by dismounted teams.

An auxiliary power unit was fitted to power the extensive communications and reconnaissance equipment. Like the BMP-1, the PRP-4 was amphibious, had NBC protection for the crew, and could create smoke by injecting diesel fuel into the exhaust outlet.

SPECIFICATIONS: PRP-4

Crew: 5
Combat weight: 13.2 tonnes
Length: 6.74m
Width: 2.94m
Height: 2.15m
Ground clearance: 0.37m
Maximum road speed: 65km/hour
Maximum road range: 600km
Armament: 1x 7.62 PKT MG

SNAR-10

Originally thought by NATO to be an artillery location radar, the SNAR-10 (known to NATO as Big Fred) was actually a battlefield surveillance radar. Its primary role was the location of stationary and moving targets in the forward edge of the battle area.

The radar antenna was mounted on a turret fitted on the rear of an MT-LB tracked vehicle. The antenna was folded forward to lie on top of the turret when in transit, and raised for use. It could detect moving targets at ranges of up to 16km, and plot artillery projectiles at up to 10km. The vehicle also had two R-123M radios, a PAB-2A aiming circle, a power generator and a TV-240 observation device for the commander. An improved version, the SNAR-10M, was introduced in 1982.

The vehicle retained the NBC protection and machine gun turret of the standard MT-LB. Unlike the standard MT-LB, however, it was not amphibious.

Specifications: SNAR-10

Combat weight: 12.6 tonnes
Length: 6.45m
Width: 2.86m
Ground clearance: 0.4m
Maximum road speed: 62km/hour
Maximum road range: 500km
Gradient: 60%
Vertical obstacle: 0.6m
Trench: 2.41m
Armament: 1x 7.62mm PKT machine gun (2,500 rounds)
Armour: 4-10mm

ARK-1 Rys

Like the SNAR-10, the ARK-1 mounted a radar at the rear of an MT-LB tracked vehicle. It retained the MT-LB's NBC protection, but omitted the machine gun turret. In 1986, the

ARK-1M was introduced, which added a generator, mounted at the rear of the vehicle.

An artillery location radar, it had a crew of four. Mortars could be detected at ranges of up to 13km, guns and howitzers up to 8km, multiple rocket launchers up to 25km, and tactical missiles at ranges of up to 30km. It could track up to three targets simultaneously.

SPECIFICATIONS: ARK-1 RYS

Combat weight: 15.7 tonnes
Length: 7.62m
Width: 2.85m
Maximum road speed: 60km/hour
Maximum road range: 500km

YA-12 & YA-13F

Both the Ya-12 and Ya-13F entered service toward the end of the Second World War. They were identical in appearance, but the Ya-13F had a petrol engine, which was slightly less powerful than the Ya-12's diesel engine.

They were of conventional design: the engine was at the front, with the cab behind, and the cargo/personnel compartment at the rear. The suspension had five road wheels, with the idler at the front, the drive sprocket at the rear, and three return rollers. Unlike the later M-2, they had a single headlamp, mounted at the bottom left of the radiator.

Specifications: Ya-12 (Ya-13F in brackets)

Crew: 1+1
Weight: 6.5 tonnes (empty) (5.7 tonnes)
    8.5 tonnes (loaded) (8.5 tonnes)
Maximum load: 2 tonnes
Towed load: 8 tonnes (5 tonnes)
Length: 4.89m
Width: 2.4m
Height: 2.2m (cab) (2.29m)
Ground clearance: 0.31m
Maximum road speed: 37km/hour (23km/hour)
Maximum road range: 290km (210km)
Gradient: 60%

M-2

Introduced after the Second World War, this was the replacement for the Ya-12 and Ya-13F. Its main distinguishing features were the two headlamps, front bumper, and higher cargo area. The Hungarian K-800 was very similar to the M-2.

The M-2 had a conventional design: the engine was at the front, with the cab behind it, and the cargo compartment at the rear. The suspension was similar to that of the SU-76, with five road wheels, idler at the front, drive sprocket at the rear, and three return rollers.

The M-2 was used to mount the Long Trough (SNAR-1) radar system.

SPECIFICATIONS: M-2

Crew: 1+1
Weight: 7.2 tonnes (empty)
Maximum load: 2 tonnes
Towed load: 6 tonnes
Length: 4.97m
Width: 2.82m
Height: 2.33m (cab)
Height: 2.45m (tarpaulin)
Ground clearance: 0.37m
Maximum road speed: 35km/hour
Maximum road range: 330km
Gradient: 60%
Vertical obstacle: 0.5m
Fording: 0.6m
Trench: 1.5m

K-800 (Hungary)

This Hungarian version of the Soviet M-2 entered service with the Hungarian army in the 1950s. Lighter than the Soviet vehicle, it also had a more powerful engine (130hp compared to the M-2's 110hp).

It had the same conventional design as the M-2, with the engine at the front, the cab behind it, and the cargo compartment at the rear. Unlike the M-2, the K-800's cab had a circular roof hatch. The suspension was similar to that of the SU-76, with five road wheels, idler at the front, drive sprocket at the rear, and three return rollers.

The K-800 was also built in Yugoslavia as the GJ-800. The Yugoslavian version had a different engine and the cab of the FAP lorry.

Specifications: K-800

Crew: 1+1
Weight: 6.4 tonnes (empty)
  8.2 tonnes (loaded)
Maximum load: 1.8 tonnes
Towed load: 8 tonnes
Length: 5m
Width: 2.4m
Height: 2.2m (cab)
Ground clearance: 0.3m
Maximum road speed: 35km/hour
Maximum road range: 300km
Gradient: 60%
Vertical obstacle: 0.5m
Fording: 0.6m
Trench: 1.5m

AT-T

The AT-T was introduced in 1950, originally used to tow heavy artillery such as the S-23 gun, 130mm KS-30 anti-aircraft gun, and the 130mm SM-4-1 mobile coastal gun. It was later used for various towing roles, and to carry specialised loads such as radars and other electronic equipment.

The engine was under the cab floor, which had a door on each side. The cargo compartment at the rear was provided with a drop tailgate and tarpaulin cover. Fuel tanks were situated under the cargo compartment, and a winch was fitted at the back.

The AT-T was used as the basis for various combat engineering vehicles, and a fully-enclosed variant carried the Track Dish radar. A lengthened version with an extra road wheel on each side was used to carry the Long Track radar.

Specifications: AT-T

Crew: 1+3
Weight: 20 tonnes (empty)
    25 tonnes (loaded)
Maximum load: 5 tonnes
Towed load: 25 tonnes
Length: 6.99m (travelling)
Width: 3.17m (travelling)
Height: 2.58m (cab)
Ground clearance: 0.43m
Maximum road speed: 35km/hour
Gradient: 60%
Vertical obstacle: 1m
Fording: 0.75m
Trench: 2.1m

AT-L & AT-LM

First introduced in 1953, the AT-L was widely used for towing anti-tank guns, tube artillery, and large mortars, until it was replaced by 6x6 lorries in the towing role. The engine was fitted at the front, with the cab behind and the cargo compartment at the rear. The cargo compartment had a drop tailgate and tarpaulin cover. The cab had a circular hatch in the right roof, and a three-part windscreen, with the outer two screens hinged at the top.

The AT-LM, introduced in 1956, replaced the original six road wheels and three return rollers with five large wheels without return rollers. The AT-L and AT-LM were used to carry electronic equipment, such as the Pork Trough and Small Yawn radars.

Specifications: AT-L & AT-LM

Crew: 1+2
Weight: 6.3 tonnes (empty)
    8.3 tonnes (loaded)
Maximum load: 2 tonnes
Towed load: 60 tonnes
Length: 5.31m (travelling)
Width: 2.21m (travelling)
Height: 2.18m (cab)
Ground clearance: 0.35m
Maximum road speed: 42km/hour
Maximum road range: 300km
Vertical obstacle: 0.6m
Fording: 0.6m
Trench: 1m

AT-S

This tracked medium artillery tractor entered service in the early 1950s, towing medium and heavy artillery, such as 152mm howitzers and 100mm anti-aircraft guns. The engine was mounted at the front, with the cab behind. There was a circular hatch on the right side of the cab roof, and two doors on each side. The cargo compartment was at the rear, and had a tailgate and tarpaulin cover. As well as its primary use as an artillery tractor, it was used to mount various electronic equipment, including radars.

Specifications: AT-S

Crew: 1+6
Weight: 12 tonnes (empty)
    15 tonnes (loaded)
Maximum load: 3 tonnes
Towed load: 16 tonnes
Length: 5.87m (travelling)
Width: 2.57m (travelling)
Height: 2.54m (cab)
Height: 2.85m (tarpaulin)
Ground clearance: 0.4m
Maximum road speed: 35km/hour
Maximum road range: 380km
Gradient: 50%
Vertical obstacle: 0.6m
Fording: 1m
Trench: 1.45m

Mazur D-350 (Poland)

The D-350 was developed in the 1950s, and was partially based on the Soviet AT-S. The initial prototypes were designated D-300, but production versions with a more powerful engine were designated D-350. It was used to tow anti-tank guns and artillery of up to 152mm calibre.

Of conventional layout, it had the engine at the front, cab in the centre, and cargo area at the rear. Two doors were fitted on each side of the cab, one to the front and one to the rear. The front windscreens could be opened horizontally, hinging at the top, and there was a square hatch in the forward part of the cab roof. The cargo area had a tailgate, removable bows, and a tarpaulin cover. The suspension had five road wheels, drive sprocket at the front, idler at the rear, and four track return rollers. A 17-tonne capacity winch, with 80m of cable, was fitted as standard.

SPECIFICATIONS: D-350

Crew: 1+8
Weight: 18.56 tonnes (loaded)
Towed load: 15 tonnes
Length: 5.81m
Width: 2.89m
Height: 2.6m (cab)
Maximum road speed: 53km/hour
Maximum road range: 490km
Gradient: 50%
Vertical obstacle: 0.6m
Fording: 0.8m
Trench: 1.45m

ATS-59

Introduced in the late 1950s as a replacement for the AT-S, the ATS-59 used a number of T-54 components. The cab was at the front, with the engine behind, projecting into the cargo compartment. The cab had a circular hatch on the right side of the roof, and a door on each side. The cargo compartment had a tailgate and tarpaulin cover.

A variant was used to tow semi-trailers carrying the SA-2 Guideline surface-to-air missile. This variant did not have a cargo compartment, instead having an attachment for the semi-trailer on the rear chassis.

SPECIFICATIONS: ATS-59

Crew: 1+1
Weight: 13 tonnes (empty)
    16 tonnes (loaded)
Maximum load: 3 tonnes
Towed load: 14 tonnes
Length: 6.28m (travelling)
Width: 2.78m (travelling)
Height: 2.3m (cab)
Height: 2.5m (tarpaulin)
Ground clearance: 0.43m
Maximum road speed: 39km/hour
Maximum road range: 350km (500km with long-range tanks)
Gradient: 50%
Vertical obstacle: 1.1m
Fording: 1.5m
Trench: 2.5m

ATS-59G

First seen in 1972, this vehicle was initially known to NATO as the M1972. An improved version of the ATS-59, it had a redesigned cab. The cab on the ATS-59G was much larger, and of the forward control type, with the cargo compartment at the rear.

Specifications: ATS-59G

Weight: 13.75 tonnes (empty)
    16.75 tonnes (loaded)
Maximum load: 3 tonnes
Towed load: 14 tonnes
Fording: 1.5m

Bumar Labedy 668 (Poland)

Based on the Soviet ATS-59G, this was used in agriculture and forestry in addition to its use as a general-purpose tractor and prime mover for artillery and anti-tank guns. It had a forward control all-steel cab, mounted over the engine. It had seating for up to five passengers in addition to the driver, with a roof hatch on the right side. The cabin had overpressure NBC protection, and could be fitted with extra defrosting equipment for use in very cold environments.

A load area behind the cab could be used to carry supplies, but could not be fitted with seats for passengers. The rear load area could be fitted with seating, or could be used for cargo. A 14.7-tonne capacity winch was fitted for recovery purposes.

Specifications: 668

Crew: 1+5 (plus 12 in the rear)
Weight: 13 tonnes (empty)
    16 tonnes (loaded)
Maximum load: 3 tonnes
Towed load: 14 tonnes
Length: 6.28m
Width: 2.78m
Height: 2.58m (cab)
Height: 2.62m (tarpaulin)
Ground clearance: 0.42m
Maximum road speed: 39km/hour
Maximum road range: 350km (500km with extra tanks)
Vertical obstacle: 1.1m
Fording: 1.1m
Trench: 2.5m

MT-S

The MT-S was introduced in the early 1980s, but few details were ever released, and it appears to have only entered limited production. The basic chassis was derived from that used for the 2S3 Akatsiya self-propelled howitzer, which was also used for other applications, such as the GMZ minelayer.

Specifications: MT-S (provisional)

Crew: 1+3
Weight: 23.5 tonnes
Length: 7.8m
Width: 3.34m
Height: 1.85m

MT-T

Introduced in the early 1980s, the MT-T used suspension components from the T-64 and a diesel engine derived from that fitted in the T-72. The cab was at the front, and the large cargo compartment at the rear, with a canvas cover. The MT-T's chassis was used as the basis for several other vehicles, including the PTS-2 amphibious ferry, MDK-3 excavator, and BAT-2 digger.

Specifications: MT-T

Crew: 1+4
Weight: 25 tonnes
Maximum load: 12 tonnes
Towed load: 12 tonnes
Length: 8.71m
Width: 3.28m
Height: 3.07m

Lorries Used as Tow Vehicles

Soviet lorry designations followed a standard formula, which began with an abbreviated form of the plant name. Before 1966, this abbreviation was followed by a number of up to three digits. The first digit related to the plant, and the second two were allotted in sequence, so that earlier designs had lower numbers.

The plant abbreviations and digits were as follows:

Gor'kiy: GAZ, first digit 0 (usually omitted)
Moscow: ZIL, first digit 1
Yaroslavl, Kremenchug: YaAZ, later KrAZ, first digit 2
Miass: Ural, first digit 3
Ul'Yanovsk: UAZ, first digit 4
Minsk: MAZ, first digit 5
Kutaisi: KAZ, first digit 6
Zaporozh'ye, Lutsk, Riga: ZAZ, first digit 9

A new designation system came into effect on 1st August 1966, although existing models kept their old designations. This new system included information on various aspects of the vehicle. The new system used the same plant abbreviation, followed by a number of four to six digits, with four being the most common.

For lorries, the first digit indicated the gross tonnage, as follows:

1: Less than 1.2 tonnes
2: 1.2 to 2 tonnes
3: 2 to 8 tonnes
4: 8 to 14 tonnes
5: 14 to 20 tonnes
6: 20 to 40 tonnes
7: Over 40 tonnes

For light vehicles or cars, the first digit referred to engine size, rather than gross tonnage:

1: Less than 1.2 litres
2: 1.2 to 2 litres
3: 2 to 4 litres
4: Over 4 litres

The second digit denoted the vehicle type:

1: Passenger cars
2: Buses
3: Lorries with sides
4: Tractors
5: Dump lorries
6: Tanker lorries
7: Vans
8: Kept for future use
9: Special vehicles

The third and fourth digits were assigned sequentially by design, usually starting with 01. Special sequences were used for ambulances, high mobility vehicles, and specially-heightened models. The fifth digit, where used, identified modifications or improvements to the basic design. The sixth digit, when used, applied to export models. A 6 denoted a standard export model, a 7 denoted models for export to the tropics. Experimental models had an E appended. This letter was omitted when the design was accepted for production.

Engines for both cars and lorries had a similar system, using three or four digits. The first digit indicated the engine's displacement and type:

1: Less than 0.75 litres
2: 0.75 to 1.2 litres
3: 1.2 to 2 litres
4: 2 to 4 litres
5: 4 to 7 litres
6: 7 to 10 litres
7: 10 to 15 litres
8: Over 15 litres
9: Gas turbine engine

The second and third were model numbers, and denoted the engine as petrol (0 to 39) or diesel (40 to 99). The fourth digit, if present, indicated modifications.

GAZ-63

The GAZ-63 was a 4x4, 1.5-tonne lorry that entered service in 1946. It remained in production until 1963, when it was replaced by the improved GAZ-63A, which remained in production until 1968. The GAZ-63 chassis was used as the basis for the BTR-40 wheeled armoured personnel carrier.

GAZ-63

The all-steel, two-seat cab was situated immediately behind the engine, with the cargo area to the rear. The cargo bay had a wooden platform, high sides, and rear tailgate. Benches were fitted, which could be folded upwards when not in use. A winch, and a tarpaulin cover with bows, could be fitted if required.

SPECIFICATIONS: GAZ-63

Crew: 1+1
Configuration: 4x4
Weight: 3.5 tonnes
    4.99 tonnes (loaded)
Maximum load: 2 tonnes

Towed load: 2 tonnes
Length: 5.8m
Width: 2.2m
Height: 2.25m (cab)
Height: 2.25m (tarpaulin)
Ground clearance: 0.27m
Maximum road speed: 65km/hour
Maximum road range: 650km
Fording: 0.8m

GAZ-66

The GAZ-66 was a 4x4, 2-tonne lorry that replaced the GAZ-63A, entering production in 1964. Early vehicles did not have a central tyre pressure regulation system, but this was fitted to all production vehicles from 1968.

GAZ-66

The cab was fitted over the engine, and hinged forward to give access to it. The rear cargo area had fixed sides and a drop tailgate. If required, a tarpaulin cover could be fitted, with five bows to fix it in place. Intended for use at temperatures from -50°C to +50°C, it was fitted with an engine pre-heater and cab heater as standard. Many vehicles were fitted with a winch.

Specifications: GAZ-66

Crew: 1+1 (plus 21 in the rear)
Configuration: 4x4
Weight: 4.09 tonnes
Maximum load: 2.3 tonnes
Towed load: 2 tonnes
Length: 5.92m
Width: 2.53m
Height: 2.49m (cab)
Height: 2.52m (tarpaulin)
Ground clearance: 0.32m
Maximum road speed: 90km/hour
Maximum road range: 1,400km
Gradient: 67%
Fording: 1.2m

YaAZ-214 & KrAZ-214

This 6x6 lorry was originally built at the Yaroslavl Plant from 1956 to 1959 and designated YaAZ-214. Production was then moved to the Kremenchug Plant, and the vehicle was renamed KrAZ-214. Production ended in 1967, when it was replaced by the KrAZ-255B.

The vehicle had the engine at the front, with the fully enclosed cab to the immediate rear and the cargo area behind the cab. The cargo area had a hinged tailgate, removable bows, and a tarpaulin. The vehicle had a tyre pressure regulation system, cab heater, engine pre-heater, and 8-tonne capacity winch.

Specifications: KrAZ-214

Crew: 1+2
Configuration: 6x6
Weight: 12.3 tonnes
     19.3 tonnes (loaded)
Maximum load: 7 tonnes
Towed load: 30 tonnes
Length: 8.53m
Width: 2.7m
Height: 2.88m (cab)
Height: 3.17m (tarpaulin)
Ground clearance: 0.36m
Maximum road speed: 55km/hour
Maximum road range: 530km
Gradient: 30%
Fording: 1m

KrAZ-255B

In 1967, this lorry replaced the KrAZ-214 in production, and remained in production until 1979. Of similar design to the earlier vehicle, it had a more powerful engine, leading to faster speed and better cross-country performance. The layout was the same, with the engine at the front, two-door cab behind, and cargo area at the rear. The cargo area had a tailgate, removable bows, and a tarpaulin. A cab heater, engine pre-heater, 12-tonne capacity winch, and suspension locking mechanism were fitted as standard.

Most roles originally fulfilled by the KrAZ-214 were taken over by the KrAZ-255B as it came into service.

KrAZ-255B

SPECIFICATIONS: KRAZ-255B

Crew: 1+2
Configuration: 6x6
Weight: 11.95 tonnes
    19.45 tonnes (loaded)
Maximum load: 7.5 tonnes
Towed load: 30 tonnes
Length: 8.65m

Width: 2.75m
Height: 2.94m (cab)
Height: 3.17m (tarpaulin)
Ground clearance: 0.36m
Maximum road speed: 70km/hour
Maximum road range: 750km
Gradient: 60%
Fording: 0.85m

KrAZ-260

In 1979, the KrAZ-260 replaced the KrAZ-255B in production. It had a conventional layout, with the engine at the front, two-door cab behind, and cargo area at the rear. The cargo area had a hinged tailgate and bows to secure a tarpaulin. It had a winch mounted under the body and a lockable differential. The KrAZ-260 had an increased payload and speed compared to the KrAZ-255B.

Specifications: KrAZ-260

Crew: 1+2
Configuration: 6x6
Weight: 12.25 tonnes
    21.48 tonnes (loaded)
Maximum load: 9 tonnes
Towed load: 30 tonnes
Length: 9.01m
Width: 2.72m
Height: 2.99m (cab)
Ground clearance: 0.37m

KrAZ-260

Maximum road speed: 80km/hour
Maximum road range: 700km
Gradient: 58%
Vertical obstacle: 0.5m
Fording: 1.2m
Trench: 0.68m

UAZ-469B

A vehicle designated UAZ-460B appeared in 1960, but did not enter production. After further development, it was designated UAZ-469B. Production began in 1972, and it entered service the following year.

The engine was at the front, with a four-door crew compartment behind. The windscreen could be folded down onto the bonnet, a removable canvas top was fitted, and the tops of the

UAZ-469B

doors could be removed. A hard top was also available. Two individual seats were fitted at the front, a bench seat for three behind, and two pairs of seats facing each other at the rear. The usual load was two people plus 600kg of cargo, or seven people and 100kg of cargo.

SPECIFICATIONS: UAZ-469B

Crew: 1+6
Configuration: 4x4
Weight: 1.49 tonnes
　　2.29 tonnes (loaded)
Maximum load: 695kg
Towed load: 600kg (2 tonnes braked)
Length: 4.03m
Width: 1.79m

Height: 2.02m
Ground clearance: 0.22m
Maximum road speed: 100km/hour
Maximum road range: 620km
Gradient: 62%
Vertical obstacle: 0.45m
Fording: 0.7m

URAL 375

Entering production in 1961, the first model of the 6x6 Ural 375 had an open cab with a canvas top. The later model could be easily identified by the fully enclosed all-steel cab, and also featured a number of automotive improvements. This was designated Ural 375D (without a winch) and Ural 375T (with a 7-tonne capacity winch). Both models had a central tyre pressure regulation system.

The cab was to the rear of the engine, with the cargo area to the rear of the cab. The cargo area had bench seats, a tailgate, removable bows, and a tarpaulin cover. A cab heater and engine pre-heater were fitted as standard.

A series of tests conducted in 1973 of a Ural 375D with a YaMZ-740 V8 diesel engine led to the Ural 4320.

SPECIFICATIONS: URAL 375

Crew: 1+2
Configuration: 6x6
Weight: 8.4 tonnes
    13.3 tonnes (loaded)
Maximum load: 4.5 tonnes

Ural 375D

Towed load: 10 tonnes
Length: 7.35m
Width: 2.69m
Height: 2.68m (cab)
Height: 2.98m (tarpaulin)
Ground clearance: 0.41m
Maximum road speed: 75km/hour
Maximum road range: 750km
Gradient: 60%
Vertical obstacle: 0.8m
Fording: 1m (1.5m with preparation)

URAL 4320

A diesel-powered development of the Ural 375D, production of this 6x6 lorry began in 1978. The new, more powerful engine increased payload and maximum speed, while simultaneously reducing fuel consumption and maintenance time. The main visible difference was the radiator shell, which was lengthened in front. Changes were made to various components, such as gear ratios, in order to maximise the benefit of the new engine.

Ural 4320

SPECIFICATIONS: URAL 4320

Crew: 1+2
Configuration: 6x6
Weight: 8.02 tonnes
Maximum load: 5.23 tonnes
Towed load: 7 tonnes
Length: 7.37m
Width: 2.5m
Height: 2.87m (cab)
Ground clearance: 0.4m
Maximum road speed: 85km/hour
Gradient: 58%
Fording: 0.7m

ZIL-157

A replacement for the ZIL-151, the ZIL-157 was in production from 1958 to 1961, with the improved ZIL-157K in production until 1966. The appearance was very similar to the earlier ZIL-151, with a slightly different cab and single rear wheels in place of the dual rear wheels of the ZIL-151.

ZIL-157

The two-door cab was at the front, immediately behind the engine, and the cargo area was to the rear of the cab. The cargo area had a wooden platform with sides, a drop tailgate, and bench seats that could be folded up when not required. Bows and a tarpaulin cover could be fitted, and a cab heater and engine pre-heater were fitted as standard. Many vehicles were fitted with a winch.

Specifications: ZIL-157

Crew: 1+1
Configuration: 6x6
Weight: 5.8 tonnes
    8.45 tonnes (loaded)
Maximum load: 4.5 tonnes
Towed load: 3.6 tonnes
Length: 6.92m
Width: 2.32m
Height: 2.36m (cab)
Height: 2.92m (tarpaulin)
Ground clearance: 0.31m
Maximum road speed: 65km/hour
Maximum road range: 510km
Gradient: 53%
Fording: 0.85m

DAC 444 (Romania)

The DAC 444 had a forward control configuration, with the cab over the engine. The steel cab had seating for up to three passengers in addition to the driver. The cab could be tilted forward to allow access to the engine. An observation hatch was fitted on the right side of the cab roof, and the spare wheel was mounted on the right side of the cab rear.

The cargo area was to the rear of the cab, and had a wooden platform, drop tailgate, removable bows, and tarpaulin cover. Folding bench seats were fitted on both sides. Optional equipment included an engine pre-heater, 6-tonne capacity winch, and a central tyre pressure regulation system.

Specifications: DAC 444

Crew: 1+3
Configuration: 4x4
Weight: 5.7 tonnes
   10.7 tonnes (loaded)
Maximum load: 4 tonnes
Towed load: 5.5 tonnes
Length: 6.46m
Width: 2.5m
Height: 2.79m (cab)
Ground clearance: 0.4m
Maximum road speed: 89km/hour
Gradient: 50%
Fording: 0.65m

Praga V3S (Czechoslovakia)

Developed in the 1950s and originally built by Praga, production shifted to Avia in 1964. It had a conventional layout, with the engine at the front, the two-man, two-door steel cab behind, and the cargo area at the rear. Fuel containers could be kept behind the front bumper, and a circular observation hatch was fitted in the right side of the cab's roof. The windscreen was split, and both halves of it could be opened. The cargo area had a tarpaulin cover with removable bows, which could be stowed in the cab when not in use. Some vehicles were fitted with a 3.5-tonne winch.

Praga V3S

SPECIFICATIONS: PRAGA V3S

Crew: 1+1
Configuration: 6x6
Weight: 5.35 tonnes
   10.65 tonnes (loaded)
Maximum load: 5.3 tonnes
Towed load: 5.5 tonnes
Length: 6.91m
Width: 2.31m
Height: 2.51m (cab)
Height: 2.92m (tarpaulin)
Ground clearance: 0.4m
Maximum road speed: 62km/hour
Maximum road range: 500km
Gradient: 60%
Fording: 0.8m

Tatra 138 (Czechoslovakia)

The Tatra 138 entered service in 1963, replacing the earlier Tatra 111. It had a conventional layout, with the engine at the front, two-door steel cab behind it, and cargo area at the rear, with drop sides and a drop tailgate. The military model, designated Tatra 138VN, differed from the civilian model with higher hinged sideboards, removable bows, tarpaulin cover, and a winch.

Tatra 138

Specifications: Tatra 138

Crew: 1+2
Configuration: 6x6
Weight: 8.74 tonnes
    20.59 tonnes (loaded)
Maximum load: 11.85 tonnes

Towed load: 22 tonnes
Length: 8.57m
Width: 2.45m
Height: 2.44m (cab)
Height: 3.2m (tarpaulin)
Ground clearance: 0.29m
Maximum road speed: 71km/hour
Maximum road range: 540km
Gradient: 35%
Fording: 1m

Towed Guns and Howitzers

The Soviet army showed little interest in self-propelled artillery during the Second World War. Multiple rocket launchers, anti-tank guns, and assault guns were mounted on tracked or wheeled vehicles, but development of self-propelled guns and howitzers for indirect fire didn't begin until the late 1960s.

Although towed weapons sacrificed cross-country mobility and crew protection, they were cheaper to produce and easier to maintain. The Soviets often used a single-carriage design for multiple weapons, increasing simplicity of manufacture. Towed weapons also had a measure of increased tactical flexibility. If the prime mover was destroyed or broke down, the weapon could be towed by another vehicle.

The last towed Soviet anti-tank gun to enter production was the 100mm MT-12. Development began of a 125mm towed gun, the 2A45 Sprut, but this never entered production. Both self-propelled and towed guns and howitzers, up to and including 152mm calibre, were supplied with anti-armour rounds, either HEAT, APHE (known as HESH or HEP in the West) or some version of kinetic AP.

152MM ML-20 GUN-HOWITZER

Introduced in 1938, the ML-20 replaced the earlier 152mm M1910/34, the new weapon having a considerably higher maximum elevation. The ML-20's carriage was also adopted for the 122mm A-19. Compared to the A-19, the ML-20's ordnance was shorter, fatter, and had a multi-slotted muzzle brake.

ML-20

The carriage was a box-section split-trail, originally fitted with a spoked wheel on either side of the small shield. The single wheels were soon replaced with dual solid wheels, and the solid rubber tyres were replaced with sponge rubber filled tyres. For transit, a two-wheeled limber was attached to the rear of the trail, and the ordnance was withdrawn to the rear and secured between the trails. The gun could be moved with the ordnance in place, but only for short distances and at slow speed.

The ML-20 fired variable-charge, case-type, separate-loading ammunition. HE-FRAG, concrete-piercing, chemical, HEAT, illuminating, and smoke projectiles were available. The AP-T round could penetrate 124mm of armour at 1,000m. It was normally towed by an AT-S or AT-T artillery tractor.

Specifications: ML-20

Calibre: 152.4mm
Barrel length: 4.93m
Weight: 7,270kg
 8,073kg (travelling)
Length: 7.21m (travelling)
Width: 2.31m (travelling)
Height: 2.26m (travelling)
Elevation/depression: +65/-2°
Traverse: 58° total
Rate of fire: 4 rounds/minute
Maximum range: 17,265m
Crew: 9

76mm M1938 Mountain Gun

Originally a Czech 75mm design (Skoda C5), the Soviets began licence production in 1938 as the M1938. It saw widespread service in the Second World War, and it served with Soviet mountain units during the Cold War.

The M1938 could be broken down into three loads for towing by animals or light vehicles, or into ten loads for man-packed transport. It had a split trail which could be used in a short or long leg configuration, and two pneumatic wheels. The shield

M1938

sloped back at a sharp angle, and could be removed if required. Armour-piercing and shrapnel rounds were developed, but it appears to have only been used to fire high-explosive rounds.

SPECIFICATIONS: M1938

Calibre: 76mm
Barrel length: 1.63m
Weight: 785kg
    1,450kg (travelling)
Height: 1.35m (0.76m without shield)
Elevation/depression: +65/-5°
Maximum range: 10,100m

122MM A-19 CORPS GUN

Introduced just before the Second World War, this was a development of an earlier gun, mounting the same recoil system and ordnance on a new carriage which allowed greater elevation. The carriage was the same as that fitted to the 152mm ML-20. The A-19 could be distinguished from the ML-20 by its longer, thinner barrel, and a counterweight in place of the ML-20's muzzle brake.

A-19

The carriage was a box-section split-trail, originally fitted with a spoked wheel on either side of the small shield. The single wheels were soon replaced with dual solid wheels, and the solid rubber tyres were replaced with sponge rubber filled tyres. For transit, a two-wheeled limber was attached to the rear of the trail, and the ordnance was withdrawn to the rear and secured between the trails. The gun could be moved with the ordnance in place, but only for short distances and at slow speed.

The A-19 fired variable-charge, case-type, separate-loading ammunition. HE-FRAG, concrete-piercing, and AP-T rounds were available. The AP-T round could penetrate 160mm of armour at 1,000m. It was towed by an AT-T, AT-L, ATS-59, or

AT-S artillery tractor, or a KrAZ-214 6x6 7-tonne or Ural 375 6x6 4.5-tonne lorry.

SPECIFICATIONS: A-19

Calibre: 122mm
Barrel length: 5.65m
Weight: 7,250kg
    8,050kg (travelling)
Length: 7.87m (travelling)
Width: 2.46m (travelling)
Height: 2.27m (travelling)
Elevation/depression: +65/-2°
Traverse: 58° total
Rate of fire: 5-6 rounds/minute
Maximum range: 20,800m
Crew: 8

122MM M-30 HOWITZER

The M-30 entered service with the Soviet army in 1939, and was the standard Soviet and Warsaw Pact divisional howitzer until it was replaced by the D-30. Each motorised rifle division had two battalions, and each tank division had three battalions. In both cases, each battalion had three batteries of six howitzers.

The split-trail carriage was identical to that of the D-1 152mm howitzer. The top half of the shield sloped to the rear, and the centre section slid upwards to allow for elevation. The howitzer could be fired without spreading the trails, but traverse was limited to 1.5° in that case. Each trail had two spades: a fixed one for use on hard surfaces, and a hinged one for use on soft

M-30

ground. Maximum towing speed was 48km/hour, and it was normally towed by a Ural 375 6x6 4.5-tonne lorry or MT-LB multi-purpose tracked vehicle.

The M-30 fired variable-charge, case-type, separate-loading ammunition. HE-FRAG and HEAT warheads were available, both of which could be fired by the newer D-30. In the 1980s, Poland upgraded some M-30s to improve their direct fire capability, designating the new weapons wz 1938/1985.

SPECIFICATIONS: M-30

Barrel length: 2.8m
Weight: 2,450 kg (travelling order)
    2,450 kg (firing position)
Length: 5.9m (travelling)
Width: 1.98m (travelling)
Height: 1.71m (travelling)
Ground clearance: 0.33m
Elevation/depression: +63.5/-3°
Traverse: 49° total
Rate of fire: 5-6 rounds/minute

Sustained rate of fire: 1.5 rounds/minute
Range: 11,800m max, 630m effective (HEAT)
Crew: 8
Unit of fire: 80 rounds

152MM M-10 HOWITZER

Introduced into service just before the Second World War, the M-10 remained in service with the Soviet army until the 1950s, and saw service with the Romanian army throughout the Cold War. Its weight made it difficult to manoeuvre, and so a new carriage was developed. This new carriage, and the addition of a double-baffle muzzle brake, resulted in the D-1 howitzer.

The upper part of the M-10's shield sloped to the rear and had chamfered corners. The carriage had dual rubber-tyred road wheels, and there was a limber, which also had rubber-tyred wheels. The recoil system was under the barrel, with the counter-recoil system above. Elevation controls were on the right, traverse on the left. The normal tow vehicle was an AT-S artillery tractor.

Ammunition was variable-charge, case-type, separate-loading. HE-FRAG, concrete-piercing, chemical, HEAT, illuminating, semi-AP, and smoke rounds were available.

SPECIFICATIONS: M-10

Calibre: 152.4mm
Barrel length: 3.7m
Weight: 4,150kg
    4,550kg (travelling)
Length: 6.4m (travelling)
Width: 2.1m (travelling)

M-10

Height: 1.9m (travelling)
Elevation/depression: +65/-1°
Traverse: 50° total
Rate of fire: 4 rounds/minute
Maximum range: 12,400m
Crew: 7

76MM ZIS-3 DIVISIONAL GUN

Introduced in 1942, this was the latest in a long line of 76mm artillery pieces. The ordnance was used as the main armament in the SU-76, although the limited elevation in the vehicle restricted the range compared to the towed gun.

The carriage was the same split-trail carriage used on the 57mm ZIS-2 anti-tank gun, with tubular trails. A double-baffle

ZIS-3

muzzle brake reduced recoil to allow the larger gun to operate on the relatively light carriage. A vertical shield was fitted, and the carriage had two rubber-tyred wheels.

Ammunition was of the fixed type. HE-FRAG, AP-T, HVAP-T, and HEAT rounds were produced. The HE-FRAG round had 710g of TNT. The AP-T round could penetrate 61mm of armour at 1,000m, or 69mm at 500m. The HVAP-T round could penetrate 58mm at 1,000m or 92mm at 500m. The HEAT round could penetrate 120mm at any range.

It was towed by a BTR-152 APC, GAZ-66 4x4 2-tonne lorry, or a ZIL-157 6x6 2.5-tonne lorry.

Specifications: ZIS-3

Calibre: 76mm
Barrel length: 3.46m
Weight: 1,116kg (travelling)
Length: 6.1m (travelling)

Width: 1.65m (travelling)
Height: 1.38m (travelling)
Elevation/depression: +37/-5°
Traverse: 54° total
Rate of fire: 15-20 rounds/minute
Maximum range: 13,290m

152MM D-1 HOWITZER

Introduced in 1943 to replace the 152mm M-10 howitzer, this used a strengthened version of the carriage and recoil system of the 122mm M-30 howitzer. The ordnance was the same as the 152mm M-10, fitted with a new double-baffle muzzle brake. It was lighter than the earlier weapon, and fired the same ammunition.

The carriage was a riveted box-section split-trail. The shield sloped to the rear at the top and included a section in the middle that slid upwards to allow the weapon to elevate. The recoil system was under the barrel, with the counter-recoil system above. Elevation controls were on the right, traverse on the left. It was normally towed by an AT-S artillery tractor, at speeds of up to 48km/hour. Two spades were fitted to each trail: a fixed one for use on hard ground, and a hinged one for use on soft ground.

Ammunition was variable-charge, case-type, separate-loading. HE-FRAG, concrete-piercing, chemical, HEAT, illuminating, semi-AP, and smoke rounds were available.

SPECIFICATIONS: D-1

Calibre: 152.4mm
Barrel length: 4.21m

D-1

Weight: 3,600kg
    3,640kg (travelling)
Length: 7.56m (travelling)
Width: 2m (travelling)
Height: 1.85m (travelling)
Elevation/depression: +64/-3°
Traverse: 35° total
Rate of fire: 4 rounds/minute
Maximum range: 12,400m
Crew: 7

57mm ZIS-2 Anti-Tank Gun

Adopted for service in 1943, this combined the carriage of a 76mm ZIS-3 divisional gun with the ordnance of a 57mm M1941 anti-tank gun. Superficially similar to the ZIS-3, it could be differentiated by the longer, thinner barrel, without a muzzle brake.

ZIS-2

Originally it was fitted with a straight-topped shield that could be folded forward, but after the Second World War many were fitted with a new shield with a wavy top, and some had fittings for an infra-red night vision device ahead of the shield.

The ammunition was interchangeable with that for the 57mm Ch-26 and ASU-57. HE-FRAG, AP-T, and HVAP ammunition was available. The AP-T round could penetrate 96mm at 1,000m or 106mm at 500m. The HVAP round could penetrate 95mm at 1,000m or 140mm at 500m. It was normally towed by a BTR-152 or a GAZ-63 4x4 2-tonne lorry.

SPECIFICATIONS: ZIS-2

Calibre: 57mm
Barrel length: 4.16m
Weight: 1,150kg

Length: 6.8m (travelling)
Width: 1.7m (travelling)
Height: 1.37m (travelling)
Elevation/depression: +25/-5°
Traverse: 56° total
Rate of fire: 25 rounds/minute
Sustained rate of fire: 10-15 rounds/minute
Maximum range: 8,400m
Crew: 7

100MM BS-3 ANTI-TANK & FIELD GUN

The largest towed anti-tank gun of the Second World War, the BS-3 was developed from the 100mm B-34 naval gun and entered service in 1944. It saw some service in the Second World War, in both the anti-tank and field gun roles. In the anti-tank role, it was a very powerful weapon, able to penetrate 170mm of armour at 1,000m. In the field gun role, it was less powerful than the 122mm A-19, but was more mobile and had a higher rate of fire. It was later replaced in the anti-tank role by the D-48 and then the T-12.

It had a shield to give some protection to the crew, a standard box-section split trail, and a double-baffle muzzle brake. Distinguishing features included dual tyres on the carriage wheels and stowage boxes on the front of the shield. The ammunition used by the BS-3 could also be fired by the KS-19 AA gun, the T-54 and T-55 tanks, and the SU-100 assault gun. Usual tow vehicles were an AT-P armoured artillery tractor or Ural 375 6x6 4.5-tonne lorry.

BS-3

SPECIFICATIONS: BS-3

Calibre: 100mm
Barrel length: 6.07m
Weight: 3,650kg
Length: 9.37m
Width: 2.15m
Height: 1.5m
Elevation/depression: +45/-5°
Traverse: 58° total
Rate of fire: 8-10 rounds/minute
Maximum range: 21,000m
Crew: 6

85MM D-44 DIVISIONAL GUN

The 85mm D-44 was developed during the Second World War as a replacement for the 76mm ZIS-3 divisional gun. Although it was developed during the war, it was not deployed until after the war ended. The barrel was a development of the 85mm gun used in the T-34/85 tank, and was virtually identical to the 85mm KS-12 anti-aircraft gun. It used fixed ammunition, which was interchangeable with that used by the SD-44 and the Czech M-52 field gun. Penetration was up to 180mm (using HVAP-T ammunition) of vertical standard armour plate at 1,000m.

A small wheel near the end of one trail made it easier to manoeuvre the weapon into position. An infra-red night vision device could be fitted to the shield. In this configuration, the gun was designated D-44-N.

The SD-44 was a variant of the D-44 with a small petrol auxiliary propulsion unit. Initial models were conversions of standard D-44s. The engine was mounted on the left trail, with fuel and ready-use ammunition carried in the trails. The engine drove the two carriage wheels, with a small castor wheel just behind the spades being used to steer. The weapon could be driven at up to 25km/hour, and could still be towed if required. It was developed for the airborne forces, and each airborne division was issued with 18 guns in three six-gun batteries.

SPECIFICATIONS: D-44

Calibre: 85mm
Barrel length: 4.7m
Weight: 1,725kg

D-44

Length: 8.35m (travelling)
Width: 1.78m (travelling)
Height: 1.42m (travelling)
Elevation/depression: +35/-7°
Traverse: 54° total
Rate of fire: 15-20 rounds/minute
Maximum range: 15,650m
Crew: 8

152MM M-18/46 HOWITZER (CZECHOSLOVAKIA)

At the end of the Second World War, there were many German 15cm Feldhaubitze 18 (15cm sFH 18) howitzers in Czechoslovakia. With the decision to standardise on Soviet ammunition, they were re-bored to allow them to fire standard Soviet 152mm rounds, as used by the M-10 and D-1. A large square shield and double-baffle muzzle brake was added, and the weapons were designated M-18/46.

The M-18/46 fired variable-charge, case-type, separate-loading ammunition. Semi-AP, HE, and HEAT rounds were available. The semi-AP round was originally developed for naval use, with a larger HE warhead than the normal APHE round, and an effective range of 510m.

The M-18/46 had a standard split-trail, box-section carriage, with a limber. Normal tow vehicle was an AT-S medium-tracked artillery tractor.

SPECIFICATIONS: M-18/46

Calibre: 152.4mm
Barrel length: 4.88m
Weight: 5,512kg
    6,304kg (travelling)
Length: 8.28m (travelling)
Width: 1.71m (travelling)
Height: 1.71m (travelling)
Elevation/depression: +45/-0°
Traverse: 60° total
Rate of fire: 4 rounds/minute
Maximum range: 12,400m
Crew: 7

85mm M-52 & M52/55 Field Gun (Czechoslovakia)

The 85mm M-52 was the Czech equivalent of the Soviet 85mm D-44, and fired the same ammunition. A slightly modified version, the M-52/55, was also developed. Both could be fitted with an infra-red night vision device.

In appearance, it was similar to the 100mm M-53. The M-52 could be differentiated by the shield's wavy top, tubular rather than box-section trails, and the lack of castor wheels. Unlike the M-53, the sides of the shield did not slope to the rear.

It had a double-baffle muzzle brake and a conventional split-trail carriage, with tubular trails and two rubber-tyred road wheels. The usual tow vehicle was a Praga V3S 6x6 5-tonne lorry, which could tow it at speeds of up to 50km/hour (10km/hour cross-country). Effective direct fire range with HVAP-T ammunition was 1,150m.

Specifications: M-52 (M-52/55 in brackets)

Calibre: 85mm
Barrel length: 5.07m
Weight: 2,095kg (2,111kg)
    2,130kg (travelling) (2,168kg)
Length: 7.52m (travelling)
Width: 1.98m (travelling)
Height: 1.52m (travelling)
Elevation/depression: +38/-6°
Traverse: 60° total
Rate of fire: 20 rounds/minute

Maximum range: 16,160m
Crew: 7

152MM D-20 GUN-HOWITZER

Developed soon after the Second World War, the D-20 used the same carriage and recoil system as the 122mm D-74 field gun. The D-20 could be distinguished from the D-74 by the shorter, thicker barrel and larger double-baffle muzzle brake. Like the D-74, the D-20 was first seen in public during the 1955 Moscow May Day Parade. The gun in the 2S3 Akatsiya self-propelled howitzer was a development of the D-20.

D-20

The shield had a sliding centre section to allow the barrel to be elevated, and the top section could be folded down to reduce overall height. When in action, the D-20 was positioned on a firing pedestal, allowing it to be quickly traversed through a full 360°. For transit, the pedestal was inverted and secured forward of the shield. The carriage was a split box-section trail, each trail having a spade and a castor wheel at the end. For transit, the spade was folded underneath and the wheel on top of the trail. It was towed by an AT-S artillery tractor or a Ural 375 6x6 4.5-tonne lorry.

The gunner's position was to the left of the ordnance. He was provided with a PG1M sight for indirect fire, and an OP4M sight for direct fire. Ammunition was case-type, variable-charge, separate-loading. HE-FRAG, AP-T, CP, chemical, HE-RAP, HEAT, illuminating, and smoke ammunition were produced. The HE-RAP round increased range to 24,000m.

Specifications: D-20

Calibre: 152.4mm
Barrel length: 5.2m
Weight: 5,650kg
    5,700kg (travelling)
Length: 8.69m (travelling)
Width: 2.4m (travelling)
Height: 1.93m (travelling)
Elevation/depression: +63/-5°
Traverse: 360° total
Rate of fire: 5-6 rounds/minute
Maximum range: 17,410m (24,000m with RAP)
Crew: 10

122mm D-74 Field Gun

The D-74 was designed to meet the same requirement as the 130mm M-46. The M-46 was considered superior, because it fired a heavier projectile to a longer distance. Nonetheless, the D-

74 entered production. Most of the weapons were exported, but it saw limited service in the Soviet army, and was first observed by the West during the 1955 May Day Parade in Moscow.

It used the same carriage as the 152mm D-20 gun-howitzer. The centre section of the shield slid upwards to allow the barrel to be elevated, and sloped slightly to the rear. When in action, the D-74 was positioned on a firing pedestal, allowing it to be quickly traversed through a full 360°. For transit, the pedestal was inverted and secured forward of the shield. The carriage was a split box-section trail, each trail having a spade and a castor wheel at the end. For transit, the spade was folded underneath and the wheel on top of the trail.

The D-74 fired variable-charge, case-type, separate-loading ammunition. HE-FRAG, APC-T, illuminating, and smoke charges were available. The usual towing vehicle was a Ural 375 6x6 4.5-tonne lorry.

Specifications: D-74

Calibre: 122mm
Barrel length: 6.45m
Weight: 5,500kg
    5,550kg (travelling)
Length: 9.88m (travelling)
Width: 2.35m (travelling)
Height: 2.75m (travelling)
Elevation/depression: +45/-5°
Traverse: 58° total
Rate of fire: 6-7 rounds/minute
Sustained rate of fire: 1.3 rounds/minute

Maximum range: 24,000m
Crew: 10

130MM M-46 FIELD GUN

Accepted for service in 1950 and first seen by the West in the 1954 May Day Parade, this weapon was ballistically similar to 130mm guns used by the Soviet navy. When travelling, a mechanism on the right trail drew the barrel back to reduce the overall length, and the spades were removed and fitted on top of the trails. The split-trail carriage was provided with a limber.

Damaged Iraqi M-46

The barrel had a pepper pot muzzle brake, with the recoil system mounted under the barrel and forward of the shield. The OP4M-35 direct fire sight had x5.5 magnification, and an APN-3 night sight was fitted, which could be used in active or passive modes. The M-46 fired case-type, variable-charge, separate-loading ammunition.

The long range and high accuracy of the M-46 meant that it was often used in the counter-battery role. It was towed by an AT-S or ATS-59 artillery tractor at speeds of up to 50km/hour.

Specifications: M-46

Calibre: 130mm
Barrel length: 7.6m
Weight: 7,700kg
    8,450kg (travelling)
Length: 11.73m (travelling)
Width: 2.45m (travelling)
Height: 2.55m (travelling)
Elevation/depression: +45/-2.5°
Traverse: 50° total
Rate of fire: 5-6 rounds/minute
Maximum range: 27,150m
Crew: 8

76.2mm Mountain Gun (Romania)

Specifically developed for the needs of Romanian mountain troops, this gun could be towed by a vehicle or horse team, or quickly disassembled into loads to be carried by eight pack animals. It had a crew of seven: commander, aimer, breech operator, loader, fuse handler, projectile handler, and charge handler. When towed, it could be brought into action within a minute. When carried by pack animals, it took six to eight minutes to be brought into action. The gun could fire smoke and HEAT, as well as standard high-explosive ammunition. When firing HEAT, maximum range was limited to 1,000m. The gun was fitted with a telescope with x3 magnification.

Specifications: 76.2mm Mountain Gun

Calibre: 76.2mm
Barrel length: 1.18m
Weight: 722kg
Length: 2.45m (travelling)
    3.1m (in action)
Width: 1.33m (travelling)
    2.65m (in action)
Height: 1.66m
Elevation/depression: +45/-15°
Traverse: 50° total
Rate of fire: 25 rounds/minute
Sustained rate of fire: 1.3 rounds/minute
Maximum range: 8,600m
Crew: 7

130mm SM-4-1 Coastal Gun

Development of the SM-4-1 began in May 1944, with factory testing in 1948 and 1949. Government testing took place in 1950 and 1951, with service acceptance in October 1951. Initially, it used the Moskva-TsN fire control system and ZALP-B radar. These were considered too inaccurate, and so work on a new fire control system and radar began in 1950. The new Burya-MT-4 fire control and Burun radar were accepted into service in 1955. The new system was designated SM-4-1B.

SM-4-1

The carriage had two axles, each with four rubber-tyred road wheels. The axles were removed when in action, and four stabilisers, two on each side of the carriage, were extended and staked to the ground. In transit, the stabilisers were mounted on the front of the shield. The slightly curved shield had a centre section that could be removed to facilitate elevation of the ordnance. The 130mm barrel had an unusual muzzle brake and a travel lock. The SM-4-1 ammunition was not interchangeable with the M-46 field gun or KS-30 anti-aircraft gun.

APHE and HE rounds were available. The APHE round could penetrate 250mm of armour at 1,000m. Usual deployment was four-gun batteries with a radar fire control system, giving it an all-weather capability. It was normally towed by an AT-T heavy tracked artillery tractor.

Specifications: SM-4-1

Calibre: 130mm
Barrel length: 7.6m
Weight: 16,000kg
    19,000kg (travelling)
Length: 12.8m (travelling)
Width: 2.85m (travelling)
Height: 3.05m (travelling)
Elevation/depression: +45/-5°
Traverse: 360° total
Rate of fire: 5 rounds/minute
Maximum range: 29,500m

100mm M-53 Field Gun (Czechoslovakia)

Developed in the early 1950s to fulfil a similar role to the Soviet 100mm BS-3, the M-53 could fire the same ammunition. It could not, however, fire the 100mm T-12's ammunition. Like the BS-3, it could be used in both the field gun and anti-tank roles.

It had a double-baffle muzzle brake, and a large diameter APN-3-5 infra-red night vision device could be fitted over the rear part of the barrel. Usual tow vehicle was a Tatra 138 6x6 12-tonne lorry, and effective anti-tank range was 1,000m.

It was visually similar to the Czech 85mm M-52 as well as the Soviet BS-3. However, the M-53 had a box-section split-trail carriage rather than the M-52's tubular trails. It had single road wheels instead of the BS-3's double wheels, and the shield had a straight top and sides that sloped to the rear, unlike the M-52. It also had a castor wheel at the end of each trail to assist in deployment.

Specifications: M-53

Calibre: 100mm
Barrel length: 6.74m
Weight: 4,210kg
    4,280kg (travelling)
Length: 9.1m (travelling)
Width: 2.61m (travelling)
Height: 2.61m (travelling)
Elevation/depression: +42/-6°
Traverse: 60° total
Rate of fire: 8-10 rounds/minute
Maximum range: 21,000m
Crew: 6

180mm S-23 Gun

Developed in the early 1950s from a naval weapon, this was first seen by the West during the 1955 May Day Parade in Moscow. Western intelligence initially believed it to have a calibre of 203mm, and so referred to it as the 203mm gun-howitzer M1955. This error was corrected after examples were captured by the Israelis.

When in action, the S-23 was supported on a base. When in transit, the base was retracted under the carriage and the barrel was traversed to the rear and attached to the trails. The carriage had split, box-section trails and four large rubber tyres filled

S-23

with sponge rubber. The long barrel had a pepper pot muzzle brake.

The S-23 fired bag-type variable charges. The HE-FRAG projectile weighed 88kg, with 10.7kg of TNT. The concrete-piercing projectile weighed 97.5kg, with 7.35kg of TNT. A rocket-assisted HE projectile was also available, which weighed 84kg and had 5.62kg of RDX and aluminium.

SPECIFICATIONS: S-23

Calibre: 180mm
Barrel length: 8.8m
Weight: 21,450kg
Length: 10.49m
Width: 3m
Height: 2.62m
Elevation/depression: +50/-2°
Traverse: 44° total
Rate of fire: 1 rounds/minute
Maximum range: 30.4km (43.8km with RAP)
Crew: 16

85mm D-48 Anti-Tank Gun

Originally seen by the West during the 1955 Moscow May Day Parade, the D-48 was initially mis-identified as a 100mm weapon. It was replaced in Soviet anti-tank formations by the T-12 in the mid-1960s, and NATO did not realise its mistake and reclassify the D-48 as an 85mm weapon until the 1970s.

The D-48 had an impressive performance, achieved by necking down 100mm ammunition to accept a new 85mm projectile. Ammunition included AP, HVAP, and HE rounds. Estimated penetration at 1,000m was 190mm with AP, 240mm with HVAP.

It had a very long barrel with a multi-perforated muzzle brake, mounted on a split-trail carriage with two wheels and a shield. A single castor wheel was fitted to assist in bringing it into and out of action. For transit, the breech was clamped between the trails. An infra-red night vision device could be fitted. It was towed by either an AT-P armoured artillery tractor or Ural 375 6x6 4.5-tonne lorry.

Specifications: D-48

Calibre: 85mm
Barrel length: 6.49m
Weight: 2,350kg
Length: 8.72m (travelling)
Width: 1.59m (travelling)
Height: 1.89m (travelling)
Elevation/depression: +35/-6°
Traverse: 54° total

Rate of fire: 15 rounds/minute
Maximum range: 18,970m
Crew: 6

57MM CH-26 AUXILIARY-PROPELLED ANTI-TANK GUN

The Ch-26 mounted a shorter version of the Ch-51M gun from the ASU-57 self-propelled anti-tank gun on a new split-trail carriage, fitted with an auxiliary propulsion unit. It could fire the same ammunition as the ASU-57, and like that vehicle was developed for use by airborne divisions. The two-cylinder petrol engine was fitted on the right side of the shield, with fuel stored in the hollow trails. The driver's seat was at the end of the trails, facing rearwards. A single road wheel was lowered to the ground before driving. A pair of boxes were fitted behind the driver's seat, containing ready-use ammunition, and an infra-red sight was often fitted on the shield. It was towed by a BTR-152 APC or driven under its own power at speeds of up to 40km/hour.

SPECIFICATIONS: CH-26

Calibre: 57mm
Barrel length: 4.07m
Weight: 1,250kg
Length: 6.11m
Width: 1.8m
Height: 1.22m
Elevation/depression: +15/-4°
Traverse: 56° total
Rate of fire: 12 rounds/minute

Maximum range: 6,700m
Crew: 5

98MM MODEL 93 MOUNTAIN HOWITZER (ROMANIA)

Like the 76.2mm gun, this was developed for the Romanian mountain troops. It had a conventional split-trail carriage, but unusually, the rear half of each trail folded upwards and lay on top of the front half when in transit. The trails were then locked together, using a locking pin that had a towing eye included. A small rubber-tyred wheel was mounted under the lock to assist with deployment.

When in action, a spade at the end of each trail helped to absorb recoil, and stakes could also be driven into the ground through the rear part of the trails if required. The carriage had two rubber-tyred wheels and a pair of handbrakes, used when positioning. Elevation and traverse were both manual, with the controls fitted on the left side. Sights for both direct and indirect fire were also fitted on the left side of the weapon. A small shield was fitted to give the crew some protection. The barrel had a multi-baffle muzzle brake, and ammunition was of the separate-loading type. HE and HEAT rounds were available.

It was normally towed by a DAC 444 4x4 2.5-tonne lorry, which also carried the crew and ammunition. It could be quickly disassembled into three loads, each of which could be transported on a carriage towed by a horse.

SPECIFICATIONS: MODEL 93

Calibre: 98mm
Weight: 1,500kg

Length: 4.25m
Width: 1.65m
Height: 1.7m
Elevation/depression: +70/-5°
Traverse: 40° total
Rate of fire: 6 rounds/minute
Maximum range: 10,800m
Crew: 8

100MM T-12 & MT-12 Anti-Tank Gun

The T-12 was developed as a replacement for the D-48 anti-tank gun, and was the first smoothbore anti-tank gun to enter service, in 1961. The decision to adopt a smoothbore barrel led to improved HEAT performance, higher muzzle velocity, and longer barrel life than an equivalent rifled barrel. The kinetic energy penetrator was very long and thin, further improving penetration. Production of an improved version, the MT-12 (also known to NATO as the T-12A), began in 1970. This had a new improved carriage, which was less prone to turning over whilst being towed. Both models had sights for indirect fire and direct fire, but indirect fire range was limited by the maximum elevation of only 20°. The T-12 was normally towed by a lorry, the MT-12 by an MT-LB.

The crew of six consisted of commander, towing vehicle driver, gunlayer, loader, and two ammunition numbers. The barrel had a perforated muzzle brake, and was clamped to the trails when in transit. The loader had to open the breech manually to load the first round, after which a semi-automatic loading system would open and close the breech, so that the loader only had to load

T-12

shells. Image intensifier night sights were fitted. A shield gave the crew some protection from small arms fire and shell splinters.

The T-12 and MT-12 both fired APFSDS, HEAT, and HE ammunition. The APFSDS round had penetration of 230mm at 500m, 140mm at 3,000m. The HEAT round could penetrate 350mm. From 1981, the MT-12 was able to fire the new AT-10 Stabber laser beam-riding ATGM, which had a maximum range of 4,000m and penetration of 550mm. The laser designator was mounted on a tripod to one side of the gun.

SPECIFICATIONS: T-12 (MT-12 IN BRACKETS)

Calibre: 100mm
Barrel length: 6.3m
Weight: 2,750kg (3,050kg)
Length: 9.48m (9.65m) (travelling)
Width: 1.8m (2.31m) (travelling)
Height: 1.57m (1.60m) (travelling)
Elevation/depression: +20/-6°
Traverse: 27° total
Rate of fire: 14 rounds/minute
Towing speed: 60km/hour (70km/hour) (road)

15km/hour (25km/hour) (cross-country)
Maximum range, APFSDS: 3,000m
HEAT: 5,995m
HE (indirect): 8,200m
Crew: 6

122MM D-30 HOWITZER

The D-30 entered service in the early 1960s, as a replacement for the M-30. Compared to the M-30, the D-30 had greater range and could be rapidly traversed through 360°. The main armament of the 2S1 was based on the D-30 ordnance.

D-30

Later production models, with several improvements, were designated D-30M. The D-30M had a double-baffle muzzle brake; a square, rather than round, baseplate; a towing lunette; and changes to the cradle, carriage, and recoil system.

In transit, the D-30 was towed muzzle-first, with the three trails of the carriage under the barrel. To deploy, two of the trails were spread so that the three trails were equidistant, and the firing jack was raised, then the trails staked into position.

The D-30 fired variable-charge, case-type, separate-loading ammunition. Some D-30 ammunition was compatible with the M-30, but it also fired a non-spinning HEAT-FS round. As well as HE-FRAG and HEAT-FS, it could fire illuminating, leaflet, flechette, and incendiary rounds.

Specifications: D-30

Calibre: 122mm
Barrel length: 4.88m
Weight: 3,150kg
   3,210kg (travelling)
Length: 5.4m (travelling)
Width: 1.95m (travelling)
Height: 1.66m (travelling)
Elevation/depression: +70/-7°
Traverse: 360°
Rate of fire: 7-8 rounds/minute
Sustained rate of fire: 1.25 rounds/minute
Maximum range: 15,400m
Crew: 7

76mm GP Mountain Gun

First reported in 1966, this was designated M1966 in the West, though it was sometimes referred to as the M1969. It had a split trail, split shield, and a short 76mm calibre barrel with no muzzle brake. The trails could fold sideways, and one was fitted with a small wheel to facilitate handling. Sights for direct and indirect fire were mounted to the left of the barrel. The axles could be lowered or raised to adjust the height of the gun, and it could be disassembled for transport.

A variety of ammunition was available, including HE-FRAG, HEAT, HVAP, and AP-T. In addition, it could use ammunition produced for the 76mm ZIS-3 Divisional Gun. The HEAT warhead could penetrate 300mm of armour. Maximum rate of fire was 15 rounds per minute, and 100 rounds per hour could be sustained. It was towed by a Ural 375 6x6 4.5-tonne or GAZ-66 4x4 2-tonne lorry.

SPECIFICATIONS: GP

Barrel length: 2.8m
Weight: 780 kg
Length: 4.8m (travelling)
Width: 1.5m (travelling)
Height: 1.4m (travelling)
Elevation/depression: +65/-5°
Traverse: 50° total
Rate of fire: 15 rounds/minute
Crew: 7

152MM 2A36 GIATSINT-B FIELD GUN

Development of the 2A36 began in 1968, to satisfy a requirement for a 152mm gun to replace the 130mm M-46. The new gun was to be used in both towed and self-propelled versions, the towed version's primary purpose being counter-battery fire.

The self-propelled gun became the 2S5 Giatsint-S, and the towed gun became the 2A36 Giatsint-B. Surprisingly, the two types did not fire the same ammunition, though they shared ballistic characteristics.

Full-scale production began in 1976, but it was not shown in public until 1985. It was towed by a KrAZ-260 6x6, KrAZ-255B 6x6 or Ural 4320 6x6 lorry, or a tracked artillery tractor such as an AT-T, AT-S, or ATS-59.

The gun was fitted with a multi-slotted muzzle brake, and had sights for both direct and indirect fire. Elevation and traverse were both manual, and an armoured shield provided some protection to the crew. A hydraulic rammer was fitted, with a manual backup. In the firing position, the front was supported on a circular jack under the forward part of the carriage. Each trail had a spade, with extra-large spades available for use on soft ground.

The usual projectile was HE-FRAG, which could be fused for high explosive or fragmentation effect. A rocket-assisted version was available, which extended the range to 40km. AP-T projectiles were available for use in direct fire against armoured targets, as well as smoke, concrete-piercing, and incendiary. The ammunition was not backward-compatible with older 152mm artillery systems.

Four braked wheels and an improved suspension allowed faster towing speeds and improved cross-country mobility compared to earlier towed artillery pieces.

Specifications: 2A36 Giatsint-B

Barrel length: 8.2m
Weight: 9,800 kg (travelling)
      9,760 kg (firing)
Length: 12.92m (travelling)
      12.3m (firing)
Width: 2.79m
Height: 2.76m
Ground clearance: 0.48m
Elevation/depression: +57/-2.5°
Traverse: 50° total
Rate of fire: 5-6 rounds/minute
Range: 27km (40km with RAP)
Crew: 8
Towing speed: 80km/hour (road)
      30km/hour (cross-country)
Unit of fire: 60 rounds

152mm Howitzer M1981 (Romania)

Developed in Romania, this had a box-section split-trail carriage. A castor wheel was fitted to each trail leg to facilitate bringing the weapon into action, and these rested on the trails when in transit. A circular firing pedestal was fitted, which would be inverted and secured ahead of the shield for transit. When deployed, the pedestal in conjunction with the castor wheels allowed rapid transit through a full 360°. A large double-baffle muzzle brake was fitted, with a circular ring around the barrel immediately behind the muzzle brake, giving the weapon a distinctive look.

The M1981 fired separate-loading ammunition. HE, HEAT, leaflet, and illuminating rounds were available. Maximum range was 24,000m with HE.

130MM GUN M1982 (ROMANIA)

This was mounted on a split-trail carriage very similar to the Romanian 152mm M1985, with a similar top carriage, shield, and recoil system. The ballistic characteristics were similar to the Soviet M-46, though it appears to have been independently developed.

The barrel had a double-baffle muzzle brake. When deployed, it rested on a circular firing jack under the front of the carriage, and a pair of spades at the end of the trails. For transit, the firing jack was swung through 180° and locked under the barrel. It fired separate-loading ammunition, which could also be fired by the Soviet M-46.

SPECIFICATIONS: M1982

Calibre: 130mm
Barrel length: 6.85m
Weight: 6,150kg
    6,200kg (travelling)
Length: 10.8m (travelling)
Width: 2.59m (travelling)
Height: 2.65m (travelling)
Elevation/depression: +45/-2°
Traverse: 58° total
Rate of fire: 7 rounds/minute

Maximum range: 27,150m
Crew: 7

152MM GUN-HOWITZER M1985 (ROMANIA)

Developed in Romania, this had a split-trail two-wheeled carriage which was very similar to the Soviet D-20. The Romanian weapon had a longer barrel, leading to a longer range. Each trail had a castor wheel to assist in bringing the weapon into and out of action. When deployed to fire, the castor wheels rested on top of the trails. In action, the weapon was supported on a circular firing jack at the front of the carriage and a pair of spades at the rear of the trails. HE-FRAG and APC-T ammunition was available.

SPECIFICATIONS: M1985

Calibre: 152.4mm
Barrel length: 8.03m
Weight: 7,500kg
  7,550kg (travelling)
Length: 11.17m (travelling)
Width: 2.53m (travelling)
Elevation/depression: +57/-5°
Traverse: 50° total
Rate of fire: 2-4 rounds/minute
Maximum range: 24,000m

152MM 2A65 HOWITZER

Introduced in 1987 and initially designated M1987 by NATO, this was the towed version of the gun fitted in the 2S19 self-propelled gun. It fired the same ammunition, and could also fire older ammunition used by the D20 towed gun-howitzer and 2S3 self-propelled gun-howitzer. It had a conventional split-trail carriage, with castor wheels at the ends of the trails to help when bringing the gun into action. These were swung around to sit on top of the trail when in action. In the firing position, the weapon rested on spades at the rear of the trails and a firing jack at the front.

The barrel had a double-baffle muzzle brake, and the weapon also had a semi-automatic breech, spring-operated ram, hydraulic counter-recoil, and a liquid-cooled recoil brake. Elevation and traverse were manual, with two speeds. Sights were fitted for direct fire and indirect fire, and pneumatic brakes were fitted.

SPECIFICATIONS: 2A65

Calibre: 152.4mm
Weight: 7,000kg
Elevation/depression: +70/-3.5°
Traverse: 54° total
Rate of fire: 7 rounds/minute
Maximum range: 24,000m
Crew: 8

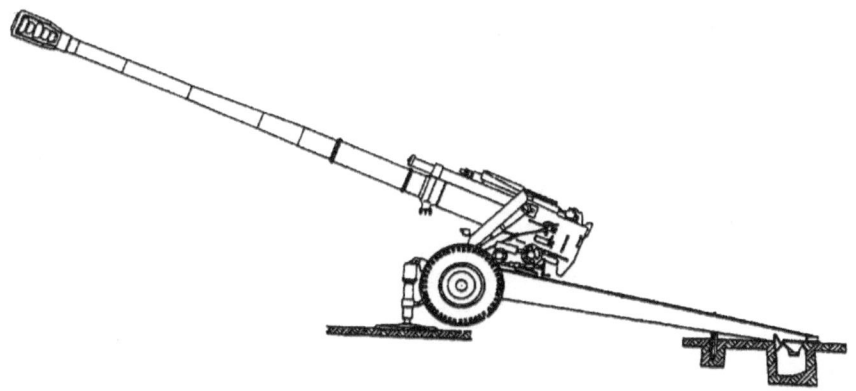

2A65

Self-Propelled Guns, Howitzers, and Mortars

During the Second World War, little interest was shown in self-propelled artillery, with only multiple rocket launchers (commonly referred to by the nickname "Katyusha") being developed as mobile systems. The only self-propelled guns were tank destroyers and assault guns designed for direct fire, rather than artillery guns and howitzers intended to provide indirect fire. Development of self-propelled guns, howitzers, and mortars started in the late 1960s, probably helped by the removal from power of Khrushchev, a firm proponent of missiles and rockets.

SU-76

In 1942, the Soviet army had an urgent need for a tank destroyer, and the SU-76 was hastily developed to meet that requirement. First used in combat in early 1943, it was found to be inadequate for the anti-tank role, and so was repurposed to infantry support. Over 12,000 vehicles were built, but production stopped in 1945.

The chassis was a longer and wider version of that used on the T-70 light tank, armed with a modified version of the ZIS-3

76mm divisional gun. Originally, it had engines on either side of the hull and a fully-armoured fighting compartment. This was not a success and only a few were built. The design was changed to have engines mounted in tandem and a partially-armoured fighting compartment, creating the SU-76M.

The hull was of all-welded construction. The driver sat at the front centre, with a single-piece hatch cover and a periscope. The engines were mounted in tandem on the right side of the hull, toward the rear, with the fuel tank to the left of the driver.

The open-topped fighting compartment was at the rear of the vehicle. A tubular frame allowed a tarpaulin cover to be fitted to give protection against inclement weather. Access was via a single door in the rear, and firing ports were fitted on either side of the fighting compartment. The commander had a vision port to the right of the armament, with the gunner's sight to the left of the gun.

The 76mm gun was mounted to the left of centre, and had a double-baffle muzzle brake. Elevation and traverse were both manual, and it fired the same types of ammunition as the PT-76 light tank. 60 rounds of ammunition were carried, and during the Second World War many vehicles carried a 7.62mm machine gun for use against aircraft.

The SU-76 did not have NBC protection, night-vision equipment, or an amphibious capability.

SPECIFICATIONS: SU-76M

Crew: 4
Combat weight: 11.2 tonnes

SU-76M

Length: 5.0m
Width: 2.74m
Height: 2.1m
Ground clearance: 0.3m
Maximum road speed: 45km/hour
Maximum road range: 360km
Gradient: 47%
Vertical obstacle: 0.65m
Armament: 1x 76.2mm gun (60 rounds)

Armour:
Hull glacis: 25mm @ 30° [Effective: 29mm]
Hull nose: 35mm @ 60° [Effective: 70mm]
Superstructure front: 25 @ 27° [Effective: 28mm]
Superstructure side: 12mm @ 17° [Effective: 13mm]
Mantlet: 14mm
Lower hull side: 16mm
Hull rear: 15mm
Belly: 10mm

ISU-122

Like the heavier ISU-152, the ISU-122 was based on the IS-2 tank chassis. The armament was mounted in an armoured superstructure at the front, with the engine and transmission at the rear. The main armament, an 122mm A-19S gun, was mounted to the right of centre, with the driver seated to the left. Elevation and traverse were both manual. A 12.7mm DShKM machine gun was mounted on the roof for anti-aircraft use. Long-range fuel tanks were fitted on the sides of the hull, at the rear.

The A-19S was a development of the towed A-19 gun, and had a rate of fire of three rounds per minute. HE-FRAG, concrete piercing, and AP-T rounds were available. The range of the HE-FRAG round was reduced by the gun's elevation to 13,400m.

In 1944, the original ISU-122 was replaced in production by the ISU-122S. This was armed with a 122mm D-25S gun, a development of the D-25 used in the IS-2, IS-3, and IS-4 heavy tanks. An improved breech compared to the A-19S meant that the rate of fire was increased to six rounds per minute. An MSh-17 gun sight was fitted for direct fire. Unlike the ISU-122, the ISU-122S had a double-baffle muzzle brake.

Specifications: ISU-122S

Crew: 5
Combat weight: 46.5 tonnes
Length: 6.8m (10.1m including gun)
Width: 3.07m
Height: 2.47m

ISU-122

Ground clearance: 0.46m
Maximum road speed: 37km/hour
Maximum road range: 150km (306km with long-range fuel tanks)
Gradient: 60%
Vertical obstacle: 1m

Armament:
1x 122mm D-25S (30 rounds)
1x 12.7mm DShKM MG (250 rounds)

Armour:
Hull glacis: 110mm @ 70° [Effective: 322mm]
Mantlet: 90mm
Upper hull sides: 90mm

Hull top: 25mm
Hull rear: 22-64mm
Belly: 19mm

ISU-152

Almost identical to the earlier SU-152, the ISU-152 was based on an IS-2 chassis, whereas the SU-152 was based on the KV-2. The 152mm ML-20S gun, a development of the ML-20, was mounted in an armoured superstructure at the front of the vehicle, to the right of centre. The gun was shorter than the one fitted on the ISU-122, and had a multi-baffle muzzle brake.

ISU-152

The driver was seated to the left of the main armament. Hand rails were fitted on the outside of the vehicle to allow infantry to be carried into action, and a 12.7mm DShKM machine gun was mounted on the roof for anti-aircraft use. The very limited on-board ammunition store of only twenty rounds meant that frequent resupply was required. Elevation and traverse were both manual, and the maximum elevation of the gun limited the range of the HE-FRAG round to 9,000m. Long-range fuel tanks were fitted on the sides of the hull, at the rear.

Specifications: ISU-152

Crew: 5
Combat weight: 46.5 tonnes
Length: 6.8m (9.05m including gun)
Width: 3.07m
Height: 2.47m
Ground clearance: 0.46m
Maximum road speed: 37km/hour
Maximum road range: 150km (306km with long-range fuel tanks)
Gradient: 60%
Vertical obstacle: 1m

Armament:
1x 152mm ML-20S (20 rounds)
1x 12.7mm DShKM MG (250 rounds)

Armour:
Hull glacis: 110mm @ 70° [Effective: 322mm]
Mantlet: 90mm
Upper hull sides: 90mm
Hull top: 25mm
Hull rear: 22-64mm
Belly: 19mm

2S1 Gvozdika

The first prototype 2S1 vehicles were built in 1969. It was accepted for service in 1970 and began volume production in

1971. The hull was made of welded steel, based on the automotive components and running gear of the MT-LB. The driver sat at the front with the engine behind him, and the turret and fighting compartment at the rear. Within the turret, the commander sat on the left, with the gunner below and in front of him, and the loader to the right. The gun had sights for indirect and direct fire.

2S1 Gvozdika

The main armament was a 2A31 122mm howitzer, based on the D-30 towed howitzer. It had a fume extractor and double-baffle muzzle brake, and a remote-controlled lock on the hull to fix the barrel in place during transit. A rate of fire of 5-8 rounds per minute could be maintained for a protracted period. 40 rounds of ammunition were carried in the vehicle, the usual load being 32 HE, six smoke, and two HEAT-FS. Standard practice during a fire mission was for ammunition to be supplied from outside the vehicle. When firing HE, the gun had a maximum range of 15.3km. The HEAT-FS warhead could penetrate around 460mm of standard steel armour. Chemical and HE-RAP ammunition was also available, the latter extending the maximum range to 21.9km.

The 2S1's suspension could be adjusted to make the vehicle shorter, a useful feature when transporting by air. The standard tracks were 400mm wide, but like the MT-LB, 670mm wide tracks could be fitted for use in snow, swampy ground, etc. The 2S1 had NBC protection, infra-red driving lights, and a small infra-red searchlight on the commander's cupola. It was fully amphibious, propelled in the water by its tracks. Before entering the water, a bilge pump was switched on, shrouds were fitted to the hull front, water deflectors were lowered at the rear, the trim vane was erected at the front of the hull, and covers were fitted around the engine air intakes. Only 30 rounds could be carried when swimming; any excess had to be removed before entering the water.

Specifications: 2S1 Gvozdika

Crew: 4 + 2 in ammunition carrier
Combat weight: 15.7 tonnes
Length: 7.26m
Width: 2.85m
Height: 2.287m
Ground clearance: 0.4m
Maximum road speed: 61.5km/hour
Maximum road range: 500km
Gradient: 77%
Vertical obstacle: 0.7m

Armament: 1x 122mm 2A31 howitzer (40 rounds)

Armour:
Hull: 15mm
Turret: 10-20mm

2S3 Akatsiya

Production of the 2S3 started in 1970, although it was not accepted for service until late 1971. The hull was based on an improved version of the SA-4 Ganef chassis, with a more powerful 520hp engine, upgraded track and suspension. The hull was welded steel, with the driver in the front to the left, the engine to his right, and the turret at the rear. The commander was seated in the left of the turret, the gunner forward and below him, and the loader on the right. The gun had sights for direct fire as well as indirect fire.

Main armament was a 2A33 152mm howitzer. Almost identical to the D-20 towed howitzer, it was fitted with a fume extractor and travelling lock, which was remotely operated by the driver from his seat. Traverse and elevation were powered, though manual controls were also provided. 33 rounds of ammunition were carried in the rear of the hull. Normally, ammunition was supplied from outside the vehicle and passed in through hatches in the rear, the internal ammunition being reserved for immediate use. HE-FRAG ammunition was most commonly used, though HEAT-FS, HE-RAP, AP-T, illuminating, smoke, incendiary, flechette, and scatter mine ammunition were also available. Maximum range was 18.5km with conventional ammunition, 24km when firing HE-RAP.

© Vitaly V. Kuzmin
2S3 Akatsiya

A 7.62mm PKT machine gun was mounted on the commander's cupola. This could be aimed and fired by remote control from inside the turret. The 2S3 had NBC protection, infra-red driving lights, a small white light/infra-red searchlight mounted forward of the commander's hatch, and a self-entrenching blade at the front of the hull. It did not have an amphibious capability.

The 2S3M, introduced in 1975, increased the on-board ammunition load to 46 rounds, 12 of which were in a rotating carousel to facilitate faster loading. The 2S3M1, introduced in 1987, added a data terminal connected to the battery commander's vehicle, allowing fire commands to be instantly displayed in the fire vehicles. It also had an improved sight and new laser-guided, rocket-assisted projectiles were available.

Specifications: 2S3 Akatsiya

Crew: 4 + 2 in ammunition carrier
Combat weight: 27.5 tonnes
Length: 7.7m (8.4m including gun)
Width: 3.25m
Height: 3.05m
Ground clearance: 0.45m
Maximum road speed: 60km/hour
Maximum road range: 500km
Gradient: 60%
Vertical obstacle: 0.7m
Trench: 3m

Armament:
1x 152mm 2A33 howitzer (33 rounds, 2S3M/M1: 46 rounds)
1x 7.62mm PKT MG (1,500 rounds)

Armour:
Hull: 15mm max
Turret: 20mm max

2S4 Tyulpan

Introduced in 1970, the 2S4 mounted a 240mm breech-loading mortar on a tracked vehicle based on the GMZ minelayer chassis. The mortar, complete with baseplate, lay along the length of the vehicle when in transit. To deploy, the mortar was rotated around a hinge at the rear of the vehicle, so that it came to rest facing away from the vehicle to the rear, with the baseplate on the ground. Elevation was from +45° to +80°, with 8° of traverse.

2S4 Tyulpan

Four men were carried in the vehicle, though a total of nine were required to load and fire the mortar. Twelve mortar bombs were carried in the vehicle, and a small hand-operated crane was fitted to the rear to facilitate loading. The mortar had a rate of fire of one round per minute, and could fire HE, chemical, and nuclear rounds. The 240mm mortar was the first Soviet artillery piece to be equipped with nuclear ammunition.

The vehicle hull had welded steel armour, with the driver at the front left and the engine to his right. To the rear of the driver was the commander, who was provided with a raised cupola, on which was mounted a 7.62mm PKT machine gun. The vehicle provided NBC protection for the crew while they were inside, though they had to exit the vehicle to operate the mortar.

SPECIFICATIONS: 2S4 TYULPAN

Crew: 4 + 5 in ammunition carrier
Combat weight: 30 tonnes
Length: 8.5m
Width: 3.2m
Height: 3.2m
Ground clearance: 0.46m
Maximum road speed: 50km/hour
Maximum road range: 500km
Gradient: 65%
Vertical obstacle: 1.1m
Armour: 15-20mm

Armament:
1x 240mm mortar (12 rounds)
1x 7.62mm PKT MG

2S5 GIATSINT-S

In 1968, development began on a new 152mm gun, which was intended to be used in both towed and self-propelled versions. Production of both towed (2A36) and self-propelled (2S5) guns began in 1976. The 2S5 had a welded steel hull, and a self-entrenching blade was mounted on the front. The engine was at the front right of the vehicle, and could use diesel or aviation fuel. The vehicle provided NBC protection when sealed, though the gun could not be operated from inside the vehicle.

The driver sat to the left of the engine, and was provided with day and passive night periscopes. The vehicle commander sat behind the driver in a slightly raised superstructure with a cupola, on which was mounted a 7.62mm PKT machine gun and

2S5 Giatsint-S in firing position

a white light/IR searchlight. The machine gun could be operated from within the vehicle. The three remaining crew members were seated in a compartment at the rear of the vehicle, entering via a ramp at the rear. They were provided with periscopes, but these periscopes did not have any night-vision capability.

The 2A37 152mm gun was mounted on the vehicle roof in an open mount at the rear, and had a multi-baffled muzzle brake. Sights for direct and indirect fire were included, and a travelling lock was used when in transit. A large spade was deployed at the rear of the vehicle before firing, to provide extra stability.

The gunlayer sat to the left of the gun, and had a simple shield to his front. 30 projectiles and charges were carried in the rear of the vehicle. The projectiles were in a carousel and the charges were in three rows of ten on a conveyor belt. Maximum rate of fire was five to six rounds per minute.

SPECIFICATIONS: 2S5 GIATSINT-S

Crew: 5
Combat weight: 28.2 tonnes
Length: 8.33m
Width: 3.25m
Height: 2.76m
Ground clearance: 0.45m
Maximum road speed: 63km/hour
Maximum road range: 500km
Gradient: 58%
Vertical obstacle: 0.7m
Trench: 2.5m
Armour: 13mm

Armament:
1x 152mm 2A37 gun (30 rounds)
1x 7.62mm PKT MG

2S7 PION

In the late 1960s, a requirement for a large calibre self-propelled gun was issued. The calibre was not specified, and after studies of various calibres, 203mm was chosen and the 2S7 entered service in 1975. The hull was welded steel, with the driver seated at the front left, and the engine in the front right. When travelling, the commander and gunner were seated in the driver's compartment. The remaining four vehicle crew members were seated to the rear of the engine (another seven crew were carried in the ammunition vehicle). An entrenching blade was fitted to the front of the hull, and an SA-14 surface-to-air missile system was carried.

2S7 Pion

The 203mm gun was mounted on top of the hull at the rear of the vehicle, with a manually operated travel lock fitted on the hull. A large spade was mounted at the rear, which was used to stabilise the vehicle before firing. Gun traverse and elevation was powered, though manual controls were provided for emergency use. Indirect and direct fire sights were provided for the gunner, who sat to the left of the gun when in action.

The standard HE-FRAG ammunition had a maximum range of 37.5km. Rocket-assisted ammunition was available, which increased maximum range to 47.5km. Concrete-piercing, nuclear, and chemical ammunition was also available. Four rounds were carried on the vehicle, with more ammunition normally carried on a lorry. An ammunition-handling system allowed a rate of fire of two rounds per minute. The vehicle had night-vision equipment and provided the crew with NBC protection when they were inside.

The 2S7M entered service in 1983. This variant carried eight rounds of ammunition on board, had improved durability, and new communications facilities that allowed firing data to be transmitted directly to the gun from the battery commander.

Specifications: 2S7 Pion

Crew: 7
Combat weight: 46.5 tonnes
Length: 13.12m including gun
Width: 3.38m
Height: 3m
Ground clearance: 0.4m
Maximum road speed: 50km/hour
Maximum road range: 650km
Gradient: 40%
Vertical obstacle: 0.7m
Trench: 2.5m
Armour: 10mm
Armament: 1x 203mm 2A44 gun (4 rounds, 2S7M: 8 rounds)

2S9 NONA

The 2S9 entered service in 1981, mounting an 120mm gun/mortar in an armoured turret on a BTR-D armoured personnel carrier. Like the BTR-D, it was amphibious, air-droppable, and had NBC protection. It could be used in the indirect and direct fire roles, with HEAT warheads available to provide an anti-tank capability.

2S9 Nona

The driver sat in the front centre of the hull, with the commander in the front left. The gunner and loader sat in the turret, the gunner on the left, the loader on the right. The turret had limited traverse of 35° either side of directly ahead.

Main armament was a 2A51 120mm gun/mortar, with a rate of fire of six to eight rounds per minute. It could fire HE, HE-

RAP, white phosphorous, smoke, and HEAT rounds. Maximum indirect fire range was 8.8km with standard rounds, increased to 13km with rocket-assisted projectiles.

SPECIFICATIONS: 2S9 NONA

Crew: 4
Combat weight: 8.7 tonnes
Length: 6.02m
Width: 2.63m
Height: 1.9m
Ground clearance: 0.1m - 0.45m
Maximum road speed: 60km/hour
Maximum road range: 500km
Gradient: 60%
Vertical obstacle: 0.5-0.8m
Trench: 2m
Armour: 16mm
Armament: 1x 120mm 2A60 gun/mortar (25 rounds)

2S19 MSTA

The 2S19 entered production and was accepted for service in 1989, as a replacement for both the 2S3 and 2S5. The suspension and running gear were based on those of the T-80 MBT, while the engine was the same as that fitted to the T-72 MBT. The driver's compartment was at the front, the turret extended over the centre and rear of the hull, and the engine was at the rear. The turret and hull were welded steel, and a self-entrenching blade was fitted at the front of the hull.

2S19 Msta

Main armament was a 2A64 152mm howitzer, which had a fume extractor, double-baffle muzzle brake, and travelling lock. Indirect and direct fire sights were fitted. The gun could fire HE-FRAG and smoke projectiles to a range of 24.7km. Turret traverse and gun elevation were powered, with manual controls for use in an emergency. 50 rounds were carried in the vehicle, though ammunition was normally supplied from outside the vehicle.

A 12.7mm NSVT machine gun and small searchlight were fitted to the roof of the turret, in front of the commander's hatch. Both could be operated remotely from within the vehicle. The 2S19 had NBC protection and passive night-vision equipment. Six smoke grenade dischargers were mounted on the turret, three on each side. A smokescreen could also be generated by injecting diesel fuel into the exhaust.

Specifications: 2S19 Msta

Crew: 5
Combat weight: 42 tonnes
Length: 7.15m (11.92m including gun)
Width: 3.38m
Height: 2.99m
Ground clearance: 0.44m
Maximum road speed: 60km/hour
Maximum road range: 500km
Gradient: 47%
Vertical obstacle: 0.5m
Trench: 2.8m
Armour: Unknown, but proof against small arms and shell splinters

Armament:
1x 152mm 2A64 howitzer (50 rounds)
1x 12.7mm NSVT MG (300 rounds)

vzor 77 Dana (Czechoslovakia)

This wheeled 152mm self-propelled gun-howitzer was developed in the late 1970s, and entered service with the Czech army in 1981. It had an eight-wheeled chassis based on components of the Tatra 813 8x8 lorry, rather than the more usual tracked chassis. The Tatra 813 had been shown to have a good cross-country capability, but wheeled chassis were much cheaper and easier to maintain than comparable tracked systems.

Since the Dana operated some distance behind the lines, tactical mobility was less important than on front-line vehicles.

The driver sat in the front compartment on the left, with the commander to his right. A large, fully enclosed turret was in the centre, with the engine at the rear. Armour was sufficient to provide protection against small arms and shell splinters. A central tyre pressure regulation system and power steering were both fitted.

The driver and commander had roof hatches and windscreens with armoured shutters. Each also had two firing ports, one to the front and one to the side. The commander operated the communication system and was provided with a night sight. The driver operated the turret locking system and stabilisers.

The 152mm gun-howitzer was fitted with a muzzle brake, and could fire the same ammunition as the Soviet 2S3 Akatsiya, as well as Czech-made ammunition. The vehicle had a fully automatic loading system, which loaded the projectile and the separate charge, and could operate at all elevations. Single shot or fully automatic fire modes could be selected by the gunner.

The Dana took two minutes to prepare for firing after coming to a halt, and required one minute to prepare to move off after the last round had been fired. Hydraulic jacks were lowered before firing to ensure a stable platform. Sights were provided for direct fire as well as indirect fire. Up to 60 rounds of ammunition could be carried, but road speed was reduced if more than 40 rounds were carried.

The turret was made up of two distinct parts, with the weapon mounted externally between them, ensuring that no fumes could enter the interior. The turret could only rotate through 225°. Each side of the turret had access doors, roof hatches, and vision devices. The gunner and loader operator were in the left half of the turret, with the ammunition handler, who set the fuses, in the right half.

A 12.7mm anti-aircraft machine gun was fitted to the turret roof on the right side, and could also be used in the direct fire role. An NBC system was fitted as standard.

Specifications: vzor 77 Dana

Crew: 5
Combat weight: 29.25 tonnes
Length: 11.16m
Width: 3m
Height: 2.85m
Ground clearance: 0.41m
Maximum road speed: 80km/hour
Maximum road range: 740km
Gradient: 60%
Vertical obstacle: 0.6m
Trench: 2m

Armament:
1x 152mm gun-howitzer (40 rounds, or 60 rounds with speed reduced to 70km/hour)
1x 12.7mm NSV MG

Mortars

During the Second World War, the Soviet Union made extensive use of mortars. The simpler construction of the smoothbore barrels used by mortars, compared to the rifled barrels of tube artillery, meant that mass production could be continued after armaments factories were overrun by the Germans. Even in peacetime, the large armies of the Warsaw Pact valued the ease of production that mortars offered.

A single mortar bomb had more explosive than a howitzer shell of the same calibre, albeit with inferior accuracy and shorter range. Mortars gave infantry commanders indirect fire support under their own command, able to stay with the infantry they supported. The Soviet Union developed mortars of very large calibres, up to 240mm. The very long barrels of the large calibre weapons mandated the use of unconventional breech-loading mechanisms, since it was simply not possible to load at the muzzle.

50mm M-38, M-39, M-40 & M-41

In the late 1930s and early 1940s, the Soviet Union developed a range of light 50mm mortars. All were conventional muzzle-loaders, but only the M-39 used variable elevation to adjust range. The others were always fired at an angle of 45 or 75 degrees. A sleeve around the base of the barrel opened or closed a number of gas ports. The more that were open, the more propellant gas was evacuated to the atmosphere, reducing propellant power and thus range. All fired HE ammunition only.

The M-38, M-39, and M-40 had base plates and bipods, but the M-41 dispensed with the bipod, having only a baseplate. An interesting variant of the M-40 was developed which had three barrels, the extra two mounted alongside the centre barrel. A lanyard was pulled to drop the bombs in all three barrels simultaneously. This variant was produced in very limited numbers, and does not appear to have been a success.

SPECIFICATIONS: M-40

Calibre: 50mm
Weight: 11.5kg
    12.25kg (travelling)
Elevation: 45 to 75°
Traverse: 5.5° total
Maximum range: 800m

SPECIFICATIONS: M-41

Calibre: 50mm
Weight: 10kg
    12kg (travelling)
Elevation: 45 to 75°
Traverse: 12° total
Maximum range: 800m

82MM M-36, M-37, M-41, M-43, & "NEW" M-37

The first Soviet 82mm mortar was the M-36, which was very similar to the US 81mm M1 mortar. The design of both weapon and ammunition was conventional, the ammunition having a primary cartridge and six increments. HE and smoke ammunition were available, and three types of sights were used: the MP-1, the MP-82, and a simple aiming circle inclinometer.

The M-37 was a modified M-36, with a circular baseplate instead of the original rectangle.

The M-41 was an attempt to improve the mobility and performance of the M-37. Instead of the conventional bipod and yoke, the M-41 had a long column supported by two short legs. At the end of each bipod leg was a very short axle, to which a wheel could be fitted. For transit, the bipod was folded along the barrel and clamped to the baseplate. The wheels would then be attached, so that the mortar could be towed. The M-41 was not a success, offering only slightly better mobility than the M-37, with significantly inferior firing stability and ballistic performance.

The M-43 was a continuation of the attempt to improve mobility that began in the M-41. It was basically the same, but the wheels were not detachable. This was also not a success, and so production was discontinued in favour of continued M-37 production.

The "new" M-37 was an M-37 with a lighter tripod and baseplate. A device was fitted to the muzzle to prevent a second round being loaded before the first had left the muzzle.

SPECIFICATIONS: M-36

Calibre: 82mm
Barrel length: 1.29m
Weight: 57.3kg
Elevation: 45 to 85°
Maximum range: 3,100m

SPECIFICATIONS: M-37

Calibre: 82mm
Barrel length: 1.22m
Weight: 56kg
Elevation: 45 to 85°
Traverse: 6° total
Rate of fire: 15-25 rounds/minute
Minimum range: 100m
Maximum range: 3,000m
Crew: 5

SPECIFICATIONS: M-41

Calibre: 82mm
Barrel length: 1.22m
Weight: 52kg
    58kg (travelling)
Elevation: 45 to 85°
Traverse: 5° total
Rate of fire: 15-25 rounds/minute
Maximum range: 2,550m
Crew: 5

107MM M-38

This was a scaled-down version of the 120mm M-38, and produced after that weapon. Being lighter and smaller, it was intended for animal transport and use by mountain troops. The complete weapon was carried on a two-wheeled trolley.

Two different HE projectiles were available, one "light" and one "heavy". The light one weighed 7.9kg and could be fired to a range of 6,300m. The heavy one weighed 9kg and could be fired to a distance of 5,150m.

Specifications: M-38

Calibre: 107mm
Barrel length: 1.67m
Weight: 170kg
    340kg (travelling)
Elevation: 45 to 80°
Traverse: 3° total
Rate of fire: 15 rounds/minute
Minimum range: 800m
Crew: 5

120MM M-38

A very successful design that formed the basis of a scaled-down 107mm weapon for mountain infantry, the M-38 was much more mobile than most mortars of its size. For transit, it was lifted onto a two-wheeled carriage, which could be towed by any suitable vehicle. Alternatively, it could be broken down into three loads for animal transport. Firing could be accomplished by either dropping the bomb onto a firing pin, or by using a trigger device. During the Second World War, the Germans used large numbers of captured M-38s, and copied it to create their own 120mm mortar.

SPECIFICATIONS: M-38

Calibre: 120mm
Barrel length: 1.86m
Weight: 280kg
Elevation: 45 to 80°
Traverse: 6° total
Maximum range: 6,000m

120MM M-43 (120-PM-43)

An incremental improvement on the very successful M-38, this had longer shock absorber cylinders. It retained the same style of baseplate and the tubular two-wheeled carriage. Like the earlier weapon, it could be easily broken down into three loads for pack transport. It fired a 15.4kg projectile to a maximum range of 5,700m, slightly less than the M-38's maximum range.

SPECIFICATIONS: M-43

Calibre: 120mm
Barrel length: 1.85m
Weight: 274.8kg
    500kg (travelling)
Elevation: 45 to 80°
Traverse: 8° total
Rate of fire: 12-15 rounds/minute

Minimum range: 460m
Maximum range: 5,700m
Crew: 6

120MM 2B11 SANI/2S12

The 2B11 was a developmental improvement of the M-43. Better materials and a redesigned carriage led to a significant reduction in weight. The basic design, however, was unchanged, retaining the smoothbore barrel resting on a conical baseplate, supported by a bipod connected via a recoil buffer mechanism. The muzzle had a system to prevent double loading.

The 2B11 was normally carried fully assembled on a two-wheeled carriage, with the baseplate attached and the bipod above the barrel. The mortar was normally carried on the back of a GAZ-66 4x4 2-tonne lorry, which had special fittings for carrying the mortar. If required, the lorry could also tow the mortar, although the carriage's very light weight limited it to short moves at slow speed. The combination of mortar and lorry was designated 2S12, and the lorry also carried the crew and a supply of ammunition.

If necessary, the mortar could be disassembled into barrel, tripod, and baseplate, for transport by pack animal. Ammunition included HE-FRAG, smoke, illumination, and incendiary bombs.

SPECIFICATIONS: 2B11 SANI

Calibre: 120mm
Weight: 210kg
    297kg (travelling)
Elevation: 45 to 80°

2B11 Sani

Traverse: 10° total (56° total by moving bipod)
Rate of fire: 12-15 rounds/minute
Minimum range: 460m
Maximum range: 7,180m
Crew: 5

160MM M-43 & M-160

The M-43 was introduced during the Second World War to provide infantry divisions with a weapon that could produce a great deal of high explosive, without making significant demands on manufacturing resources.

The long barrel meant that breech-loading wasn't feasible. Instead, the barrel pivoted around trunnions close to the centre of the barrel. The M-160 replaced the wartime M-43. It was virtually identical in design, but was heavier, with a longer barrel and much greater range. The M-43 fired a 40.8kg bomb; the M-160 a 41.5kg bomb.

Specifications: M-43

Calibre: 160mm
Barrel length: 3.03m
Weight: 1,170kg
    1,270kg (travelling)
Elevation: 45 to 80°
Traverse: 25° total
Rate of fire: 3 rounds/minute
Minimum range: 630m
Maximum range: 5,150m
Crew: 7

Specifications: M-160

Calibre: 160mm
Barrel length: 4.55m
Weight: 1,300kg
    1,470kg (travelling)

Elevation: 50 to 80°
Traverse: 24° total
Rate of fire: 2-3 rounds/minute
Minimum range: 750m
Maximum range: 8,040m
Crew: 7

240MM M-240

First seen by the West at a Moscow parade in 1953, it was given the designation M1953. Tactical limitations, including needing a long time to prepare for either action or transit, meant that it was replaced by the 2S4 where possible once the latter system came into service.

The M-240 was breech-loaded, and had a frame with shock absorbers and a two-wheeled carriage. The sights were carried separately, and only fitted when firing. The shock absorbers protected the sights from the vibrations caused by firing. A boom was fitted to provide firing stability, and a pair of winches were fitted to assist with changing from firing to travelling configuration.

Elevation was from 45° to 65°, which translated into a minimum range of 800m and maximum range of 9,700m. Sights, elevation, and traverse gears were all mounted to the left of the barrel, which had a removable towing lunette at the muzzle. It was normally towed by an AT-P, AT-L, or AT-S, with the crew of 11 carried on the tow vehicle. Ammunition and other equipment were carried on separate vehicles.

The mortar had to be deployed on firm ground for firing. To prepare for firing, the towing lunette was removed, the baseplate lowered to the ground and packed with earth. The barrel was moved to a horizontal position for loading. Time to prepare for action was at least 25 minutes, and preparing to move took almost as long.

The 240mm F-864 mortar bomb weighed 131kg, with a 32kg warhead. It was transported to the mortar on a two-wheeled trolley, and loaded by a team of five. Two men on each side used large grips to lift the bomb, while the fifth man was at the rear, keeping the bomb steady. Rate of fire was around 1 per minute.

In the 1980s, a laser-guided projectile was developed, which could be fired by both the M-240 and 2S4 mortars. Although it was successfully trialled in Afghanistan, it never entered volume production.

SPECIFICATIONS: M-240

Calibre: 240mm
Barrel length: 5.34m
Weight: 4,150kg
Length: 6.51m
Width: 2.49m
Height: 2.21m
Elevation: 45-65°
Traverse: 18° total
Rate of fire: 1 round/minute
Maximum range: 9,700m
Crew: 11

82MM 2B9 VASILYEK

Introduced in the early 1970s, the Vasilyek was an 82mm automatic mortar capable of both direct and indirect fire. The complete system was known as the 2K21 and included a transport vehicle based on the GAZ-66 4x4 2-tonne lorry. The mortar was carried under a canvas cover on the cargo area. Two ramps were fitted to assist with loading and unloading.

2B9 Vasilyek

A variable-charge system was used in the indirect fire role, with up to three charges used when firing at high angles. A separate, fixed charge was used in the direct fire role. The mortar had a water-cooled barrel for sustained fire, which allowed a sustained rate of fire of 120 rounds per minute.

Although it could be muzzle-loaded like a traditional mortar, it was normally breech-loaded using a clip containing four rounds, which could be fired in two seconds. These rapid bursts of fire meant a greater quantity of explosive landing on the target in a shorter time, increasing the shock effect. When operating in a sustained fire role, the loader could link the first clip with following clips during firing, forming a continuous belt.

HE-FRAG and HEAT rounds were available. The HE-FRAG round weighed 3.1kg, and the HEAT round could penetrate 100mm of standard armour. The weapon was mounted on a wheeled carriage with a split trail. Traverse was 60°, 30° either side, with elevation from -1° to +85°.

In Afghanistan, some Vasilyeks, with their wheels removed, were mounted on the rear deck of MT-LBs. An improved version, the 2B9M, entered service in 1983.

Specifications: 2B9 Vasilyek

Weight: 645kg
Length: 4.12m (travelling)
Width: 1.58m (travelling)
Height: 1.18m
Elevation/depression: +85/-1°
Traverse: 60° total
Rate of fire: 170 rounds/minute
Sustained rate of fire: 120 rounds/minute
Maximum range: 4,270m
Crew: 5-6

120mm 2B16 Nona-K Gun/Mortar

The 120mm 2B16 combined the characteristics of a gun and mortar, in a weapon system that had no Western equivalent. It was listed as a howitzer in the Conventional Armed Forces in Europe Treaty, possibly because of its unique nature. The 2B16 was the towed version, the 2S9 a self-propelled version mounted in a turret on a BTR-D chassis. Developed in the 1970s, the 2B16 entered service in 1986.

2B16 Nona-K

The 2B16 had a split-trail carriage. Each trail had a spade and a castor wheel to facilitate bringing the weapon into action. For transit, the trails were locked together, then the upper assembly was rotated over the trails and locked into place. The usual tow vehicle was a GAZ-66 4x4 2-tonne lorry, which would also carry the crew and some ammunition. It could be towed short distances by a UAZ-469B 4x4 695kg light vehicle.

When deployed for action, the wheels were raised clear of the ground and the weapon rested on a circular baseplate. The weapon itself was the same 2A51 as mounted in the 2S9, firing the same 120mm ammunition. It had a rifled barrel and a large double-baffle muzzle brake to reduce recoil. A shield provided some protection to the crew from small arms and shell splinters.

It could fire HE, HE-RAP, white phosphorous, smoke, and HEAT rounds. Sights were provided for both direct and indirect fire.

SPECIFICATIONS: 2B16 NONA-K

Calibre: 120mm
Weight: 1,200kg
Length: 5.9m
Width: 1.79m
Elevation/depression: +80/-10°
Traverse: 60° total
Rate of fire: 8-10 rounds/minute
Maximum range: 8,700m (12,800m with RAP)
Crew: 5

82MM 2B14 PODNOS

Developed in the early 1980s, the 2B14 was a completely new design, rather than an evolutionary development of existing designs. It was used by airborne, special forces, and light infantry units.

The general design was a conventional, bipod-mounted, smoothbore, muzzle-loaded mortar. A device to prevent double loading was available, but not normally used. Modern materials and maufacturing methods led to a reduction in weight compared to the earlier M-37. It could be broken down into loads small enough for it to be carried by the four-man crew.

2B14 Podnos

Specifications: 2B14

Calibre: 82mm
Weight: 41.88kg
Elevation: 45 to 85°
Traverse: 8° total (360° on baseplate)
Rate of fire: 24-30 rounds/minute
Minimum range: 80m
Maximum range: 3,200m
Crew: 4

Czech Mortars

The Skoda works in Czechoslovakia produced a number of mortar designs during and after the Second World War. Some of these were rather unusual, such as the 305mm design, development of which stopped at the end of the war. The B24 was an 120mm design that saw service with at least some Warsaw Pact armies. A short version, for use by airborne and mountain troops, was produced in 1948, and fired the same ammunition as the B24.

The M-48 and M-52 were both 82mm designs, with performance comparable to the Soviet M-37, and firing the same ammunition. They could be broken down into three loads for transportation.

Recoilless Guns

After the Second World War, recoilless guns had a brief period of prominence. They offered the possibility of firing a large calibre projectile to a good distance. The low muzzle velocity meant that kinetic-energy AP rounds were of no use, but chemical-energy warheads such as HEAT were effective at any speed. The combination of a large calibre recoilless gun firing HEAT warheads resulted in a potent and relatively light anti-tank weapon. They became largely obsolete with the introduction of anti-tank guided missiles, which offered greater accuracy at longer range.

82mm SPG-82

The SPG-82 entered service at the end of the Second World War. It had a long barrel with a flared muzzle and a small two-wheeled carriage. A sizeable shield protected the crew from the back-blast of the rocket-propelled rounds, but did not provide protection from enemy fire. Normally fired from the carriage, it could be dismounted and fired from the shoulder, if a second man helped to support the weight.

The SPG-82 could fire HE and HEAT ammunition, both of which weighed 5kg. Two sets of iron sights were fitted, one for each type of ammunition.

Specifications: SPG-82

Calibre: 82mm
Weight: 38kg
Length: 2.15m
Maximum range: 200m (anti-tank)
    700m (HE)
Armour penetration: 230mm
Crew: 2

82mm B-10

This was a smoothbore recoilless gun that fired a fin-stabilised projectile resembling a mortar bomb. For transit, it was carried on a two-wheeled carriage. A bar was fitted to the muzzle to allow it to be dragged into position. For firing, the carriage was removed and the tripod was lowered from beneath the barrel, although it could be fired from the wheeled carriage if necessary.

It was fitted with an optical sight, but the sight had no range-finding capability. It was gradually phased out of use by most Soviet units from the early 1960s, but remained in use with the parachute battalions of the airborne divisions for some years after. HEAT and HE ammunition were available, weighing 3.6kg and 4.5kg respectively.

Artillery of the Warsaw Pact

B-10

Specifications: B-10

Calibre: 82mm
Weight: 87.6kg (travelling)
Length: 1.68m (travelling)
Rate of fire: 6-7 rounds/minute
Maximum range: 400m (anti-tank)
    4,500m (HE)
Armour penetration: 240mm

107mm B-11

Introduced alongside the B-10, which was supplied to battalion anti-tank platoons, the B-11 was issued to regimental anti-tank companies. Like the B-10, it was a smoothbore weapon, fitted with a two-wheeled carriage for transit. Normally fired from a tripod, it could be fired from the wheeled carriage in emergency, at the cost of reduced accuracy.

B-11

Primarily intended for anti-tank use with a HEAT round, it also had sights for indirect fire with an HE round. Like the B-10, it was gradually phased out of use by most Soviet units from the early 1960s, replaced with 57mm anti-tank guns as an interim measure until SPG-9s were available. The HEAT and HE rounds weighed 9kg and 13.6kg respectively.

SPECIFICATIONS: B-11

Calibre: 107mm
Weight: 305kg (travelling)
Length: 3.31m
    3.56m (travelling)
Rate of fire: 6 rounds/minute

Maximum range: 450m (anti-tank)
    6,650m (HE)
Armour penetration: 380mm

73MM SPG-9 KOPYE

Introduced in the late 1960s, the SPG-9 was a light anti-tank gun mounted on a tripod, with a four-man crew. Light enough to be carried by two soldiers, it could also be towed on a small two-wheeled carriage or mounted on a vehicle. A lighter version, the SPG-9D, could be carried by one man, and was used by air assault and airborne units. The PGO-9M optical sight was provided for direct fire, but PGO-K9 optical sights and PGN-9 night sights were also available. A device sometimes seen above the barrel was initially thought by NATO to be a spotting rifle, but was later confirmed to be a sub-calibre training device.

Afghan soldiers loading an SPG-9

The SPG-9 fired fin-stabilised HEAT and HE-FRAG ammunition. The propellant charge was contained in an extension behind the folded fins, and fell away from the rest of the projectile after leaving the muzzle. A rocket motor inside the projectile ignited twenty metres from the muzzle, accelerating the projectile to full velocity. This combination produced a high muzzle velocity of 435m/s and a final velocity of 700m/s. The HEAT round could penetrate 400mm of armour, at a maximum range of 1,300m. The HE-FRAG round had an explosive charge of 753g of TNT, with a range of 4,500m.

Specifications: SPG-9 Kopye

Calibre: 73mm
Weight of launcher: 47.5kg
Weight of tripod: 12kg
Length of launcher: 2.11m
Height of launcher: 399-900mm
Elevation: 25°
Maximum range: 1,300m (direct fire)
    4,500m (indirect fire)
Armour penetration: 400mm
Crew: 4

82mm T-21 Tarasnice (Czechoslovakia)

The T-21 was a smoothbore gun firing fin-stabilised ammunition. It was mounted on a pair of small-diameter steel wheels. It could be fired while mounted on the wheels, or while held on a shoulder. It was also seen mounted on OT-62 armoured personnel carriers. Only used in the direct fire role, it fired a 2.13kg HEAT warhead.

T-21

Specifications: T-21 Tarasnice

Calibre: 82mm
Weight: 17.3kg
    20kg (travelling)
Length: 1.47m (travelling)
Maximum range: 457m
Armour penetration: 228mm

82mm M-59 & M-59A (Czechoslovakia)

The M-59 and M-59A were virtually identical, being differentiated only by the M-59A's radially finned section over the chamber, which helped to dissipate heat. They had a carriage with two rubber-tyred wheels, and could be towed behind an APC (commonly the OT-810). They were also observed mounted on or carried inside OT-62 APCs. A bar across the muzzle allowed two men to tow the weapon using a harness. HEAT and HE warheads were provided, and they were used in both direct and indirect fire roles. A ranging rifle could be utilised when they were used for direct fire.

M-59A

Specifications: M-59 and M-59A

Calibre: 82mm
Weight: 385kg
Length: 4.6m (travelling)
Maximum range: 1,200m (direct fire)
    6,657m (indirect fire)
Armour penetration: 250mm

Multiple Rocket Launchers

The Soviet Union pioneered the use of self-propelled multiple rocket launchers (MRL) during the Second World War, when they were officially known as Guards Mortars, but commonly known by the nickname Katyusha. The ease of construction compared to tube artillery (which requires complex tools for rifling barrels) meant that mass production was possible even after the Germans overran many of the armaments factories. The ability to deliver a large quantity of explosive in a short time made them ideal for laying down suppressive fire to minimise the effectiveness of enemy anti-tank systems and artillery.

Most multiple rocket launcher systems were mounted on lorries or other vehicles. This allowed them to move immediately after firing to avoid counter-battery fire, a significant problem given the large launch signature and long time to reload. The few towed systems sacrificed this advantage in order to save weight, facilitating their use in airborne units.

BM-24

The BM-24 entered service in 1951. It had a crew of six and mounted twelve 240mm rockets on an elevating launcher with limited traverse. Elevation and traverse was manual, and two stabilising jacks had to be lowered before launch. The launch frames were arranged in two rows of six, mounted on the rear of a ZIL-151 6x6 chassis. Steel plates were fitted above the cab and fuel tanks to protect them from the blast when the rockets were fired. The system could fire two types of HE rocket: the M-24F with 27.4kg of explosive, and the M-24FUD, which had a lighter payload of 18.4kg but extended the range from 6km to 10.6km. It could also fire MS-24 and MS-24D rockets, fitted with chemical warheads.

BM-24

In 1956, a new rocket, the MD-24F, was introduced. This had a maximum range of 17.5km.

The BM-24T variant entered service in 1956. It used the AT-S artillery tractor as the base for the launch vehicle, and was issued to tank divisions, with the wheeled BM-24 going to motor rifle divisions. The BM-24 had open frame launchers, the BM-24T enclosed tubes.

SPECIFICATIONS: BM-24 VEHICLE

Weight: 9.2 tonnes
Length: 6.71m
Width: 2.32m
Height: 2.91m
Maximum road speed: 65km/hour
Range: 430km
Number of launchers: 12
Reload time: 3-4 minutes
Traverse: 140°
Elevation: 0 to +65°

SPECIFICATIONS: BM-24T VEHICLE

Weight: 15.24 tonnes
Length: 5.87m
Width: 2.57m
Height: 3.1m
Maximum road speed: 35km/hour
Range: 380km
Number of launchers: 12
Reload time: 3-4 minutes
Traverse: 210°
Elevation: 0 to +45°

Specifications: BM-24 Rocket

Rocket calibre: 240mm
Warhead weight: 46.9kg
Rocket length: 1.18m
Rocket weight: 112.5kg
Rocket range: up to 17.5km, depending on rocket type

BMD-20

Development of a 200mm rocket for what was to become the BMD-20 started in 1945. Several changes to the requirements led to delays. Trials were carried out in 1951, and the BMD-20 entered service in 1952, mounting four 200mm rockets in a single row on the back of a ZIL-151 6x6 chassis. Two jacks were lowered before firing to improve stability of the launch platform. The rockets were housed in open framework tubes on a manually operated mounting with limited traverse. The rockets had 30kg HE-FRAG warheads and a maximum range of 19km.

Specifications: BMD-20

Weight: 8.7 tonnes
Length: 7.2m
Width: 2.3m
Height: 2.85m
Maximum road speed: 60km/hour
Range: 600km
Rocket calibre: 200mm
Number of launchers: 4
Warhead weight: 30kg

Rocket length: 3.11m
Rocket weight: 91.4kg
Rocket range: 19km
Reload time: 10 minutes
Traverse: 200°
Elevation: 0 to +50°

BM-14

The BM-14 (also known as BM-14-16) entered service in 1952 as a replacement for the wartime BM-13. It had sixteen 140mm rockets, in two rows of eight, on a mounting with limited traverse. Elevation and traverse was manual, and the mounting was fitted on a ZIS-151 6x6 chassis. A remote firing mechanism was provided, allowing the operator to fire the rockets from up to 60m away from the vehicle. Initially only HE-FRAG warheads were available, but smoke (WP) and chemical warheads were introduced in 1955. Later models used ZIL-157 (BM-14M) and ZIL-131 (BM-14MM) chassis in place of the original ZIS-151.

BM-14

In 1959, the BM-14-17 was introduced, which had 17 launch tubes on a GAZ-63A 4x4 chassis. A towed variant, the RPU-14, was produced for use with the airborne forces. This had 16 tubes in four rows of four, mounted on a carriage similar to that used by the D-44 85mm gun. It was replaced by the BM-21V.

SPECIFICATIONS: BM-14-16 VEHICLE

Weight: 8.2 tonnes
Length: 9.92m
Width: 2.3m
Height: 2.65m
Maximum road speed: 60km/hour
Range: 600km
Number of launchers: 16
Traverse: 200°
Elevation: 0 to +52°

SPECIFICATIONS: BM-14-17 VEHICLE

Weight: 5.3 tonnes
Length: 5.41m
Width: 1.93m
Height: 2.24m
Maximum road speed: 65km/hour
Range: 650km
Number of launchers: 17
Traverse: 210°
Elevation: 0 to +47°

SPECIFICATIONS: BM-14 ROCKET

Rocket calibre: 140mm
Warhead weight: 18.8kg

Rocket length: 1.08m
Rocket weight: 39.6kg
Rocket range: 9.8km
Reload time: 4 minutes

BM-25

The BM-25 entered service in 1957, and had six liquid-fuelled 255mm rockets in open-frame launchers. The launchers were mounted in two rows of three on a KrAZ-214 6x6 chassis. Before firing, two stabilisers were lowered and armoured shutters were fitted over the windscreens. A tarpaulin normally covered the launch assembly while in transit.

Specifications: BM-25

Weight: 18.15 tonnes
Length: 9.82m
Width: 2.7m
Height: 3.5m
Maximum road speed: 55km/hour
Range: 530km
Rocket calibre: 250mm
Number of launchers: 6
Rocket length: 5.82m
Rocket weight: 455kg
Rocket range: 30km
Reload time: 10-20 minutes
Traverse: 6°
Elevation: 0 to +55°

BM-21 Grad

Developed during the mid-to-late 1950s, the BM-21 entered service in 1963, with the designation BM-21 (known in the West as BM-21a). Each division was equipped with a battalion of 12 launchers, and each army or front had three battalions. In wartime, all battalions were to be increased in size to 18 launchers.

BM-21 Grad

The launch vehicle was based on a Ural-375D 6x6 chassis, fitted with an elevating, rotating assembly on the rear bed, carrying 40 launch tubes in four rows of ten. The launch assembly was rotated forward for travelling. Stabilisers were fitted to each side of the vehicle at the rear and were lowered to the ground before firing. The cabin contained all the equipment needed to prepare and fire the rockets, which could be fired individually, in a salvo, or by selective ripple. A remote-control unit was provided, allowing the crew to fire the rockets from a distance of up to 60m from the vehicle. Initially only HE-FRAG warheads were available, but incendiary and chemical warheads were subsequently developed.

Later, the Ural-4320 6x6 chassis was used as the base vehicle, and this variant was given the designation BM-21-1. This version also had an automated fire control system and a satellite navigation system.

In 1969, the BM-21V was developed for use by airborne forces. This was much lighter, mounting a 12-tube launcher on a GAZ-66B 4x4 chassis. Like the BM-21, two stabilisers had to be lowered before firing, and rockets could be fired individually or in a salvo. In order to facilitate air transport and dropping by parachute, the cab was collapsible, the steering wheel was telescopic, and the doors and windscreen could be removed. There were tie-down points for attaching the vehicle to a pallet for dropping by parachute.

The BM-21b Grad-1 entered service in 1976 as a lightweight, regimental-level system for use in independent MRL batteries. The basic arrangement was the same as the original BM-21, but with 36 launch tubes (the lower two rows had eight tubes each instead of 10) mounted on the rear of a ZIL-131 chassis. This variant fired a different rocket with shorter range but more effective warhead (the HE-FRAG warhead was preformed, and the incendiary warhead carried more incendiary elements).

Specifications: BM-21 Grad

Weight: 13.7 tonnes
Length: 7.35m

Width: 2.69m
Height: 2.85m
Maximum road speed: 75km/hour
Range: 480km
Rocket calibre: 122mm
Number of launchers: 40
Warhead weight: 19.4kg
Rocket length: 3.22m
Rocket weight: 77.5kg
Rocket range: 20.5km
Reload time: 10 minutes
Traverse: 180°
Elevation: 0 to +55°

Specifications: BM-21B Grad-1

Weight: 10.5 tonnes
Length: 6.9m
Width: 2.5m
Height: 2.48m
Maximum road speed: 80km/hour
Range: 525km
Rocket calibre: 122mm
Number of launchers: 36
Warhead weight: 18.4kg
Rocket length: 2.87m
Rocket weight: 66kg
Rocket range: 20km
Reload time: 10 minutes
Traverse: 180°
Elevation: 0 to +55°

BM-27 Uragan

Development of the BM-27 was completed in 1975, and it was accepted for service in the same year. It was sometimes mistakenly referred to as the BM-22 in the West. It was deployed in regiments (three battalions) or brigades (four battalions) at army or front level. Each battalion had 12 launch vehicles, but in wartime would receive an extra six. Each battalion had a Kapustnik-B automated fire control system, comprising a commander's vehicle based on the BTR-80 chassis, a chief of staff vehicle based on a Ural-4320 chassis, three battery command vehicles based on BTR-80 chassis, and three battery senior officer vehicles based on the Ural-4320 chassis. The Kapustnik-B included systems for reconnaissance, initial battalion orientation, location fixing, weather reconnaissance, ballistic tracking, communications, and data transfer.

The BM-27 launch vehicle was based on the same ZIL-135LM 8x8 chassis as the FROG-7 tactical ballistic missile. The crew compartment was not armoured, but did provide NBC protection. 16 tubes were arranged in three rows on an elevating mount at the rear with limited traverse. The top row had four tubes, while the lower two rows had six tubes each. Launch preparation and firing equipment were in the cab, where the operator could choose between firing a full salvo or individual rockets. Before firing, two stabilisers were lowered and a steel shutter was fitted over the windscreen.

The 9T452 transloader vehicle was based on the same chassis as the launch vehicle. Each one carried 16 rockets in two stacks, either side of a hydraulic crane fitted in the centre of the rear

BM-27 Uragan

deck. For loading, the launcher was traversed to one side and put into the horizontal position.

SPECIFICATIONS: BM-27 URAGAN

Weight: 20 tonnes
Length: 9.63m
Width: 2.8m
Height: 3.23m
Maximum road speed: 65km/hour
Range: 570km
Rocket calibre: 220mm
Number of launchers: 16
Warhead weight: 51.7kg
Rocket length: 4.83m
Rocket weight: 280kg
Rocket range: 35km

Reload time: 20-30 minutes
Traverse: 60°
Elevation: 0 to +55°

BM-30 Smerch

Development of the BM-30 started during the late 1970s, and the system entered service in 1987. The launch vehicle was based on the MAZ-543A 8x8 chassis, with a 12-round elevating, rotating launcher. The launch tubes were arranged as a row of four on top, with a pair of 2x2 blocks underneath, one on each side of the elevating assembly. Two stabilisers were fitted, which had to be lowered before firing. The cabin contained the launch preparation and firing equipment. The rockets could be fired individually or as a salvo. Each launch vehicle had an associated 9T234-2 transloader vehicle, based on the same MAZ-543A chassis, with 12 reload rockets and a hydraulic crane to facilitate loading.

BM-30s were organised into batteries of four launchers, with three batteries to a battalion. Each battery had a command vehicle and a staff vehicle, both based on the KamAZ-4310 6x6 chassis. These vehicles contained communications equipment, digital computers, and the Vivariy automated fire control system.

The rockets had a flight-control system to allow them to correct their trajectory in flight, leading to greatly improved accuracy, claimed to be 0.21% of range. High explosive and cluster munition warheads were available.

BM-30 Smerch

SPECIFICATIONS: BM-30 SMERCH

Weight: 43.7 tonnes
Length: 12.1m
Width: 3.05m
Height: 3.05m
Maximum road speed: 60km/hour
Range: 850km
Rocket calibre: 300mm
Number of launchers: 12
Warhead weight: 92.5kg
Rocket length: 7.6m
Rocket weight: 800kg
Rocket range: 70km
Reload time: 36 minutes
Traverse: 60°
Elevation: 0 to +55°

BM 9A51 Prima

The BM 9A51 was developed in the early to mid-1980s, and entered service in 1987. It was primarily assigned to divisions, in battalions of 12 vehicles, which would be expanded to 18 vehicles in wartime, but was sometimes found at army or front level in place of the BM-21.

The BM 9A51 used the same Ural-4320 6x6 chassis as the BM-21-1, but mounted 50 launch tubes in a rotating, elevating mount on the rear. The tubes were arranged in five rows of 10, within a box structure. Two stabilisers were fitted on the sides, toward the rear, which had to be lowered before firing. Aiming and launching could be controlled from within the cab, or from outside the vehicle, using a remote-control unit. 72 reloads were carried on a 9T232M transloader vehicle, also based on the Ural-4320 chassis. Reloading took around 10 minutes.

The BM 9A51 could fire the same 122mm rockets as the BM-21, but a new rocket, the 9M53F, was developed specifically for it. This rocket had a HE-FRAG warhead that separated and descended below a small parachute, then detonated several yards above the ground. The combination of air burst and near-vertical descent due to the use of a parachute resulted in a wider blast radius than the more usual ground burst. If required, the fuse could be set to enable conventional operation, with the warhead remaining with the rocket and detonating on contact with the ground.

Specifications: BM 9A51 Prima

Weight: 13.9 tonnes
Length: 7.35m
Width: 2.43m
Height: 2.68m
Maximum road speed: 85km/hour
Range: 990km
Rocket calibre: 122mm
Number of launchers: 50
Warhead weight: 26kg
Rocket length: 3.04m
Rocket weight: 70kg
Rocket range: 20.5km
Reload time: 10 minutes
Traverse: 58°
Elevation: 0 to +55°

RM-51 (Czechoslovakia)

The RM-51, sometimes referred to as the RM-130, entered service with the Czech army in 1956. It mounted 32 rockets on the back of a Praga V3S 6x6 lorry in four rows of eight. The 130mm rockets were spin stabilised, and the launcher had to be traversed to one side before firing, since the unarmoured cab had no protection from back blast. Stowage boxes for spare rockets were fitted on either side of the hull, under the launcher.

The standard version was used by Czechoslovakia and exported to Bulgaria, Cuba, and Egypt. The Austrian army used the RM-51 launcher mounted on Steyr 680 M3 6x6 lorries, and

RM-51

the Romanian army used it mounted on Soviet ZIL-151 or ZIL-157 lorries.

SPECIFICATIONS: RM-51

Weight: 8.9 tonnes
Length: 6.91m
Width: 2.31m
Height: 2.92m
Maximum road speed: 62km/hour
Range: 440km
Rocket calibre: 130mm
Number of launchers: 32
Warhead weight: 2.3kg

Rocket length: 0.8m
Rocket weight: 24.2kg
Rocket range: 8.2km
Reload time: 2 minutes
Traverse: 240°
Elevation: 0 to +50°

RM-70 (Czechoslovakia)

First observed by the West at a 1972 parade, the RM-70 was based on a Czech Tatra 813 8x8 lorry. It had the same launcher as the Soviet BM-21 at the rear of the vehicle, but unlike the Soviet vehicle, an extra set of 40 rockets was carried between the launcher and the cab, to allow for rapid reloading. The cab was fully armoured, providing the crew with protection from small arms fire and shell splinters, and the Tatra chassis provided much better cross-country capability than the Ural-375D 6x6 chassis used by the BM-21. A central tyre pressure regulation system was fitted, allowing the driver to adjust the tyre pressure according to the ground being crossed.

An improved version, the Mod 70/85, was introduced in the mid-1980s. This used the more modern Tatra T815 VNN 8x8 chassis, with the same launcher and reloads. The cab was not armoured, but it did have a central tyre pressure regulation system and NBC protection for the crew of four.

Specifications: RM-70 (RM-70/85 in brackets)

Weight: 25.3 tonnes (25 tonnes)
Length: 8.8m (9.6m)
Width: 2.55m (2.53m)
Height: 2.96m (3.03m)
Maximum road speed: 75km/hour (60km/hour)
Range: 1,100km (1,000km)
Rocket calibre: 122mm
Number of launchers: 40
Warhead weight: 19.4kg
Rocket length: 3.22m
Rocket weight: 77.5kg
Rocket range: 20.5km
Reload time: 35 seconds
Traverse: 125° left, 70° right
Elevation: 0 to +55°

140mm RPU-14

Designed for use by airborne troops, the RPU-14 mounted sixteen 140mm rocket tubes, in four rows of four, on a simple two-wheeled, split-trail carriage. Normally towed by a GAZ-66 4x4 lorry, eighteen were issued to each Soviet airborne assault division, organised into a battalion of three batteries. It was later replaced by the BM-21V, which was based on a GAZ-66B chassis.

The RPU-14 fired the same spin-stabilised rocket as the Polish WP-8 and the widely deployed BM-14-16 and BM-14-17 lorry-mounted MRLs. The same rocket, mounted on a single-round tripod launcher, was supplied to some guerrilla forces. High explosive and smoke warheads were used.

RPU-14

Specifications: RPU-14

Calibre: 140mm
Barrels: 16
Weight: 1,835kg (loaded)
Length: 4.04m (travelling)
Width: 1.8m (travelling)
Height: 1.6m (travelling)
Elevation/depression: +48/0°
Traverse: 30° total
Crew: 5
Rocket calibre: 140mm
Warhead weight: 18.8kg
Rocket length: 1.08m
Rocket weight: 39.6kg
Rocket range: 9.8km
Reload time: 4 minutes

140MM WP-8 (POLAND)

The WP-8 mounted eight 140mm rocket tubes in two rows of four on a simple two-wheeled, split-trail carriage. Like the Soviet RPU-14, it was designed for use with airborne troops, specifically the Polish 6th Pomeranian Air Assault Brigade. The brigade had a battery of six WP-8 launchers and two batteries of D-30 howitzers (twelve in total) in its composite artillery battalion.

WP-8

The WP-8 fired the same spin-stabilised rocket as the Soviet RPU-14 and the widely deployed BM-14-16 and BM-14-17 lorry-mounted MRLs. High explosive and smoke warheads were used. It could be towed by a light vehicle, the UAZ-469 being commonly used.

SPECIFICATIONS: WP-8

Calibre: 140mm
Barrels: 8
Weight: 687.6kg (loaded)
Length: 3.29m (travelling)
Width: 1.63m (travelling)
Height: 1.2m (travelling)
Elevation/depression: +47/-12°
Traverse: 28° total
Crew: 5
Rocket calibre: 140mm
Warhead weight: 18.8kg
Rocket length: 1.08m
Rocket weight: 39.6kg
Rocket range: 9.8km
Reload time: 2 minutes

Tactical Ballistic Missiles

When Khrushchev came to power following Stalin's death, he ordered major cuts in conventional forces, as he intended to rely on nuclear missiles for defence. The new leader was a great believer in the relatively new technology of missiles, and this led to greater use of missiles throughout the Soviet military, as it was easier to secure funding for missile systems than for gun systems. Under Khrushchev, the Soviet Union sought to build up its nuclear missile forces at all levels, from tactical systems to intercontinental ballistic missiles.

FROG-1

The first two vehicles of the FROG (Free Rocket Over Ground) series, the FROG-1 and FROG-2, entered service in 1955. The FROG-1 carried a rocket with a solid fuel engine and a maximum range of 25.7km. It could be fitted with a tactical nuclear warhead or a 1,200kg HE-FRAG warhead. The launch vehicle was based on a modified IS-2 tank chassis.

Specifications: FROG-1

Vehicle weight: 36 tonnes
Vehicle length: 9.33m

Vehicle width: 3.07m
Vehicle height: 3m
Vehicle road speed: 30km/hour (41km/hour without a rocket)
Vehicle road range: 150km
Missile length: 10.2m
Missile diameter: 612mm
Missile weight: 3,200kg
Missile range: 25.7km
Missile CEP: 700m

FROG-2

The FROG-2 had a non-amphibious chassis based on that of the PT-76 light tank. It carried a solid fuel powered rocket with a maximum range of 17.5km. The rocket was fitted with a conventional high explosive warhead.

FROG-2

Specifications: FROG-2

Vehicle weight: 16.4 tonnes
Vehicle length: 9.4m
Vehicle width: 3.18m
Vehicle height: 3.05m
Vehicle road speed: 20km/hour (40km/hour without a rocket)
Vehicle road range: 250km
Missile length: 9.01m
Missile diameter: 324mm
Missile weight: 1,760kg
Missile range: 17.5km
Missile CEP: 770m

FROG-3/4/5

The FROG-3, FROG-4 and FROG-5 were given different designations by NATO, but were in fact the same system, with different warheads on the rockets. They entered service with the Soviet army in 1960, under the designation 2K6 Luna. The chassis was based on that of the FROG-2. The vehicles weighed 18.8 tonnes and had a maximum speed of 40km/hour. The rockets could be fitted with HE-FRAG (FROG-3), chemical (FROG-4), or tactical nuclear (FROG-5) warheads.

The launch vehicles were reloaded from ZIL-157 6x6 lorries, each towing a trailer with two reload rockets, and a separate crane lorry to lift the rockets onto the launch vehicles. Each launch vehicle had a crew of 11.

FROG-3

SPECIFICATIONS: FROG-3/4/5

Vehicle weight: 18.8 tonnes
Vehicle length: 10.5m
Vehicle width: 3.1m
Vehicle height: 3.05m
Vehicle road speed: 40 km/hour
Missile length: 10.6m
Missile diameter: 540mm
Missile weight: 2,280kg
Missile range: 45km–61km depending on warhead
Missile CEP: 800m

FROG-7

In 1964, a new missile system was accepted for service, designated FROG-7a by NATO. This was a solid fuel powered rocket mounted on a wheeled TEL vehicle based on the ZIL-135LM 8x8 chassis. A range of different warheads were available. As well as high explosive, chemical, and nuclear warheads, a leaflet-dispensing warhead was produced. An air-mobile version, with the rocket mounted on a self-propelled trailer, did not got past the prototype stage. The FROG-7b entered service in 1968, with improvements to the rocket and a longer warhead, increasing rocket length from 8.95m to 9.4m. Cluster munition warheads, with 42 HE bomblets, were available for the FROG-7b. There were three types of nuclear warhead for the FROG-7: the AA-22 and AA-38 had selectable yields of 3, 10 or 22kT; and the AA-52 had a selectable yield of 5, 10, 20 or 200kT. The HE warhead carried 450kg of explosive.

FROG-7

Unlike previous vehicles, the FROG-7 TEL had an on-board hydraulic crane for loading rockets. Reloads were carried on a similar vehicle, with three rockets on each. It took around 15-30 minutes to prepare to fire, and around 20 minutes to reload. Maximum flight time was around 160 seconds, with the engine burning for 7-11 seconds.

SPECIFICATIONS: FROG-7 (FROG-7B IN BRACKETS)

Vehicle weight: 19 tonnes
Vehicle length: 10.69m
Vehicle width: 2.8m
Vehicle height: 3.35m
Vehicle road speed: 65 km/hour
Vehicle road range: 650 km
Missile length: 8.95m (9.4m)
Missile diameter: 0.5m
Missile weight: 2,432 - 2,450kg
Missile range: 70km
Missile CEP: 400m

SS-1 SCUD

The SS-1b Scud A entered service in 1957. Unlike the FROG series, it employed gyroscopes to provide a rudimentary guidance system. Guidance commands were only issued during powered flight and the missiles were unguided once the rocket ran out of fuel, after around 80 seconds. This resulted in poor accuracy, especially at longer ranges. The SS-1b was carried on a TEL vehicle with a tracked chassis derived from the IS-3 tank. Maximum range was 150km.

The SS-1c Scud B entered service in 1961, initially mounted on the same TEL vehicle as the SS-1b, though in 1965, a new wheeled TEL based on the MAZ-543 was introduced. This model

SS-1c Scud B

had an improved rocket with a new engine. Maximum range was increased to 300km, and accuracy was improved. Nuclear, chemical, and HE warheads were available. The launch sequence could be controlled from the TEL, but was normally done from a command vehicle. Time to prepare and launch was around one hour.

SPECIFICATIONS: SS-1B SCUD A

Vehicle weight: 38 tonnes
Vehicle length: 12.5m
Vehicle width: 3.2m
Vehicle height: 3.32m
Vehicle road speed: 37km/hour
Missile length: 10.7m
Missile diameter: 0.88m
Missile weight: 4,400kg

Missile range: 180km
Missile CEP: 3km

SPECIFICATIONS: SS-1C SCUD B

Vehicle weight: 29 tonnes
Vehicle length: 13.58m
Vehicle width: 3.02m
Vehicle height: 3.7m
Vehicle road speed: 70km/hour
Missile length: 11.25m
Missile diameter: 0.88m
Missile weight: 5,900kg
Missile range: 300km
Missile CEP: 450m

SS-12 SCALEBOARD

The SS-12 Scaleboard was the longest-ranged ballistic missile to serve with the Soviet ground forces. It entered service in 1969, mounting a single missile inside a container on the same MAZ-543 chassis as the SS-1c Scud B. In 1979, a new missile, the SS-12M Scaleboard B (initially known in the West as the SS-22) began to replace the original missiles. The TEL was the same, but accuracy was improved. Under the terms of the 1987 INF Treaty, these missiles were destroyed between August 1988 and July 1989.

SS-12 Scaleboard

SPECIFICATIONS: SS-12 SCALEBOARD (SS-12M IN BRACKETS)

Vehicle weight: 30.8 tonnes
Vehicle length: 13.15m
Vehicle width: 3.02m
Vehicle height: 3.5m
Vehicle road speed: 70km/hour
Missile length: 12.78m
Missile diameter: 1.01m
Missile weight: 9,800kg
Missile range: 800km (900km)
Missile CEP: 750m (370m)

SS-21 Scarab

The SS-21 Scarab entered service in 1976, as a replacement for the FROG-7. The TEL was a six-wheeled vehicle with amphibious capability and NBC protection for the crew, with the missile contained in a temperature-controlled unit until launch. The missile was powered by a solid fuel rocket motor, and was guided throughout the entire flight. The crew could perform all tasks related to targeting and launching the missile from within the cab. High explosive, chemical, and nuclear warheads were available, with the AA-60 nuclear warhead having a selectable yield of 5, 10, 20 or 200kT. In 1989, the Scarab B was introduced, with a longer range and better accuracy. A separate transloader vehicle carried two additional missiles, and had a crane for loading missiles onto the launch vehicle.

SS-21 Scarab

Specifications: SS-21 Scarab (Scarab B in brackets)

Vehicle weight: 18.15 tonnes
Vehicle length: 9.48m
Vehicle width: 2.78m

Vehicle height: 2.35m
Vehicle road speed: 60 km/hour
Vehicle road range: 650km
Missile length: 6.4m
Missile diameter: 0.65m
Missile weight: 2,000kg (2,010kg)
Missile range: 70km (120km)
Missile CEP: 160m (95m)

SS-23 Spider

The SS-23 Spider entered service in 1980, replacing the SS-1c Scud B. The TEL vehicle was based on the 8x8 BAZ-6944 chassis. It had NBC protection for the crew and was fully amphibious, propelled in the water by a pair of water jets. When in transit, the missile was contained within the vehicle. The crew did not need to leave the cab to prepare and launch the missile, which took around 5-10 minutes.

The missile had a single solid fuel rocket motor, with inertial and active radar terminal guidance, providing a high level of accuracy. It missile was difficult to intercept, and the high level of accuracy meant that use against moving or hardened targets was feasible. A transporter-loader was based on the same chassis, and carried a single reload missile with a loading crane. High explosive (450kg), chemical, submunition, and nuclear (AA-60, as used on SS-21) warheads were available.

When the INF Treaty was signed in 1987, the United States claimed that the SS-23 was covered by the treaty, since they had estimated the range to be at least 500km. The Soviet Union maintained that maximum range was less than 500km and that

SS-23 Spider

the system was therefore not covered. None the less, as a gesture of goodwill, all existing systems were destroyed and work on an improved version was cancelled.

SPECIFICATIONS: SS-23 SPIDER

Vehicle weight: 24.7 tonnes
Vehicle length: 11.76m
Vehicle width: 3.13m
Vehicle height: 3m
Vehicle road speed: 70 km/hour
Vehicle road range: 700km
Missile length: 7.5m
Missile diameter: 0.9m

Missile weight: 4,500 - 5,000kg
Missile range: 50-480km
Missile CEP: 30-150m

Glossary

AA: Anti-Aircraft
AFV: Armoured Fighting Vehicle
AP: Armour Piercing
AP: Armour-Piercing
APC: Armoured Personnel Carrier. An armoured vehicle used to transport infantry, usually lightly armed and armoured
APC-T: Armour-Piercing Capped Tracer
APDS: Armour Piercing Discarding Sabot. A type of kinetic energy anti-tank round fired from rifled guns
APFSDS: Armour Piercing Fin Stabilised Discarding Sabot. A type of kinetic energy anti-tank round, usually fired from smoothbore guns
APFSDS: Armour-Piercing Fin Stabilised Discarding Sabot. A type of kinetic energy anti-tank round, usually fired from smoothbore guns
APHE: Armour-Piercing High Explosive. Known in the West as HESH (High Explosive Squash Head) or HEP (High Explosive, Plastic), it had a thin metal outer shell containing plastic explosive. On impact, the plastic explosive squashed against the target before exploding.
AP-T: Armour-Piercing Tracer
ARV: Armoured Recovery Vehicle

ATGM: Anti-Tank Guided Missile
ATGW: Anti-Tank Guided Weapon
Bangalore torpedo: One or more tubes filled with explosive, used to clear obstacles
BMD: Boevaya Mashina Desantnaya (Airborne Combat Vehicle)
BMP: Boevaya Mashina Pekhota (Infantry Combat Vehicle)
BRM: Boevaya Razvedyvatnaya Mashina (Combat Reconnaissance Vehicle)
CEP: Circular Error of Probability. A measure of accuracy, the CEP was the radius of a circle within which 50% of projectiles would fall
CP: Concrete-Piercing
ECCM: Electronic Counter-Counter Measures
ECM: Electronic Counter Measures
ERA: Explosive Reactive Armour
FASCAM: Family of Scatterable Mines. A generic term for a set of artillery-developed mines developed by the US army
GSFG: Group of Soviet Forces Germany. The Soviet forces based in East Germany
HEAT-FS: High Explosive Anti-Tank - Fin Stabilised
HEAT-FS: High Explosive Anti-Tank, Fin-Stabilised. A HEAT round stabilised by fins rather than by spin imparted from a rifled barrel. Usually fired from smoothbore guns.
HEAT: High Explosive Anti-Tank. A form of chemical energy anti-tank warhead commonly used on anti-tank missiles
HEAT: High Explosive Anti-Tank. A form of chemical energy anti-tank warhead, it fired a jet of super-heated molten metal into the target.
HE-FRAG: High Explosive Fragmentation
HE: High Explosive

HE-RAP: High Explosive — Rocket Assisted Projectile. A HE projectile with a small rocket motor to boost range
HE-RAP: High Explosive Rocket Assisted Projectile. A HE projectile with a small rocket motor to boost range
HESH: High Explosive Squash Head. A form of chemical energy anti-tank warhead, particularly favoured by the British army
HVAP: High Velocity Armour-Piercing
HVAP-T: High Velocity Armour-Piercing Tracer
IFF: Identification Friend or Foe. A system to automatically identify friendly aircraft
IFV: Infantry Fighting Vehicle. Similar to an APC, but with greater armament, intended to provide support to the dismounted infantry
Lunette: A ring used to attach a weapon to a vehicle for towing
MBT: Main Battle Tank
MCLOS: Manual Command Line-Of-Sight. First generation anti-tank missile guidance system, which required the operator to manually steer the missile to the target
MG: Machine gun
MRL: Multiple Rocket Launcher
Muzzle brake: A device fitted to the muzzle of a gun to redirect propellant gasses, reducing recoil
NBC: Nuclear, Biological, and Chemical
RAP: Rocket Assisted Projectile. A projectile with a small rocket motor to boost range
SACLOS: Semi-Automatic Command Line-Of-Sight. Second generation anti-tank missile guidance system, which simply required the operator to keep the target in the system's sight
SAM: Surface-to-Air Missile
SPG: Self-Propelled Gun

TELAR: Transporter, Erector, Launcher, and Radar. A TEL vehicle with integrated radar

TEL: Transporter, Erector, Launcher. A vehicle on which one or more missiles were transported, and from which the missiles were launched

WP: White Phosphorous

Image Credits

T-34/85: Vitaly V. Kuzmin (CC-BY-SA 4.0 International)
T-10M: Alex-engraver (CC-BY-SA 3.0 Unported)
T-54: Vitaly V. Kuzmin (CC-BY-SA 4.0 International)
T-55: John Kearney
T-62: John Kearney
T-64BV: Andrew Bossi (CC-BY-SA 2.5 Generic)
T-72A: Vitaly V. Kuzmin (CC-BY-SA 4.0 International)
T-80U: Vitaly V. Kuzmin (CC-BY-SA 4.0 International)
TR-85: Brigada 15 Mecanizată (www.bg15mc.ro) (CC-BY-SA 3.0 Unported)

BMP-1: Vitaly V. Kuzmin (CC-BY-SA 4.0 International)
BMP-2: Vitaly V. Kuzmin (CC-BY-SA 4.0 International)
BMP-3: Vitaly V. Kuzmin (CC-BY-SA 4.0 International)
BMD-1: Vitaly V. Kuzmin (CC-BY-SA 4.0 International)
BMD-2: Vitaly V. Kuzmin (CC-BY-SA 4.0 International)
Dismounting from an MLI-84: MAPN (CC-BY-SA 3.0 Unported)

BTR-40: Bukvoed (CC-BY-SA 3.0 Unported)
BTR-50P: ShinePhantom (CC-BY-SA 3.0 Unported)
BTR-70: Vitaly V. Kuzmin (CC-BY-SA 4.0 International)

BTR-D prepared for parachute drop: Vitaly V. Kuzmin (CC-BY-SA 4.0 International)
MT-LB: Vitaly V. Kuzmin (CC-BY-SA 4.0 International)
TAB-77: Locotenent-Colonel Dragoș Anghelache (CC-BY-SA 3.0 Unported)

SU-100: Vitaly V. Kuzmin (CC-BY-SA 4.0 International)
ASU-57 with Ch-51 gun: Vitaly V. Kuzmin (CC-BY-SA 4.0 International)
ASU-85: Vitaly V. Kuzmin (CC-BY-SA 4.0 International)
2P26: High Contrast (CC-BY-SA 3.0 Germany)
2P27: Vitaly V. Kuzmin (CC-BY-SA 4.0 International)
IT-1: Vitaly V. Kuzmin (CC-BY-SA 4.0 International)
9P149: Vitaly V. Kuzmin (CC-BY-SA 4.0 International)

BRDM-1 with extra wheels lowered: Vitaly V. Kuzmin (CC-BY-SA 4.0 International)
BRM: Vitaly V. Kuzmin (CC-BY-SA 4.0 International)

ZSU-57-2: VargaA (CC-BY-SA 4.0 International)
ZSU-23-4 Shilka: Vitaly V. Kuzmin (CC-BY-SA 4.0 International)
2S6M: Vitaly V. Kuzmin (CC-BY-SA 4.0 International)
SA-4 Ganef: ShinePhantom (CC-BY-SA 3.0 Unported)
SA-6 Gainful: Vitaly V. Kuzmin (CC-BY-SA 4.0 International)
SA-8 Gecko: Sevda Babayeva (CC-BY-SA 3.0 Unported)
SA-12 Gladiator: Vitaly V. Kuzmin (CC-BY-SA 4.0 International)
SA-13 Gopher: Srđan Popović (CC-BY-SA 4.0 International)

BTR-ZD: Serge Serebro, Vitebsk Popular News (CC-BY-SA 3.0 Unported)
M53/59: Kaufi (CC-BY-SA 3.0 Unported)

MTU-20: Vitaly Kuzmin (Creative Commons Attribution-Share Alike 4.0 International)
MT-55A: Srđan Popović (Creative Commons Attribution-Share Alike 4.0 International)
MTU-72: Vitaly Kuzmin (Creative Commons Attribution-Share Alike 4.0 International)
TMM-3: David Holt (Creative Commons Attribution-Share Alike 2.0 Generic)
PMP pontoon: Bin im Garten (Creative Commons Attribution-Share Alike 3.0 Unported)
GSP vehicle unit: (Creative Commons Attribution-Share Alike 3.0 Unported)
PTS-M: Gwafton (Creative Commons Attribution-Share Alike 3.0 Unported)
PTS-2: Vitaly Kuzmin (Creative Commons Attribution-Share Alike 4.0 International)
BMK-T: ShinePhantom (Creative Commons Attribution-Share Alike 3.0 Unported)
KH-200: Kerim44 (Creative Commons Attribution-Share Alike 3.0 Unported)
NZhM-56: Vitaly Kuzmin (Creative Commons Attribution-Share Alike 4.0 International)

GMZ-2: Vitaly Kuzmin (Creative Commons Attribution-Share Alike 4.0 International)

GMZ-3: Vitaly Kuzmin (Creative Commons Attribution-Share Alike 4.0 International)
PMR-3: Mike1979 Russia (Creative Commons Attribution-Share Alike 4.0 International)
IMP mine detector: Johan Fredriksson (Creative Commons Attribution-Share Alike 3.0 Unported)

IRM: Vitaly Kuzmin (Creative Commons Attribution-Share Alike 4.0 International)

VT-34: Vikiped at Russian Wikipedia (Creative Commons Attribution-Share Alike 3.0 Unported)
BREM-1: Vitaly Kuzmin (Creative Commons Attribution-Share Alike 4.0 International)
BREM-2: Vitaly Kuzmin (Creative Commons Attribution-Share Alike 4.0 International)
MTP-1: Scott at Flickr (Creative Commons Attribution-Share Alike 2.0 Generic)
WZT-3: Pibwl (Creative Commons Attribution-Share Alike 3.0 Unported)

BAT-M: Vitaly Kuzmin (CC-BY-SA 4.0 International)
BTM: Vitaly Kuzmin (CC-BY-SA 4.0 International)
PZM-2: User:Cooper6 (CC-BY-SA 3.0 Unported)

GAZ-63: Vitaly V. Kuzmin (CC-BY-SA 4.0)
GAZ-66: High Contrast (CC-BY)
KrAZ-255B: LutzBruno (CC-BY-SA 3.0)
KrAZ-260: Vitaly V. Kuzmin (CC-BY-SA 4.0)
ZIL-157: ShinePhantom (CC-BY-SA 3.0)

ML-20: Vitaly V. Kuzmin (CC-BY-SA 3.0)
M1938: Сайга20К (CC-BY-SA 3.0)
A-19: Balcer~commonswiki (CC-BY-SA 3.0)
M-10: Kovako-1 (CC-BY-SA 3.0)
D-1: Alex Zelenko (CC-BY-SA 4.0)
D-44: Michael Rivera (CC-BY-SA 4.0)
D-20: ShinePhantom (CC-BY-SA 3.0)
SM-4-1: ShinePhantom (CC-BY-SA 3.0)

ISU-122: Taw (CC-BY-SA 3.0)
ISU-152: Vitaly V. Kuzmin (CC-BY-SA 4.0)
2S1 Gvozdika: Vitaly V. Kuzmin (CC-BY-SA 4.0)
2S3 Akatsiya: Vitaly V. Kuzmin (CC-BY-SA 4.0)
2S4 Tyulpan: Vitaly V. Kuzmin (CC-BY-SA 4.0)
2S5 Giatsint-S in firing position: Parutip (CC-BY-SA 3.0)
2S7 Pion: Vitaly V. Kuzmin (CC-BY-SA 4.0)

120mm 2B16 Nona-K Gun/Mortar: Smell U Later (CC-BY-SA 3.0)
120mm 2B11 Sani/2S12: Vitaly V. Kuzmin (CC-BY-SA 4.0)
82mm 2B14 Podnos: Vitaly V. Kuzmin (CC-BY-SA 4.0)
82mm B-10: Pibwl (CC-BY-SA 3.0)
107mm B-11: Zala (CC-BY-SA 4.0)
82mm T-21 Tarasnice (Czechoslovakia): Bukvoed (CC-BY-SA 3.0)
82mm M-59 & M-59A (Czechoslovakia): Jozef Kotulič (CC-BY-SA 4.0)

BM-24: Bukvoed (CC-BY-SA 3.0)

BM-14: (CC-BY 3.0)
BM-30 Smerch: Vitaly V. Kuzmin (CC-BY-SA 4.0)
RM-51: Tourbillon (CC-BY 3.0)
140mm RPU-14: Vlad (**Военный музей**) (CC-BY-SA 3.0)
140mm WP-8 (Poland): Kerim44 (CC-BY-SA 4.0)

FROG-3: Leonidl (CC-BY-SA 3.0)
FROG-7: Vitaly V. Kuzmin (CC-BY-SA 4.0)
SS-12 Scaleboard: Vitaly V. Kuzmin (CC-BY-SA 4.0)
SS-21 Scarab: Gulustan (CC-BY-SA 3.0)

DIGITAL REINFORCEMENTS: FREE EBOOK

To get a free ebook of this title, simply scan the code below, or go to www.shilka.co.uk/dr and enter code **WPBX45**.

The free ebook can be downloaded in several formats: Mobi (for Kindle devices & apps), ePub (for other ereaders & ereader apps), and PDF (for reading on a computer). Ereader apps are available for all computers, tablets and smartphones.

About Russell Phillips

Russell Phillips writes books and articles about military technology and history. His articles have been published in Miniature Wargames, Wargames Illustrated, and the Society of Twentieth Century Wargamers' Journal. Some of these articles are available on his website. He has been interviewed on BBC Radio Stoke and The Voice of Russia.

To get advance notice of new books, join Russell's mailing list at www.rpbook.co.uk/list. You can leave at any time.

For a full listing of Russell's books, go to www.rpbook.co.uk/books.

Find Russell Phillips Online

Website: www.rpbook.co.uk
Twitter: @RPBook
Facebook: RussellPhillipsBooks
Goodreads: RussellPhillips
E-mail: russell@rpbook.co.uk
Join Russell's mailing list: www.rpbook.co.uk/list

Index

Introduction	1
Tanks	7
T-34/85	8
T-44	10
IS-3	12
IS-10/T-10	15
PT-76	17
T-54	19
T-55	22
T-62	25
T-64	28
T-72	31
T-80	35
TR-77-580 (Romania)	38
TR-85 (Romania)	39
Infantry Fighting Vehicles	41
BMP-1	41
BMP-2	44
BMP-3	47
BMD-1	48
BMD-2	51
BMD-3	52
BMP-23 (Bulgaria)	54
MLI-84 (Romania)	56
Armoured Personnel Carriers	59
BTR-40	59
BTR-152	61
BTR-50P	63

BTR-60P..65
BTR-70..68
BTR-80..70
BTR-D...72
MT-LB...74
OT-810 (Czechoslovakia)...76
OT-62 (Czechoslovakia/Poland)..78
OT-64/SKOT (Czechoslovakia/Poland)....................................81
PSZH-IV (Hungary)..84
TAB-71 (Romania)..86
TAB-77 (Romania)..87
MLVM Mountaineers Combat Vehicle (Romania)..............89
Anti-Tank Vehicles...91
SU-100..92
SU-122-54..94
ASU-57...95
ASU-85...96
2P26..98
2P27..99
2P32..101
9P110..102
IT-1...104
9P124..106
9P122..107
9P148..109
9P149..111
Reconnaissance Vehicles..113
BRDM-1..113
BRDM-2..115
BRM..117

BRM-23 (Bulgaria)..119
FÚG (Hungary)..120
Self-Propelled Anti-Aircraft Weapons............................123
BTR-40A & BTR-152A..123
ZSU-57-2...125
ZSU-23-4 Shilka..126
2S6...128
SA-4 Ganef...130
SA-6 Gainful..132
SA-8 Gecko...134
SA-9 Gaskin..136
SA-10 Grumble..138
SA-11 Gadfly..139
SA-12 Gladiator...141
SA-13 Gopher..142
BTR-ZD..144
M53/59 (Czechoslovakia)...146
River Crossing..149
Snorkelling...150
Swimming..152
Vehicle-Launched Bridges..153
    MTU-54...154
    MT-34 (Czechoslovakia)...155
    MTU-20...156
    BLG-60 (Poland/DDR)..158
    MT-55A (Czechoslovakia)..159
    MTU-72...161
    KMM..163
    TMM...164
    AM-50 (Czechoslovakia)...166

SMT-1 (Poland)..166
Pontoon Bridges..168
    LPP..168
    TMP..169
    TPP...170
    PMP..170
    PVD-20...172
    TZI..173
    PPS...173
    DPP-40...173
    LPB (DDR)...174
    PP-64 (Poland)...175
    LMS (Czechoslovakia)....................................176
    SMS (Czechoslovakia)....................................176
    PR-60 (Romania)...177
Amphibians and Ferries..178
    K-61..178
    GSP...179
    PTS..181
    PMM-2..182
    PTS-2..182
Bridging Boats...183
    BMK-70 and BMK-90......................................184
    BMK-130..185
    BMK-150..186
    BMK-T..187
    BB-120 (DDR)...188
    KH-200 (Poland)...189
    Mo-108, Mo-111, Mo-930 (Czechoslovakia)..........190
Line of Communication Bridges...........................191

PVM, LVM, TVM Suspension Bridges....................192
MARM..193
SARM..193
BARM..193
NZhM-56..194
RMM-4...195
REM-500..195
SP-19 Self-Propelled Pontoon Bridge..................196
TMS (Czechoslovakia)...196
MS-1 (Czechoslovakia)..196
DMS-65 (Poland)...197
ESB-16 (DDR)...197
SBG-66 (DDR)...197
SB-30 and SB-45 (DDR)......................................198

Mine Warfare... 199
   Minelaying..199
      Helicopter Minelaying Equipment........................200
      GMZ and GMZ-2...200
      GMZ-3..202
      PMR-2, PMR-3, and PMZ-4.................................203
      UMZ...205
      MLG-60 (DDR)...205
   Mine Detection...206
      VIM-625 and VIM-695 Portable Mine Detectors. 206
      VIM-203M Metallic Mine Detector......................207
      UMIV-1 Portable Mine Detector..........................207
      IMP Portable Mine Detector.................................207
      DIM Vehicle-Mounted Mine Detector..................208
      VISF Model 1946 Portable Mine Detector (Bulgaria)209
      M62 Portable Mine Detector (Bulgaria).................209

M-10 and M-11 Portable Mine Detectors (Czechoslovakia) 210
MSG 64 Portable Mine Detector (DDR)..................210
Mine Clearance..210
PT-54, PT-54M, and PT-55 Mine Rollers............211
KMT-4 Mine Plough..212
KMT-5 Mine Plough and Rollers.........................213
KMT-6 Mine Plough..214
KMT-7 Mine Plough and Rollers.........................214
KMT-8 Mine Plough..214
KMT-10 Mine Plough..215
MTK Armoured Mine-Clearing Vehicle.................216
MTK-2 Armoured Mine-Clearing Vehicle............216
ITB-2, SPZ-2, and SPZ-4..217
BDT...217
UZ-1 and UZ-2 Bangalore Torpedoes...................218
PW-LWD (Poland)..218
Tank-Mounted Rollers and Ploughs (Czechoslovakia)219
Trailer-based system (Czechoslovakia)...................220
Armoured Engineer Vehicles...221
IMR Combat Engineer Vehicle..................................221
IMR-2 Combat Engineer Vehicle..............................222
IRM Engineer Reconnaissance Vehicle...........................223
ADZM Engineer Vehicle..226
MT-LB Engineer Vehicles...226
Recovery and Repair Vehicles..229
T-34 ARVs..229
IS-T...230
BTS-1..230
BTS-2..230

BTS-3	231
T-54 (A) and T-54 (B) (DDR)	231
BREM-64	231
BREM-1	232
BREM-2	234
BREhM-D	236
BTR-50PK(B)	237
MTP-1 (Bulgaria)	237
AD-090 Wheeled Recovery Vehicle (Czechoslovakia)	238
VT-34 (Czechoslovakia)	239
VT-55A (Czechoslovakia)	239
VT-72B (Czechoslovakia)	241
VPV (Czechoslovakia)	242
SU-76 Armoured Workshop Vehicle (DDR)	242
WPT-TOPAS (Poland)	243
WZT-1 (Poland)	245
WZT-2 (Poland)	245
WZT-3 (Poland)	246
Earth-Moving Equipment	**249**
BAT Digger	249
BAT-2 Digger	251
BTM and BTM-TMG Digger and Ditcher	252
PZM and PZM-2 Digger and Ditcher	253
MDK-2 and MDK-3 Excavator	254
E-305V Single-Bucket Crane Shovel	256
DOK Bulldozer (Czechoslovakia)	256
Artillery Vehicles	**259**
MT-LBus	259
PRP-3	262
PRP-4	262

SNAR-10 263
ARK-1 Rys 264
Ya-12 & Ya-13F 265
M-2 266
K-800 (Hungary) 267
AT-T 268
AT-L & AT-LM 269
AT-S 270
Mazur D-350 (Poland) 271
ATS-59 273
ATS-59G 274
Bumar Labedy 668 (Poland) 274
MT-S 275
MT-T 276

Lorries Used as Tow Vehicles 277
GAZ-63 279
GAZ-66 281
YaAZ-214 & KrAZ-214 282
KrAZ-255B 283
KrAZ-260 285
UAZ-469B 286
Ural 375 288
Ural 4320 289
ZIL-157 291
DAC 444 (Romania) 292
Praga V3S (Czechoslovakia) 293
Tatra 138 (Czechoslovakia) 295

Towed Guns and Howitzers 297
152mm ML-20 Gun-Howitzer 298
76mm M1938 Mountain Gun 299

122mm A-19 Corps Gun...301
122mm M-30 Howitzer..302
152mm M-10 Howitzer..304
76mm ZIS-3 Divisional Gun..305
152mm D-1 Howitzer..307
57mm ZIS-2 Anti-Tank Gun..308
100mm BS-3 Anti-Tank & Field Gun...310
85mm D-44 Divisional Gun...312
152mm M-18/46 Howitzer (Czechoslovakia).........................313
85mm M-52 & M52/55 Field Gun (Czechoslovakia).........315
152mm D-20 Gun-Howitzer...316
122mm D-74 Field Gun...317
130mm M-46 Field Gun..319
76.2mm Mountain Gun (Romania)..320
130mm SM-4-1 Coastal Gun..321
100mm M-53 Field Gun (Czechoslovakia)............................323
180mm S-23 Gun...324
85mm D-48 Anti-Tank Gun...326
57mm Ch-26 Auxiliary-Propelled Anti-Tank Gun.........327
98mm Model 93 Mountain Howitzer (Romania)..............328
100mm T-12 & MT-12 Anti-Tank Gun..................................329
122mm D-30 Howitzer..331
76mm GP Mountain Gun...332
152mm 2A36 Giatsint-B Field Gun...333
152mm Howitzer M1981 (Romania)..335
130mm Gun M1982 (Romania)..336
152mm Gun-Howitzer M1985 (Romania).............................337
152mm 2A65 Howitzer..337
Self-Propelled Guns, Howitzers, and Mortars....................341
    SU-76...341

    ISU-122...344
    ISU-152...346
    2S1 Gvozdika...347
    2S3 Akatsiya..350
    2S4 Tyulpan...352
    2S5 Giatsint-S..354
    2S7 Pion..356
    2S9 Nona..359
    2S19 Msta...360
    vzor 77 Dana (Czechoslovakia)..........................362
Mortars... 365
    50mm M-38, M-39, M-40 & M-41.......................365
    82mm M-36, M-37, M-41, M-43, & "New" M-37...........367
    107mm M-38...369
    120mm M-38...369
    120mm M-43 (120-PM-43)................................370
    120mm 2B11 Sani/2S12......................................371
    160mm M-43 & M-160.......................................373
    240mm M-240...374
    82mm 2B9 Vasilyek..376
    120mm 2B16 Nona-K Gun/Mortar.....................377
    82mm 2B14 Podnos..379
    Czech Mortars..380
Recoilless Guns..383
    82mm SPG-82..383
    82mm B-10..384
    107mm B-11..385
    73mm SPG-9 Kopye...387
    82mm T-21 Tarasnice (Czechoslovakia)............388
    82mm M-59 & M-59A (Czechoslovakia)............389

Multiple Rocket Launchers..391
    BM-24..391
    BMD-20..394
    BM-14..395
    BM-25..397
    BM-21 Grad..398
    BM-27 Uragan..401
    BM-30 Smerch..403
    BM 9A51 Prima..405
    RM-51 (Czechoslovakia).....................................406
    RM-70 (Czechoslovakia).....................................408
    140mm RPU-14...409
    140mm WP-8 (Poland).......................................411
Tactical Ballistic Missiles..413
    FROG-1..413
    FROG-2..414
    FROG-3/4/5..415
    FROG-7..417
    SS-1 Scud...418
    SS-12 Scaleboard..420
    SS-21 Scarab...422
    SS-23 Spider..423
Glossary...427
Image Credits..431
Digital Reinforcements: Free Ebook.............................437
About Russell Phillips..439
    Find Russell Phillips Online................................439

www.ingramcontent.com/pod-product-compliance
Lightning Source LLC
Chambersburg PA
CBHW031053080526
44587CB00011B/672